The Book of the Play

*A volume in the series*

Massachusetts Studies in Early Modern Culture

Edited by Arthur F. Kinney

# The Book of the Play

## Playwrights, Stationers, and Readers in Early Modern England

EDITED BY

MARTA STRAZNICKY

UNIVERSITY OF MASSACHUSETTS PRESS
AMHERST & BOSTON

Printed in the United States of America
LC 2006003038
ISBN 1-55849-532-0 (library cloth ed.); 533-9 (paper)
Designed by Jack Harrison
Set in Garamond No. 3 by Bookcomp, Inc.
Printed and bound by The Maple-Vail Book Manufacturing Group

Library of Congress Cataloging-in-Publication Data

The book of the play : playwrights, stationers, and readers in early modern England / edited by Marta Straznicky.
p. cm. — (Massachusetts studies in early modern culture)
Includes bibliographical references and index.
ISBN 1-55849-532-0 (library cloth : alk. paper) —
ISBN 1-55849-533-9 (pbk. : alk. paper)
1. English drama—17th century—History and criticism.
2. Drama—Publishing—England—History—17th century.
3. Books and reading—England—History—17th century.
4. Book industries and trade—England—History—17th century.
5. English drama—Early modern and Elizabethan, 1500–1600—History and criticism.
6. Drama—Publishing—England—History—16th century.
7. Books and reading—England—History—16th century.
8. Book industries and trade—England—History—16th century.
I. Straznicky, Marta. II. Series.
PR653.B66 2006
822'.409—dc22
2006003038

British Library Cataloguing in Publication data are available.

# CONTENTS

# ILLUSTRATIONS

# The Book of the Play

INTRODUCTION

# Plays, Books, and the Public Sphere

MARTA STRAZNICKY

In early modern usage, the "book" of a play was the printed or manuscript text as distinct from the play in performance. The term is used across a range of institutional and rhetorical settings, from the Stationers' Company, where licenses to print dramatic texts identify the licensed material as the "book" of a particular play, to records from the Revels Office, where the "book" is censored and approved for performance, to the playhouse, where the "book" is used to guide performance, to printers' and authors' prefaces to published plays, where the matter presented for reading is specifically understood as the "book" of a previously performed stage play. In these and other examples, the consistent usage of the term "book" to distinguish between a play in performance and a playtext indicates that the reading of drama (whether in the context of play production, censorship, pedagogy, or private leisure) was a recognized cultural practice in early modern England that only partially intersected with the culture of playgoing.

At some level, scholars have always acknowledged this alternative mode of reception, but play-reading itself as a historical practice has been marginalized by critical inquiries and procedures that, even when they are directly engaged with the history of early modern playtexts, have focused either on the process by which plays move from page to stage, or on the book trade in terms of production, regulation, and distribution alone. For the first half of the twentieth century, the New Bibliographers examined the production of printed plays in ways that simultaneously created an archive about play-reading practices, cataloguing as they did the material forms of playtexts and matters of publication history that also carry information about marketing, readership, and interpretation: it is no accident that one of their monumental achievements, W. W. Greg's *Bibliography of the English Printed Drama*, is indispensable to many of the essays in this volume. But crucial as their work has been to the revisionary history of drama as a species of print culture, the New Bibliographers themselves took no interest in plays as reading material. In fact, Greg's conception of the "book" of the play had exclusively to do with the nature and use of dramatic manuscripts in the playhouse. As Paul Werstine has shown, Greg fundamentally misrepresented the early modern usage of the term "book" when he took it to refer only to manuscripts of playhouse provenance.[1] This in turn enabled him to produce the category of "promptbook," which became decisive in setting the course of textual studies of early modern plays for much of the twentieth century, but it also had the effect of focusing scholarship on the transmission of drama from manuscript to print rather than on its reception in either medium.

Reception was, perhaps unsurprisingly, at the center of the interpretive tradition against which early-twentieth-century bibliographers defined themselves. Beginning early in the nineteenth century with the work of such towering figures as Coleridge and Charles Lamb, criticism of early modern drama engaged itself directly with the issue of whether plays—particularly the plays of Shakespeare—are best realized in actual physical performance or in the theater of the mind.[2] The question was decided, of course, unequivocally in favor of reading: "For the principal and only genuine excitement ought to come from within—from the moved and sympathetic imagination; whereas, where so much is addressed to the mere external senses of seeing and hearing the spiritual vision is apt to languish, and the attraction from without will withdraw the mind from the proper and only legitimate interest which is intended to spring from within."[3] As James Redmond points out, Coleridge's seemingly extreme view on this matter was in fact orthodox in the nineteenth century, finding expression among the most important and influential writers of the time, including Hazlitt, Byron, Scott, and Browning.[4] So entrenched was the idea that Shakespearean drama found its "proper" and "legitimate" form only in the mind of the reader that when English literature became institutionalized as a subject of university study later in the century, Shakespeare was easily appropriated by English departments and taught as a species of poetry. Throughout much of the twentieth century, in fact, the study of early modern drama was fundamentally estranged from performance, its controversies focused entirely around the issue of what it is that criticism ought to be doing with the words *on the page*. This intensely literary approach to drama developed highly nuanced and sophisticated methods of reading, but its fundamental ahistoricism meant that the matter of what Shakespeare's contemporaries may have been doing with the words on the page was never raised.

Ironically, it is in the area of performance-oriented criticism, especially as this is inflected by New Historicism, that a nascent conception of the significance of a history of play reading may be found. In a sense, this should not be surprising, since even the most antitheatrical of Romantic writers understood that the power of drama in reading was precisely that it could replicate the experience of performance. Charles Lamb, for example, pronounced that "the Lear of Shakespeare cannot be acted. . . . The greatness of Lear is not in corporal dimension, but in intellectual. . . . On stage we see nothing but corporal infirmities and weakness, the impotence of rage; while we read it, we see not Lear, but we are Lear."[5] What Lamb most valued was the inhabiting of Shakespearean character that reading enabled; in rejecting performance, he rejected merely the mediation that watching a play forced upon him. Lamb's existential conception of reading as performance is of course open to criticism on many fronts, but he gives voice here to the same generative power of enactment that informs much of the polemic for a performance-oriented approach to drama.[6] But performance criticism adds a crucial angle to the argument for enactment: it sets reception in the theater, in a social and cultural *context* that reaches beyond the solipsistic (and implicitly apolitical) imagination of the reader as constructed by Lamb.

Restoring the theatrical to the enactment of early modern drama thus restores drama to politics, a move that is, not coincidentally, at the very core of New Historicism. The New Historicist reassessment of the politics of early modern drama was from the beginning informed by an understanding that early modern political culture was itself fundamentally performative, and being performative meant that every instance of cultural experience involved an actor and an audience. Much New Historicist work has therefore concerned itself with the way in which early modern drama either represents or is itself a means of negotiation between subjects, specifically between subjects who bear authority and those who (seemingly) do not. At the center of such investigations is a concern to map the historically specific "ideological work" *performed* in and by theatrical representation. Within this framework, the theater itself has come to be characterized as a nascent form of the early modern public sphere, its entrepreneurial organization promoting the growth of a cultural practice uniquely capable of mounting open and cross-class critiques of political orthodoxy. As Douglas Bruster and Alexandra Halasz have shown, in this the theater intersected with the marketplace of print, and together the two institutions became a forum for public debate that proved crucial to the formation of the early modern subject and state.[7]

In light of the advances that have been made in our understanding of how theatrical and print cultures engaged the process of political change, it is all the more striking that the reception of early modern *printed* drama, not to mention manuscript drama, has been almost completely overlooked. But the archive of early modern printed drama is itself a vast source of information on how theater and print converged as cultural practices. From the earliest appearance of printed plays in England, the relationship between text and performance is constructed more often in terms of interchange, complementarity, and congruence than of opposition or competition, and readership thereby straddles *both* the theatrical and the reading publics.[8] *Pace* Stephen Orgel, the early modern play could be play and book at one and the same time.[9] This is not to say, however, that reading plays was meant to be a straightforward replication of playgoing, for the consumption of playtexts in spaces and institutional contexts (closets, households, academies, etc.) that were construed as *private* meant that, unlike playgoing, playreading as a cultural practice could draw on two otherwise disparate sources of authority and legitimation, the elite (private) and the popular (public). It is the fact of a *play* being a *book* that enables early modern consumers of printed drama both to be positioned and to position themselves in two overlapping and mutually constitutive public spheres.

At a more concrete level, attending to early modern plays in terms of their cultural impact *as books* is crucial to understanding the place of drama in society quite simply because books is what the surviving texts most fundamentally are. This is not to suggest that printed drama offers us no access to the history of performance, but it is to urge us to account for the fact that that access—for every published play—is decisively mediated by the culture of print.[10] In recent years, the study of early modern English print culture has been revitalized by such seminal work in book history as Lucien Fèbvre and Henri-Jean Martin's *Coming of the Book: The Impact of Printing, 1450–1800*, and this development has dovetailed with ongoing debates about the rationale, objectives, and procedures of textual scholarship. If the field of book history has a distinct mark in early modern scholarship, it is in this conjunction of textual and cultural studies known as the New Textualism. Work done in this line of thought takes the "materiality of the text" as a crucial component of social, political, and intellectual history.[11] Although it is focused primarily on textual problems surrounding the plays of Shakespeare, the New Textualism has greatly expanded what it is possible to know about the "historicity of texts" in general: not only, as was the case with the early New Historicist work that coined this term, the intersection *at the level of content* between writing and politics, but also the traces of cultural, commercial, and political contest that are embedded in texts as material objects, especially *as books.* Whether and to what extent these contests and the place of drama within them replicate the ideological struggles in which performed drama participated is an issue that has barely begun to be posed but will clearly have a profound impact on how we understand the matrix of relations between theater, text, and the public sphere. It is this larger endeavor that both postulates and demands a history of play-reading.

For the materials of such a history one can turn to a bewildering array of sources: probate and household inventories, wills, library catalogues, royal proclamations and edicts, pedagogical manuals, the registers and court books of the Stationers' Company, histories of individual print shops, booksellers' and publishers' catalogues, diaries, personal correspondence, account books of various kinds, literacy rates, verbal and pictorial representations of play-readers (most significantly in prefaces and dedications to plays, but also in conduct manuals, antitheatrical tracts, sermons, ballads, and jest-books, among many others), marginalia, dramatic theory, the material features of playbooks themselves (format, typography, arrangement of text, ink, paper, binding, etc.), and the recirculation of dramatic texts in other discursive forms, genres, and formats such as miscellanies and commonplace books, both printed and manuscript.[12] Marshaling such a varied range of materials, each of which requires specialized research and interpretive skills, into a cohesive history of play-reading is obviously an enormous undertaking, one that may well never reach completion. But certain key first steps, both methodological and substantive, have been taken. The printing conventions for early modern drama have been set in the lines of development running from medieval communal theater as well as elite classical drama.[13] Some elements of typographic design have been analyzed in relation to communities of readers.[14] The marketing of plays to a reading public has been examined.[15] The business practices of certain print shops have been reconstructed,[16] as has the commercial context of play publication generally.[17] Attitudes to play-reading have been assembled from prefatory matter and from public and private library catalogues.[18] The place of play-reading in relation to political culture in the Civil War period has been studied.[19] And, perhaps most notably, the impact of print on advancing the authority of playwrights and the cultural status of drama is now well established.[20] Most of this work has not been specifically focused on the history of play-reading, but all of it helps to configure the matrix within which such a history might emerge: that is, the relationship between the material forms of playtexts, their production and modes of circulation, and their interpretations, uses, and appropriations by various reading publics.

Difficult as it is to draw general conclusions from so many isolated studies, it is beyond doubt that the parameters for thinking about printed drama have been redefined. Peter Blayney has made perhaps the largest single contribution in his reassessment of the economics of play publication, showing that, compared with the full range of texts being printed in this period, drama was commercially negligible. Blayney's findings, however, have been revised by Alan Farmer and Zachary Lesser, who consider the figures for play publication in terms of reprint rates and within the narrower field of "speculative" publications, that is, books that were not printed on command, under monopoly, or for overtly propagandist aims.[21] Within this market share, Farmer and Lesser have found that printed plays were indeed popular commodities, with reprint rates at more than twice the rate for speculative books in general. What is significant about these results is that the market for printed drama was based on reprints rather than first editions, suggesting that the demand for plays was less dependent on theatrical popularity than has been assumed, and that plays had a longer "shelf life" than any other speculative publication. This goes a long way toward overturning Blayney's much-quoted assertion that playbooks "never accounted for a very significant fraction of the trade in English books,"[22] although his broader argument does change radically the long-standing view that actors jealously guarded their literary property from thieving printers.[23]

In addition, our understanding of playwrights' attitudes toward publication has been transformed. In three closely related studies, Douglas

Brooks, David Scott Kastan, and Lukas Erne have demonstrated that publication did not undermine the theater business, and that professional playwrights (including theater shareholders like Shakespeare) not only were not averse to seeing their plays in print, but also wrote plays with the intention of meeting the specific interests and requirements of readers as well as theatergoers. Finally, poststructuralism has forced a complete reassessment of the rationale, objectives, and procedures of early modern textual scholarship, with the result that playtexts are understood not as inherently corrupt vehicles of authorial intentions but as material objects that record the specific cultural, intellectual, and political conditions that prevailed *at the time of printing*. This work has had the greatest impact on editorial theory and methodology, particularly in relation to Shakespeare, whose textually most complex plays have begun appearing in multiple-text editions that represent variant texts as equally significant, and significantly different, witnesses to early modern theatrical and print culture.

Each of these developments in the study of early modern printed drama has major implications for our understanding of the theater's impact on the public sphere, chiefly that that impact was conducted through two congruent but distinct media, the playhouse and the printing house. If we now know that the commercial incentive for publishing drama was based more in emergent "classics" than current stage drama, that playwrights relied on print to validate their status as authors, that theater companies had more to gain than to lose by having stage plays circulating in print, and that individual playtexts themselves intersect with theatrical culture in different ways, then the question of which plays are printed, who is buying them, why they are spending money on this particular commodity, and how and in what contexts the plays are read—in short, the question of the reception of plays *in reading*—becomes crucial to understanding the place of drama in the early modern public sphere. After a quarter-century of research on the role of the theater in the social and political struggles of early modern England, we know that the theater both was and was perceived to be a crucial contributor to the development of an intellectual culture that fostered meaningful public debate. Attending the theater and watching a play was thus one means of access to the public sphere. Reading was another; and reading a *play*, especially a play that had also been performed in the public theater, was distinct yet again in that it integrated two modes of public engagement.

The essays that follow are focused on this matter of how and to what effect reading the "book" of the play intersected with theatrical culture and with the public sphere. As a group, they consolidate recent work in textual, bibliographic, and cultural studies of printed drama; individually, each of them advances our understanding of play-reading as a cultural practice with distinct material embodiments, discursive forms, social settings, and institutional affiliations. Part One, "Real and Imagined Communities," includes four studies of communities of play-readers and the terms in which they are distinguished from the reading public at large. The term "curteous readers," for example, commonly found in printers' and authors' addresses, functions rhetorically to identify a specific, self-identifiably elite interpretive community. Cyndia Clegg surveys this and other terms of address in prefaces to readers of published plays to determine who early modern dramatists and publishers conceived their readers to be. Taking a cue from Jonson, Clegg examines the stratification of play-readers into contrasting categories, be they explicitly so designated (as in Jonson's "ordinary" and "extraordinary" readers), or implicitly in terms of education and interpretive skills. Although she does identify a certain degree of overlap between play-readers and playgoers, she discovers that plays which in performance were pitched to different kinds of audiences did not in print envision significantly different readerships. Regardless of a play's original venue, the trope of reader as judge, and especially as one entitled to exercise "free" judgment, is ubiquitous and identifies the play-reader more as belonging to a community of discerning readers and even political agents than to a community of amusement-seeking spectators. Also important is Clegg's finding that readers are generally not envisioned as consumers, an interesting counterpart to Blayney's argument that play publication was not a reliably profitable undertaking and one that suggests a significant difference between the position of printed and performed drama within an emergent market economy.

Clegg's analysis of the rhetorical constructions of play-readers is complemented in Lucy Munro's essay tracing three separate readings of a single play, Edward Sharpham's *The Fleer* (1607). Taking as evidence of reading such matters as bookbinding, manuscript annotation, and republication, Munro reveals that *The Fleer* was not always read in the ways imagined or prompted by the publisher's address to the reader. Sir John Harington's copy of the play is bound with other titles having thematic links or belonging to related theatrical repertories, thus confirming the publisher's construction of the play's intended readers as discerning individuals capable of placing drama within the larger field of print culture. The subsequent publication, however, of several runs of dialogue from *The Fleer* in a jest-book reveals that the play could also be read strictly for its comic material, the effect of which alters considerably given that the original staging by boy actors is not part of its presentation in print. In her analysis of the reproduction of ten jokes from *The Fleer* in *Conceits, Clinches, Flashes, and Whimzies* (1639), Munro shows how genre can affect meaning and how readers and publishers can recycle dramatic material in forms that substantially alter the manner in which they are interpreted. Finally, Munro examines a copy of *The Fleer* that is marked for performance and finds evidence of yet another manner of reading, one that almost completely eliminates the political plot in reshaping the play for another stage. Although this reading of the play in a sense returns *The Fleer* to performance, it is conspicuously unlike the kind of reading Harington may have engaged in as he read the play, some fifty years earlier, in light of the theatrical repertory to which it then belonged. Munro's essay thus demonstrates the necessity, as Roger Chartier has urged, of recognizing "that forms produce meaning, and that even a fixed text is invested with new meaning and being [*statut*] when the physical form through which it is presented for interpretation changes."[24]

In the third essay I return to the evidence of prefatory rhetoric to examine the construction of women as readers of printed drama. I find that when women are envisioned as readers of plays, a peculiarly physical relationship between the body of the reader and the book of the play emerges. While male readers were represented as engaging their intellects in the act of reading, women were variously reading through the body: they are said to be "enfebled" by the material, shown "dandling" playbooks on their laps, or enticed with promises of being "eased" and "refreshed" by male authors. Although this evidence of the gendered nature of play-reading resonates with what is known about cultural constructions of women theatergoers, it also sheds new light on women as patrons of drama: while warnings about the physical danger of playgoing for women were explicitly designed to keep them out of the theaters, the embodiment of women's play-reading was not always admonitory. The difference between the way women's bodies were inscribed in the cultures of reading and playgoing might be traced to differences in the economics of theater and of the book trade, the latter relying more heavily on "niche" marketing and therefore representing less of a social and cultural threat. But also, the specifically domestic, private setting of recreational reading could have licensed women's pleasure in a way that was unimaginable in the public sphere. To explore this possibility, I extend the analysis of prefatory rhetoric to consider women as book owners and find no evidence of conflict around their buying, reading, and even collecting drama. There is, then, a striking continuity between rhetoric and practice in the case of women's play-reading, a continuity—precisely because it is anchored in positive conceptions of female bodily pleasure—that urges us to consider how women's literacy may have had liberating effects in private and public spheres alike.

The final essay in Part One is an analysis of how play-reading was mobilized for overtly partisan ends in the period of the Civil War. Elizabeth Sauer examines a seventeenth-century translation of Buchanan's *Baptistes sive Calumnia* (1577), *Tyrannicall-Government Anatomized* (1643), a pro-parliamentary play ordered to be printed by the House of Commons Committee Concerning Printing in 1642/3. Sauer argues that this play belongs to the tradition of politicized closet drama that was in large part initiated by Buchanan himself and found its most influential English adherents in the work of dramatists allied with the Sidney circle. For Buchanan and the Sidney writers, closet drama was an inherently antiestablishment form, its critique of absolutism and the corruption of kings licensed and even intensified by its isolation from the collective experience of playgoing. For the Civil War government, dramatic form intended at once for private reading and broad public circulation was, ironically, serviceable in much the same way, replicating in print an arena for political thought that positioned the reader in private and public realms simultaneously. The revolutionary parliament has long been viewed as fundamentally antitheatrical, its ordinance against stage plays seeming to carry an all-out condemnation of the theater as a site of public assembly and the formation of public opinion; but the adoption in parliamentary writings of dramatic conventions and performative effects suggests a more savvy and resourceful application of available media than previous criticism has allowed. In her analysis of the reading protocols embedded in the pro-parliamentary play *Tyrannicall-Government Anatomized*, Sauer demonstrates just how amenable printed drama—and closet drama in particular—was to the formation of a distinctly republican political community. Not surprisingly, it is Milton who is most frequently credited with writing the play.

The essays in Part Two, assembled under the heading "Play-Reading and the Book Trade," consider the impact of play-reading on the public sphere through the evidence of play publication. Zachary Lesser examines the use of black-letter typeface in dramatic publication in an attempt to determine the extent to which it can be taken as an indicator of "popular" culture and readership. Beginning with a survey of scholarly work on black letter, Lesser finds that the paradigm within which the typeface has been studied is itself suffused with nostalgia: either the "folk" are seen nostalgically to have a unified and coherent identity and culture that can be discerned through black-letter texts; or, alternatively, all early modern readers are seen to participate in a broadly accessible common culture, defined in large part by black-letter texts and nostalgically seen as free from distinction, struggle, and conflict. Lesser argues instead that black-letter type (like all material features of books) is not an index but a signifier that must be read with the full range of interpretive skills we typically bring to bear on language: black letter served many functions and carried many meanings (some of them apparently contradictory) within the bibliographic codes available to early modern stationers. Examining the career of the ballad publisher John Wright, and particularly his multiple editions of *The Shoemaker's Holiday*, Lesser argues that in the early modern period one of the central meanings of black letter was precisely this nostalgia for a unified culture and a unified England, a nostalgia that—like all nostalgia—in fact suppressed conflict and contest in the public sphere. Reading *The Shoemaker's Holiday* in black letter, as thousands of people did while it was in print, was thus a way of experiencing a "popular" culture that did not, in fact, exist.

The second essay in Part Two examines how the emerging news trade of the 1620s and 1630s affected the market for and the reading of printed drama in Caroline England. Alan Farmer shows that during this period, as the news trade was expanding and the visibility of news increasing, acting companies and stationers offered an unprecedented number of plays addressing contemporary political events. To Ben Jonson, this was a deplorable trend. In *The Staple of News*, which was first performed in February 1625/6 and published in 1631, Jonson satirizes the corruption of the news trade and the theater's imitation of it. He purposely constructs an image of the theater that resembles the play's Office of the Staple of News. Customers are drawn to both places for the news they can acquire there and for the commodities they can buy—short manuscripts at the Staple, the performance of Jonson's play in the theater. In the printed edition of *The Staple of News*, Jonson inserted an address "To the Readers" instructing them not to mistake the play's news for actual news as the original theatrical audience had done. And, as Farmer reveals, it appears that Jonson had good reason to worry about the designs of his readers. If we attend to the plays that were printed during the 1620s and 1630s and note how they were marketed, we can see stationers publishing plays that represented and commented on foreign and domestic politics and positioning them to appeal to readers of news. As Farmer demonstrates, then, the news trade did indeed turn the theater into a staple of news, as Jonson feared it would, and its plays into dramatic newsbooks. During these two decades at least, there was a striking continuity between playhouse and printing house as arenas of public information and debate on current affairs.

Peter Berek's analysis of the use of generic terms on the title pages of printed plays reveals another link between drama and the broader culture of reading and demonstrates yet again the importance of considering printed drama in relation to other kinds of books as well as to theatrical performance. Berek begins by questioning the commonplace association of plays designated by genre with "literary" rather than theatrical texts. In an earlier publication, Zachary Lesser and Alan Farmer have shown that this kind of stratification did indeed occur in the use of author designations on title pages.[25] Berek finds, however, that from 1616 on, there is no significant difference in the likelihood of indoor or outdoor plays, plays for children's or adult companies, being designated by genre. Examining the title page of Jonson's folio and the presentation of individual plays within the volume, Berek reveals that genre seems to be working in two ways at once: it elevates plays by associating them with classical literary precedent while at the same time linking them to a tradition not just of readership but also of performance. Despite this ambivalence, following the appearance of Jonson's volume, generic terms take on some of the glamour of Jonson's term "works," resurfacing again in the most significant dramatic publications of the century, Shakespeare's folio of 1623 and the 1647 Beaumont and Fletcher folio, where—in conjunction with author designations—they serve more to position the drama within a literary tradition than to recall its theatrical prehistory. Berek thus links the increasing use and prestige of generic designations not to theatrical venue or company status but rather to practices that are internal to the book trade. Not surprisingly, then, the trend toward using generic designations migrates from drama to other forms of writing, a theatricalization of public discourse that Berek convincingly attributes to the influence of stationers rather than authors or, indeed, the theater itself.

In her study of the masque in print, Lauren Shohet also identifies a rupture between the culture of performance and the culture of reading. While court masque was an elite, private, densely emblematic performance form saturated with insider knowledge, it was also delivered consistently into a nascent public sphere through print. Sometimes print even supplanted performance: King James canceled the 1623 performance of the controversial *Neptune's Triumph*, but the masque was published in quarto nonetheless. Critics have taken James's cancellation of this performance to demonstrate absolutist power closing down policy debates, but Shohet reveals that the masque's publication (which was in no way subject to censorship) brings the policy debate to an even broader audience, an audience of readers who can afford a threepenny pamphlet. A similar case can be made for all masques in print. Shohet examines the publication history of masque, provenance records, marginal annotations, and prefaces to readers to reveal the sometimes contrasting, sometimes complementary significance of masque for its two audiences: the elite circles who experienced them in performance and in reading, and the public readership who received masques through text alone. Shohet argues that approaching masque as a print form intended for reading extends its cultural significance beyond its producers and performance contexts and shows that in print, masque texts served as a node of interchange between closed aristocratic culture and an emergent public sphere.

In the final essay in Part Two, Douglas Brooks returns to an analysis of prefatory rhetoric, this time in relation to printing as a vehicle for the formation of dramatic authorship. Focusing on a peculiar contradiction in Brome's *The Antipodes* (1640) between the play's thematic privileging of performance over reading and the author's preface to the reader, which wrests control over the play from the actors who had shortened it for performance, Brooks traces the impact print had on eclipsing performance as the medium in which the dramatist could legitimately lay claim to having "fathered" his text. The conceptual and metaphorical ties between printing and parenting that Brooks uncovers lead in turn to a reassessment of the significance of the play-*reader* in the formation of whatever cultural authority is carried by printed drama, an authority Brooks demonstrates had migrated by the 1640s from the collaborative conditions of performance to the individualized agency of the author. In this context, the closing of the theaters in 1642 is more important as the beginning of a new era in play publication and readership than as the end of a performance tradition.

The emphasis in all of these essays is on the reading of plays *in print*, but a fuller picture of the impact of dramatic texts on early modern culture would emerge if manuscript plays were considered. The number of surviving dramatic manuscripts from this period is negligible compared with what has survived in print, but the practices to which they belong are an important component of early modern theatrical and literary culture.[26] Much of the work that has been done on dramatic manuscripts has been concerned with classifying the surviving documents into those that bear evidence of playhouse use and those that do not. Although the relative value and validity of the two types of dramatic manuscript have been vigorously debated, the emphasis has until very recently focused almost exclusively on playhouse manuscripts and the traces of authorial activity they carry. But examining them from the point of view of readership, and considering without prejudice the "literary" along with the theatrical manuscripts, reveals a range of uses for textual drama that overlaps very little with the printed archive. In their physical and literary characteristics—the presence of multiple hands, the use of rules and other divisions, the placement of directions for stage action, the evidence of revision, and so on—theatrical manuscripts indicate a restricted circulation among playwrights, actors, bookkeepers, censors, and playhouse scribes, what we might call a professional readership that had a strictly pragmatic approach to the texts in hand. Except for the early Tudor interludes, which were advertised on their title pages as scripts for future performances, there is very limited evidence that printed plays from the 1590s on were used with this sort of practical application by professional actors.[27] The reading of playhouse manuscripts therefore represents a cultural practice that, if not unique to the theater, is certainly qualitatively different from the kinds of play-reading documented in the chapters that follow.

Even more suggestive as a counterexample to the reading of plays in print is the evidence of dramatic manuscripts that were circulated outside the playhouse. This category of play has been almost completely neglected in the scholarship because it has no direct bearing on the process by which playtexts move from stage to (printed) page, but it indicates that playtexts could be directed at exclusive, specialized readerships that were distinct from the reading public reached by print. We know that private transcripts of plays were made and that they circulated in coterie circles, and in one specific case the very existence of such a manuscript is explicitly set against the public circulation of drama on stage and in print: a scribal transcript of Middleton's notorious *A Game at Chess*, one of six surviving manuscript copies, claims to be an exclusive commodity that "nor stage, nor stationers stall can showe."[28] Prepared by the professional scribe Ralph Crane, this manuscript attests to the existence of a commercial trade in dramatic manuscripts. T. H. Howard-Hill cautions that any such trade was extremely limited and that the Middleton example may be nothing more than the ad hoc attempt of an entrepreneurial scribe to capitalize on the demand for texts of a play that had been banned for public consumption.[29] Whether or not there was a broad commercial context for the circulation of manuscript drama, the fact remains that the reader of such a play is positioned at the intersection of a public sphere in which the debate about state politics has moved into a commercial entertainment industry as well as a private sphere (in the sense of a restricted manuscript circulation, of affluence, of personal connections with authorial and scribal communities) in which the impact of that very move becomes intensified, ironically, by the exclusivity of the medium. This aspect of manuscript culture has been much discussed for lyric poetry but remains almost entirely unstudied for drama.[30]

In addition to the readership of manuscript drama, there are many other aspects of the topic of this volume that remain to be explored. The matter of patronage, for example: How did the patronage practices specific to print culture complement, displace, or conflict with royal and aristocratic patronage of performed drama?[31] More work needs to be done on the function of plays in the business practices and strategies of individual printers and, more broadly, the agency of printers as cultural brokers. If publishing drama was commercially a risky undertaking, what other motivations did stationers have? How much of the impact of printed drama on the public sphere is attributable to the commercial, political, or even aesthetic designs of printers and publishers? As for play-readers, there are other identifiable communities (not to mention individuals) that should be studied in full, most obviously apprentices, citizens, and Inns of Court students, each of which presumably brought a completely different set of interpretive skills to bear on drama than did the others. Or did they? We know frustratingly little about the extent to which the stratification of playgoing audiences was replicated in the market for printed drama, and what little we know suggests a more homogeneous reading "public" than the famously heterogeneous "public" theater audience. And if our knowledge of drama in performance comes almost entirely through print, how do we account for the fact that the extant plays represent only 40 percent of the theatrical repertories?[32] What does it mean that this 40 percent survived in print while the remaining 60 percent did not?

The essays gathered here touch on many of these issues, and while they have necessarily focused on selected communities of readers, publication histories, and ideologies and practices of reading, they do demonstrate the importance of textual reception to conceptualizing the place of drama in the early modern public sphere. While play-reading was undoubtedly a more exclusive practice than playgoing, it could function to form socially and politically distinct communities, to circulate news and opinion in the guise of "popular" or "elite" culture, to legitimize pleasure, to invest writing with authority. In some of these functions, it reproduced the energetics of theater; in others, it reinvented them. As the essays in this volume demonstrate, we can no longer assume that play-reading was simply an extension of playgoing. The more we know about the reception of early modern drama in its various textual forms, the better we understand its overall cultural and political significance.

## NOTES

1. Paul Werstine, "Plays in Manuscript," in *A New History of Early English Drama*, ed. John D. Cox and David Scott Kastan (New York: Columbia University Press, 1997), 484–85.

2. For a survey of this issue in the eighteenth and nineteenth centuries, see Michael Dobson, "Shakespeare on the Page and the Stage," in *The Cambridge Companion to Shakespeare*, ed. Margreta de Grazia and Stanley Wells (Cambridge: Cambridge University Press, 2001), 235–49. For much of the twentieth century, the question of the relevance of performance to an understanding of Shakespeare's plays has divided the scholarly community. Some key works in this debate are Robert S. Knapp, *Shakespeare: The Theater and the Book* (Princeton: Princeton University Press, 1989); Harry Berger, *Imaginary Audition: Shakespeare on Stage and Page* (Berkeley: University of California Press, 1989); W. B. Worthen, *Shakespeare and the Authority of Performance* (Cambridge: Cambridge University Press, 1997); and Robert Weimann, *Author's Pen and Actor's Voice: Playing and Writing in Shakespeare's Theatre* (Cambridge: Cambridge University Press, 2000).

3. *Coleridge on Shakespeare*, ed. Terence Hawkes (Harmondsworth: Penguin Books, 1969), 119. Cited from James Redmon, "The Mind's Eye, the Worthy Scaffold, the Real

Thing: How to Read a Shakespeare Play," in *Reading Plays: Interpretation and Reception*, ed. Hanna Scolnicov and Peter Holland (Cambridge: Cambridge University Press, 1991), 59.

4. Redmond, "The Mind's Eye," 59–60.

5. Charles Lamb, "On the Tragedies of Shakespeare, Considered with Reference to Their Fitness for Stage Representation," in *Miscellaneous Prose by Charles and Mary Lamb*, ed. E. V. Lucas (London: Methuen, 1912), 185. Hereafter cited parenthetically in the text.

6. For an astute analysis of the relationship between text and performance, and a critique of the tendency to read printed text as evidence of performance practice, see Janette Dillon, "Is There a Performance in This Text?" *Shakespeare Quarterly* 45 (1994): 74–86.

7. Douglas Bruster, "The Structural Transformation of Print in Late Elizabethan England," in *Print, Manuscript, and Performance: The Changing Relations of the Media in Early Modern England*, ed. Arthur F. Marotti and Michael D. Bristol (Columbus: Ohio University Press, 2000), 49–89; Alexandra Halasz, *The Marketplace of Print: Pamphlets and the Public Sphere in Early Modern England* (Cambridge: Cambridge University Press, 1997).

8. See Julie Stone Peters, *Theatre of the Book, 1480–1880: Print, Text, and Performance in Europe* (Oxford: Oxford University Press, 2000), 237–53. On dramatic publication in the pre-Shakespearean period, see Greg Walker, "Playing by the Book: Early Tudor Drama and the Printed Text," in *The Politics of Performance in Early Renaissance Drama* (Cambridge: Cambridge University Press, 1998), 6–50.

9. Stephen Orgel's claim that "if the play is a book, it's not a play" implies a strict division between drama on stage and page that is contested by many of the essays in this volume. Orgel's comment is from "What Is an Editor?" *Shakespeare Studies* 24 (1996): 23.

10. For a critique of "performance" editions of early modern plays, and of the theory generally that printed drama represents with some authenticity early modern performance practice, see Dillon, "Is There a Performance in This Text?"; Laurie E. Osborne, "Rethinking the Performance Editions: Theatrical and Textual Productions of Shakespeare," in *Shakespeare, Theory, and Performance*, ed. James C. Bulman (London: Routledge, 1996), 168–86; and Margaret Jane Kidnie, "The Staging of Shakespeare's Drama in Print Editions," in *Textual Performances: The Modern Reproduction of Shakespeare's Drama* (Cambridge: Cambridge University Press, 2004), 158–77.

11. Lucien Fèbvre and Henri-Jean Martin, *The Coming of the Book: The Impact of Printing, 1450–1800*, trans. David Gerard (London: Verso, 1990). Some of the seminal studies in the area of the New Textualism as it relates to drama are Margreta de Grazia and Peter Stallybrass, "The Materiality of the Shakespearean Text," *Shakespeare Quarterly* 44 (1993): 255–83; Leah Marcus, *Unediting the Renaissance: Shakespeare, Marlowe, Milton* (New York: Routledge, 1996); Laurie E. Maguire, *Shakespearean Suspect Texts: The "Bad" Quartos and Their Contexts* (Cambridge: Cambridge University Press, 1996); Laurie E. Maguire and Thomas Berger, eds., *Textual Formations and Reformations* (Newark: University of Delaware Press, 1998); Marotti and Bristol, eds., *Print, Manuscript, and Performance*; Michael Steppat, ed., *The Renaissance Text: Theory, Editing, Textuality* (Manchester: Manchester University Press, 2000); Douglas A. Brooks, *From Playhouse to Printing House: Drama and Authorship in Early Modern England* (Cambridge: Cambridge University Press, 2000); David Scott Kastan, *Shakespeare and the Book* (Cambridge: Cambridge University Press, 2001); Lukas Erne, *Shakespeare as Literary Dramatist* (Cambridge: Cambridge University Press, 2003); and Ann Thompson and Gordon McMullan, eds., *In Arden: Editing Shakespeare* (London: Arden Shakespeare,

2003). For an overview of this approach, see Alan Farmer, "Shakespeare and the New Textualism," in *The Shakespearean International Yearbook,* ed. W. R. Elton and John M. Mucciolo, vol. 2, *Where Are We Now in Shakespearean Studies?* (Aldershot: Ashgate, 2002), 158–79.

12. These and other forms of evidence for the history of reading are discussed in three of the most influential briefs for the approach: Robert Darnton, "First Steps toward a History of Reading," *Australian Journal of French Studies* 23 (1986): 5–30, Roger Chartier, "Texts, Printing, Readings," in *The New Cultural History*, ed. Lynn Hunt (Berkeley: University of California Press, 1989), 154–75; and Chartier, "Laborers and Voyagers: From the Text to the Reader," *diacritics* 22.2 (1992): 49–61.

13. T. H. Howard-Hill, "The Evolution of the Form of Plays in English during the Renaissance," *Renaissance Quarterly* 43 (1990): 112–45; Walker, "Playing by the Book"; and Paul J. Voss, "Printing Conventions and the Early Modern Play," *Medieval and Renaissance Drama in England* 15 (2002): 98–115.

14. G. K. Hunter, "The Marking of *Sententiae* in Elizabethan Printed Plays, Poems, and Romances," *The Library,* ser. 5, 6 (1951): 171–88; Mark Bland, "The Appearance of the Text in Early Modern England," *Text* 11 (1998): 91–154; Zachary Lesser, "Walter Burre's *The Knight of the Burning Pestle*," *ELR* 29 (1999): 22–43; Douglas A. Brooks, "*King Lear* (1608) and the Typography of Literary Ambition," *Renaissance Drama,* n.s. 30 (2001): 133–59.

15. James P. Saeger and Christopher Fassler, "The London Professional Theater, 1576–1642: A Catalogue and Analysis of the Extant Printed Plays," *Research Opportunities in Renaissance Drama* 34 (1995): 63–109; Paul J. Voss, "Books for Sale: Advertising and Patronage in Late Elizabethan England," *Sixteenth Century Journal* 29 (1998): 733–56; Alan Farmer and Zachary Lesser, "Vile Arts: The Marketing of English Printed Drama, 1512–1660," *Research Opportunities in Renaissance Drama* 39 (2000): 77–165.

16. W. Craig Ferguson, *Valentine Simmes* (Charlottesville, Va.: Bibliographical Society of the University of Virginia, 1968); Peter W. M. Blayney, *The Texts of King Lear and Their Origins*, vol. 1, *Nicholas Okes and the First Quarto* (Cambridge: Cambridge University Press, 1982); Michael Brennan, "William Ponsonby: Elizabethan Stationer," *Analytical and Enumerative Bibliography* 7 (1983): 91–110; Gerald D. Johnson, "John Busby and the Stationers' Trade," *The Library*, ser. 6, 7 (1985): 1–15; James K. Bracken, "Books from William Stansby's Printing House, and Jonson's Folio of 1616," *The Library*, ser. 6, 10 (1988): 18–29; Akihiro Yamada, *Thomas Creede: Printer to Shakespeare and His Contemporaries* (Tokyo: Meisei University Press, 1994); Paulina Kewes, "'Give Me the Sociable Pocket-Books': Humphrey Moseley's Serial Publication of Octavo Play Collections," *Publishing History* 38 (1995): 5–21; Kirk Melnikoff, "Richard Jones (fl. 1564–1613): Elizabethan Printer, Bookseller, and Publisher," *Analytical and Enumerative Bibliography* 12 (2001): 153–84. See also David M. Bergeron, "Printers' and Publishers' Addresses in English Dramatic Texts, 1558–1642," *Explorations in Renaissance Culture* 27 (2001): 131–60.

17. See in particular Peter W. M. Blayney, "The Publication of Playbooks," in Cox and Kastan, *New History of Early English Drama*, 383–422.

18. T. A. Birrell, "Reading as Pastime: The Place of Light Literature in Some Gentlemen's Libraries of the Seventeenth Century," in *Property of a Gentleman: The Formation, Organisation, and Dispersal of the Private Library, 1620–1920*, ed. Robin Myers and Michael Harris (Winchester: St Paul's Bibliographies, 1991), 113–31; Heidi Brayman Hackel, "'Rowme' of Its Own: Printed Drama in Early Libraries," in Cox and Kastan, *New History of Early English Drama*, 113–30; and Hackel, "'The Great Variety of Readers' and Early Modern Reading Practices," in *A Companion to Shakespeare*, ed. David Scott Kastan (Oxford: Blackwell, 1999), 139–57. On drama and literary culture more

generally, see Barbara A. Mowat, "The Theater and Literary Culture," in Cox and Kastan, *New History of Early English Drama*, 213–30; and John Pitcher, "Literature, the Playhouse, and the Public," in *The Cambridge History of the Book in Britain*, vol. 4, *1557–1695*, ed. John Barnard and D. F. McKenzie, assisted by Maureen Bell (Cambridge: Cambridge University Press, 2002), 351–75.

19. Louis B. Wright, "The Reading of Plays during the Puritan Revolution," *Huntington Library Bulletin* 6 (1934): 73–108; A. H. Tricomi, "Philip, Earl of Pembroke, and the Analogical Way of Reading Political Tragedy," *Journal of English and Germanic Philology* 85 (1986): 332–45; David Scott Kastan, "Performances and Playbooks: The Closing of the Theatres and the Politics of Drama," in *Reading, Society, and Politics in Early Modern England*, ed. Kevin Sharpe and Steven N. Zwicker (Cambridge: Cambridge University Press, 2003), 167–84.

20. See chiefly Brooks, *From Playhouse to Printing House*; Kastan, *Shakespeare and the Book*; and Erne, *Shakespeare as Literary Dramatist*.

21. Alan B. Farmer and Zachary Lesser, "The Popularity of Playbooks Revisited," *Shakespeare Quarterly* 56 (2005): 1–32.

22. Blayney, "Publication of Playbooks," 385.

23. Much of the revisionist work on the bad quartos has also contributed to this shift. See Paul Werstine, "Narratives about Printed Shakespeare Texts: 'Foul Papers' and 'Bad' Quartos," *Shakespeare Quarterly* 41 (1990): 65–86; and Maguire, *Shakespearean Suspect Texts*.

24. Chartier, "Laborers and Voyagers," 50–51.

25. Farmer and Lesser, "Vile Arts."

26. Werstine, "Plays in Manuscript"; William B. Long, "'Precious Few': English Manuscript Playbooks," in Kastan, *Companion to Shakespeare*, 414–33.

27. For example, the Cholmeley Players' performance of *Pericles* in Yorkshire in 1609 using a printed quarto; and there is a copy of a printed edition of Lodge and Greene's *A looking glass for London* that has been marked up as a playbook. On the *Pericles*, see Barbara A. Mowat, "The Theater and Literary Culture," in Cox and Kastan, *A New History of Early English Drama*, 218–22; on *A looking glass*, see H. R. Woudhuysen, *Sir Philip Sidney and the Circulation of Manuscripts, 1558–1640* (Oxford: Clarendon Press, 1996), 140–41.

28. Thomas Middleton, *A Game at Chess*, Bodleian Library MS. Malone 25; cited from N. W. Bawcutt, "Ralph Crane's Transcript of *A Game at Chess, Bodleian Manuscript Malone 25*," in *Collections*, vol. 15 (Oxford: Malone Society, 1993), 20. On the transcription of plays for private readers, especially in the context of a commercial manuscript trade, see T. H. Howard-Hill, "'Nor Stage, Nor Stationers Stall Can Showe': The Circulation of Plays in Manuscript in the Early Seventeenth Century," *Book History* 2 (1999): 28–41.

29. Howard-Hill, "'Nor Stage, Nor Stationers Stall Can Showe,'" 32–35.

30. On the social and political contexts of manuscript circulation of lyric poetry, see the overview by Harold Love and Arthur F. Marotti, "Manuscript Transmission and Circulation," in *The Cambridge History of Early Modern English Literature*, ed. David Loewenstein and Janel Mueller (Cambridge: Cambridge University Press, 2002), 55–80.

31. See, however, David M. Bergeron, "The King's Men's King's Men: Shakespeare and Folio Patronage," which appears, suggestively, in *Shakespeare and Theatrical Patronage in Early Modern England*, ed. Paul Whitfield White and Suzanne Westfall (Cambridge: Cambridge University Press, 2002), 45–63.

32. Saeger and Fassler, "London Professional Theater," 67.

PART ONE

# Real and Imagined Communities

ONE

# Renaissance Play-Readers, Ordinary and Extraordinary

CYNDIA SUSAN CLEGG

The 1616 folio edition of *The Workes of Beniamin Jonson* has long served literary theorists, historians, and critics as the critical moment in English literary history when the early modern English dramatist ascended from the stage to the page and took up the mantle of "author" by collaborating with his publisher-printer, William Stansby, to create an authoritative text on which the reader could rely. According to William W. E. Slights, "Jonson always felt that his work had a better chance of being properly understood by a reading audience. Publishing his *Works* in 1616 measurably increased his chances of being taken seriously as a dramatic poet."[1] Jonson, the story goes, carefully revised, edited, and proofread his plays for a discerning literary audience.[2] Posterity not only has accorded Jonson the "literary" status he sought, but has likewise conferred it upon his contemporaries, including William Shakespeare and Christopher Marlowe, neither of whom appears to have shown much interest in "readerly" editions of their plays. Indeed, from the eighteenth century until the last part of the twentieth century, schools and scholars took far greater interest in the literary character of English Renaissance drama than they did in its performance, as witnessed by the place of drama in the literary curriculum and the extraordinary efforts of textual scholars to create editions of the plays that reflected authorial intention.[3]

Recent trends in dramatic criticism have called upon us to reconsider both the premises and consequences of arguments about dramatic literature and authorship in the English Renaissance. Dramatic authors have become "playwrights," or collaborators, or even "author functions," and we have come to appreciate the inherent instability of early modern printed texts derived from multiple dramatic and print productions.

David Scott Kastan maintains that neither the persistent effort "to act as if the works we have read have a reality independent of the physical texts in which we engage them" nor the academy's pervasive commitment to a "stage-centered" pedagogy can satisfactorily envision playtexts as anything other than "the object of our own desires." The alternative Kastan poses is not to eliminate altogether a performative approach to the study of drama but to give weight to the printed texts in all their varied historical iterations as equally central to understanding the drama.[4] What Kastan is proposing is not reintroducing close reading and textual analysis as it was performed by New Critics in the mid-twentieth century, but instead attending to the material forms in which sixteenth-century plays appeared as a means of understanding the drama.

Recent attention to the material book, to printing house practices, and to reading practices is helping us to refine our understanding of both dramatic authors and the nature of their relationships with the stage and the printed page, but it has yielded remarkably little insight into contemporary literary audiences for Renaissance drama, at least before the theaters were closed in 1642.[5] While it might be tempting to assume that scholars have been dilatory in studying dramatic reading practices, the status of the printed playtext in its own time may instead be the reason why we know less about play-readers than playgoers. According to Peter Blayney, between 1560 and 1642 printed plays represented a fraction of the trade in English books, and only eleven plays written for the English stage and three closet dramas ever sold in sufficient editions to be regarded as "best-sellers."[6] Some of Blayney's statistics and categories have been critiqued by Alan Farmer and Zachary Lesser, but his work does serve as a useful caution to those who overestimate (and have overestimated) the literary importance of drama for Shakespeare and Jonson and their contemporaries.[7] But as Farmer and Lesser's work has shown, between 1560 and 1642 printers apparently believed that there was a sufficient number of readers (albeit perhaps only a quirky few) interested enough in drama to warrant regularly printing plays performed—both successfully and unsuccessfully—on the London stage, as well as plays performed only at court. Otherwise, they would not have invested in the labor and paper necessary to produce the quarto playbooks that appeared with some regularity and in editions large enough to warrant the production costs.[8]

Who were the quirky few who frequented the booksellers' stalls looking for playbooks? Certainly they were not the kind of readers that Sir

Thomas Bodley envisioned for the national library he created, which excluded plays from all the printed books that were to be collected.[9] Bodley, however, may have misjudged. Education and class offer no sure measure of the reading audience of plays, even if Jonson feared having as his folio's reader "some clerk-like serving-man."[10] Existing records of book ownership, as Heidi Brayman Hackel has shown, attest to the breadth of the play-reading audience—even if, as Blayney suggests, it lacked depth.[11] Recent studies of reading in early modern England have done much to uncover reading practices and theorize the reader. The evidence of reading practices—actual accounts found in diaries, commonplace books, marginalia, and letters or fictional accounts found in contemporary literature—helps us understand how readers engaged with their texts, but the character of play-readers still remains elusive beyond the identifiable markers of gender, class, reading tastes, and annotative practices.[12] Were they as serious-minded as Jonson would have them? Were they of the "Great Variety" (including those who could barely read, envisioned by Heminge and Condell) who bought books and probably didn't read them? Were any play-readers, like Kevin Sharpe's Sir William Drake, intent on drawing upon reading resources to make meaning of contemporary events and personal affairs?[13] Did plays provide a textual space similar to what Annabel Patterson has found in Holinshed's *Chronicles,* where "all Englishmen" could freely exercise their judgment?[14] Or was the play-reader, like the other English Renaissance readers Wendy Wall found envisioned by book prefaces, a "voyeur, one who partakes of forbidden discourse and is complicit in stealing a glance at clandestine words"?[15]

In an attempt to answer these questions, I turn to the evidence of the material book—to prefaces of printed plays, specifically addresses and letters to readers—to determine how early modern dramatists and their publishers at least conceived of their readers. I sometimes agree with Wall that "printed plays can be said to have borrowed the discourse of privacy central to the production of printed poetic forms."[16] I have found that most of the time, however, they did not envision a reader at all, or if they did, they endowed him (or even her) with a far greater range of discerning attributes than has previously been imagined.[17] In what follows I characterize the variety of readers, query the distinctions between these readers and those of "best-selling" plays, and, finally, seek to establish the changes between readers of the earliest printed plays and those who were the plays' only audiences.

Before describing the varieties of readers envisioned by early modern publishers, however, I want to revisit a few texts printed in close proximity to one another—Shakespeare's *Troilus and Cressida* (1609) and two by Ben Jonson, *Catiline His Conspiracy* (1611) and *Sejanus His Fall* (1605)—which may be considered "readerly," that is, divorced from performance and published only with readers in mind.[18] In the printer's address to the reader of *Troilus and Cressida* (1609), a play probably not commercially performed before it appeared in print, "A neuer writer" addresses his reader as "euer" and "eternall," commending the play to him because "It deserues such a labour, as well as the best Commedy in Terence or Platus." The allusion to the Latin authors envisions, if not an elite reader, at least one possessed of a grammar school education, and certainly one juxtaposed against the playgoing audience, who are "dull and heauy-witted worldlings, as were neuer capable of the witte of a Commedie." In a curious reversal of the confidence Shakespeare's sonnets express in the poet's ability to immortalize his subject, here the "ever" and "eternal" reader perpetuates the author's fame:

> And beleeue this, that when he is gone, and his Commedies out of sale, you will scramble for them, and set up a new English Inquisition. Take this for a warning, and at the perrill of your pleasures losse, and Iudgements, refuse not, nor like this the lesse, for not being sullied, with the smoaky breath of the multitude; but thanke fortune for the scape it hath made amongst you.

Like the epistle to *Troilus and Cressida*, those to *Catiline* and *Sejanus* envision educated readers, but Jonson's are of a worthier sort who will understand Latin annotations and possess a critical interest in classical unities. Rather than drawing a distinction between a crass audience and a discerning reader, however, Jonson finds any reader suspect, even if he is "extraordinary." Readers exercise judgment. If they are ordinary, they meddle and "molest" the writer, even with "foolish praise"; if extraordinary, they possess the knowledge to judge well—but still they judge. Even so, for these three "readerly" dramatic texts, the epistles empower the reader to sustain the "author's" fame.[19]

Given the high critical esteem that Jonson's readerly plays have garnered—and the relative disdain plays printed earlier have received—we might expect epistles to readers to envision very different reading audiences for readerly and popular plays. For readerly plays, one would expect an audience to be characterized as discerning, as caring about the text's authority; but what kinds of readers would dare to cast their eyes on the common products of rapacious stationers? According to Wall, "Renaissance prefaces repeatedly call attention to the impropriety of the printed texts they introduce," and in doing so "cast the reader into the role of voyeur, one who partakes of forbidden discourse and is complicitous in stealing a glance at clandestine words."[20] Even printed plays "can be said to have borrowed the discourse of privacy central to the production of printed poetic forms."[21] Wall's identification of the reader of plays as a voyeur is apropos—but primarily for plays by one dramatist, Thomas Heywood. As Douglas Brooks points out, "no playwright in the period wrote more about the vicissitudes of dramatic authorship than Heywood, and the perils of publication he documented have been frequently quoted."[22] Indeed, of the over two hundred sixteenth- and seventeenth-century editions of plays I examined, outside of the Shakespeare folio, Heywood's plays with their wordy addresses to readers almost single-handedly create and sustain the trope of the voyeuristic reader. It is primarily to Heywood that the notorious discourse of the purloined play belongs. Here the text appears mangled by insensible stationers, and the reluctant author likens his writings to sexual indiscretions whose issue he finally legitimizes and exposes to a "private reading."[23] As responsible as he is for envisioning the reader as voyeur, Heywood also employs another of his age's most common characterization of readers. "Censure I intreat as fauourably," he proclaims, "as it is exposed to thy view freely."[24] Even for Heywood, the reader is less often a voyeur than a virtuous judge—in Heywood's case a judge called upon to excuse sexual excesses: "But curteous Reader, I can onely excuse him in this, that this is the *Brazen Age*."[25]

Casting readers as judges is the most pervasive trope by far in epistles to printed plays in the English Renaissance. Readers of plays by Lyly, Marlowe, Shakespeare, Jonson, Middleton, Dekker, Massinger, Webster, Fletcher, and Brome not only received the compliment of being "Jvditiovs" but also were invited to judge freely. The notion of free judgment so often repeated has many implications. The 1591 preface to Lyly's *Endymion* refers to the reader's "indifferent judgment."[26] "Indifferent" in this sense does not mean "unconcerned" but rather "unprejudiced"; it is the word Spenser uses in book 5 of the *Faerie Queene* to characterize the most elevated kind of judgment exercised by Mercilla, one of the work's avatars of Queen Elizabeth. The political implication of "free" likewise requires consideration. The 1622 edition of *Othello* characterizes the reader as possessing "liberty of judgment," and even Heywood offers one of his plays to the reader's "free" view.[27] The reader of plays, like Sir William Drake in Kevin Sharpe's *Reading Revolutions,* was free to read what he wished and to judge freely what he read. This notion of judgment may have derived in part from the kind of humanist education that most men of the propertied and aristocratic classes received. In *Rhetoric, Prudence, and Skepticism in the Renaissance*, Victoria Kahn demonstrates that a humanist education did not intend to effect the reader's instruction by inculcating good examples but instead sought to cultivate his ability to discern moral distinctions, that is, to produce the faculty of judgment.[28] Sharpe, too, reminds us that humanism recognized "the independence and power of readers . . . to construct their own meaning," and furthermore, that such independence of mind cannot properly be divorced from political perception.[29] The pervasiveness of the trope of free judgment in characterizing the readers of plays insists, then, that many playwrights and printers envisioned not just an educated audience but one not remarkably different from the "Englishmen all" who read Holinshed's *Chronicles* as a textual space that politically empowered them.

One particular preface—to Marlowe's *Tamburlaine*, parts one and two (1590 and 1597)—identifies its readers as the same men who engaged in more serious reading. It is addressed "To the Gentlemen Readers: and others that take pleasure in reading Histories" and conveys the printer's "hope" that "they [the plays] wil be now no lesse acceptable vnto you to read after your serious affaires and studies, then they haue bene (lately) delightfull for many of you to see." Implying the gravity of the reading audience, the epistle announces that the printed play omits "fond and friuolous Iestures [gestures]" that had appeared on the stage which would mar "so honourable & stately a historie." Both the "eloquence of the Authour" and "the worthinesse of the matter it selfe" are set before the readers' "learned censures."[30]

In many epistles the judicious reader's independence and power is closely associated with his complicity in constructing meaning. John Marston's "generall Reader" of *The Wonder of Women, or The Tragedie of Sophonisba* (1606)—referred to as "equall Reader"—is called upon to judge the play without prejudice and told that "if ought shall displease thee thanke they selfe, if ought shall please thee thanke not only me."[31] The "Vnderstanding Gentrie" who have embraced "the copious vent of three Editions" of *Philaster* receive the stationer's compliment in the

1634 edition that they alone are the play's "skilfull Triers and Refiners" and the actors but "laboring Miners."[32] Both *The White Divel* (1612) and *The Deuils Law-case* (1623) convey John Webster's preference for readers who possess the faculty of understanding over the "vncapable multitude" who frequent theaters.[33]

Not all complicit readers, however, appear benign. John Marston explains how *The Malcontent* (1604) had been formerly misconstrued—"some have bin most vnadvisedly over-cunning in misinterpreting me"—and attempts to fix the printed text's reception by informing his reader that he, the author, has "willingly erred" in creating fictions that would not "draw any disgrace to any, dead or living."[34] Ben Jonson is, of course, notorious for using prefatory materials to control the reception of his printed plays. More than any other playwright, Jonson holds his readers (and playgoing audiences) in contempt for the injudicious freedom they may in their complicity exercise. At best, as in the epistles to *Catiline* and *Sejanus*, Jonson seeks merely to restrict the reader's freedom. Sometimes in these Jonson merely places himself "aboue such molestations" of censure as the reader might perform.[35] In the case of *Volpone* (1607), however, the reader who misjudges the play becomes the butt of Jonson's satire: "If thou dar'st bite this Foxe, then read my ri'mes; / Thou guilty art of some of these foule crimes."[36]

As most of these examples suggest, dramatic authors and their publishers understood play-readers to be elite males. Pointed exceptions, however, do exist. One of the earliest of these appears in prefatory materials to *The Shoemakers Holiday, or The Gentle Craft* (1600), whose readers Dekker identifies as "all good Fellowes, Professors of the Gentle Craft, of what degree soeuer" and "Kind Gentlemen, and honest boone Companions."[37] "Of what degree soeuer" registers an inclusivity that embraces the non-elite guild member, the man about town, and, perhaps, women. In general use, "boone Companions" meant the same thing as "good Fellowes." Since the epistle has already greeted the "good Fellowes," the honest and good ("boone") companions of the "Kind Gentlemen" may be women, especially since "honest" (chaste) is more often used as a compliment to women than to men. Heywood's 1634 comedy *A Mayden-head Well Lost* definitely imagines a female reader, one that might be deterred by the play's title:

> Courteous Reader, (of what sexe soever) let not the Title of this Play any way deterre thee from the perusal thereof: For there is nothing herein contained, which doth deuiate either from Modesty, or good Manners.[38]

By the Restoration, the prefatory materials presume the female reader. The 1661 edition of Richard Brome's *The Royall Exchange* opens its address from "The Stationer to the Readers" with "Gentlemen and Ladies."[39]

Admitting women into the league of play-readers may have derived from the restraint on playing during the Civil War, which itself evoked frequent comment in prefatory epistles. Most of the numerous plays published while the theaters were closed refer to the tragic times and register a longing for the playhouse, but none more than the 1647 edition of Beaumont and Fletcher's *Comedies and Tragedies.*

> And now Reader in this Tragicall Age where the Theater hath been so much out-acted, congratulate thy owne happinesse, that in this silence of the Stage, thou hast a liberty to reade these inimitable Playes, to dwell and converse in these immortall Groves, which were only shewed our Fathers in a conjuring glasse, as suddenly removed as represented, the Landscape is now brought home by this optick, and the Presse thought too pregnant before, shall be now look'd upon as greatest Benefactor to Englishmen, that must acknowledge all the felicity of witt and words to this Derivation.[40]

Not coincidentally, I think, this edition provides the most explicit recognition of women as an important part of dramatic readership. Even though the "Stationer to the Readers" begins "Gentlemen," when it explains that the book includes no formerly printed plays, it offers the rationale that "it would have rendred the Booke so Voluminous, that Ladies and Gentlewomen would have found it scarce manageable, who in Workes of this nature must first be remembred" (A4). This indicates not just that women read plays but that they may have been the drama's most important readers. Addressing itself to "gentlemen" at the same time that the Beaumont and Fletcher volume's publisher so readily recognizes women among the book's readers argues that women, while absent from so many other preliminaries, may still have been thought a significant part of the reading audience. One reason why epistles neglect to mention female readers is suggested in the next sentence of the Beaumont and Fletcher text. Immediately after mentioning the ladies and gentlewomen, the play's publisher, Humphrey Moseley remarks, "Besides, I considered those former Pieces had been so long printed and re-printed, that many Gentlemen were already furnished; and I would have none say, they pay twice for the same Booke" (A4). While women may have read plays, men, this indicates, bought the books.[41]

Identifying readers as consumers, although present in the epistle to Beaumont and Fletcher's plays, is less prevalent and of less significance for envisioning the Renaissance play-reader than it might at first appear. The weight given to this association derives from the dominant role the 1623 Shakespeare folio's "To the great Variety of Readers" has played in figuring dramatic readers and stationers alike as financially motivated:

> From the most able, to him that can but spell: There you are number'd. We had rather you were weighd. Especially, when the fate of all Bookes depends vpon your capacities: and not of your heads alone but your purses. Well! It is now publique, & you will stand for your priuiledges wee know: to read, and censure. Do so, but buy first. That doth best commend a Booke, the Stationer saies.[42]

Certainly a brash statement of mercantile interests, this characterization of readers as buyers is the exception rather than the rule. Admittedly, the publisher of Beaumont and Fletcher's plays does remind his reader, "Heretofore when gentlemen desired but a Copy of any of these Playes, the meanest piece here (if any may be called Meane where every one is Best) cost them more then foure times the price you pay for the whole volume" (A3). Richard Brome's publisher, however, subtly couches his interest in remuneration in a compliment to his readers:

> There are published already of his Playes, the Northern Lass, the Antipodes, the Sparagus-garden, the Merry Beggers, the Lancashire Witches, beside the 5 Playes lately published in a Volume. The good acceptance of all which encourages me to publish this, being no way inferiour to the rest. . . . Your kinde entertainment of this will enable me to make known to the World divers more of the same Authors works of this kind, which have not yet seen light; for my ayme is . . . by delighting thee to profit my self.[43]

Other than these examples, very few prefaces even mention the reader's finances—or the publisher's.

Of far greater stated importance to dramatic publishers than financial gain was the desire to perpetuate the fame and immortality of the playwrights whose works they published. We have already seen how the publisher of *Troilus and Cressida* relied on his reader to ensure Shakespeare's legacy. Perpetuating their authors' fame especially concerned publishers during the time the theaters were closed, and doing so, as the preliminaries to the editions of Beaumont and Fletcher and Richard Brome make clear, depended on the reader. The readers of Beaumont and Fletcher's *Comedies and Tragedies* are told that the book, "the greatest Monument of the Scene that Time and Humanity have produced [,]

. . . must Live, not only the Crowne and sole Reputation of our owne, but the stayne of all other Nations and Languages" (A3). On the page opposite the frontispiece's engraved portrait of Richard Brome in the 1653 edition of *Five New Playes*, a poem to the reader remarks, "Wee thinke Brome dead, hee's drawne so to the life / That by's owne pen's done so ingeniously / That who reads it, must think hee nere shall dy."[44] Prefatory remarks to the 1657 edition of Thomas Middleton's *More Dissemblers besides Women* and *Women Beware Women* express confidence that Middleton's name "would prove as great an Inducement for thee to Read, as me to print them," and calls upon the reader "to continue the Author in his deserved Esteem."[45] This interest in immortality, however, does not belong only to collections printed when the theaters were closed. The 1632 edition of Lyly's *Sixe Court Comedies* begins its "To the Reader":

> Reader, I haue (for the loue I beare to Posteritie) dig'd vp the Graue of a Rare and Excellent Poet, whom Queen Elizabeth then heard, Graced, and Rewarded. These Papers of his, lay like dead Lawrels in a Churchyard; But I haue gathered the scattered branches vp, and by a Charme (gotten from Apollo) made them greene againe, and set them vp as Epitaphes to his Memory.[46]

To ensure Lyly's longevity, the printer envisions the reader as the playwright's intimate friend:

> When Old Iohn Lilly, is merry with thee in thy Chamber, Thou shalt say, Few (or None) of our Poets now are such witty Companions: and thanke mee, that brings him to thy Acquaintance. Thine. Ed. Blount

This special relationship envisioned between readers and the playwrights whose reputations depend for a time on the act of reading may be seen as registering a change in the status of the printed play and its author as well. Starting in the 1620s, if we can accept the witness of prefatory materials, plays begin to be regarded by their publishers as literary texts, and playwrights become celebrated in some of the same ways as other authors.

Before we consider the specific nature of these changes, it will be useful to look generally at the character and frequency of epistles to readers. Only 22 percent (54) of the 248 editions of the Huntington Library's printed plays that I examined contained addresses to the readers. I examined multiple editions of plays that are generally regarded as being the product of the most important sixteenth- and early-seventeenth-century playwrights or their collaborations (Beaumont and Fletcher, Brome, Chapman, Dekker, Heywood, Jonson, Ford, Kyd, Lyly, Marlowe, Marston, Massinger, Middleton, Rowley, Shakespeare, Shirley, and Webster). In addition, I examined editions of the two anonymous plays that Peter Blayney identifies as "best-sellers"—*Mucedorus and Amadine* (1598) and *How a Man May Choose a Good Wife* (1602). Apparently, the popularity of a play had absolutely nothing to do with whether or not it had an epistle to the reader. Of the eleven plays Blayney lists as best-sellers (*Mucedorus, Dr. Faustus, The Spanish Tragedy, Henry IV, Part 1, Richard III, Richard II, If You Know Not Me* [Heywood], *Philotas* [Daniel], *How a Man May Choose a Good Wife* [anonymous], *Philaster,* and *Brennoralt*), only the last one recognizes the reader at all. (*Mucedorus,* however, raises the curious possibility that readers are also expected to perform the play by heading up the list of dramatis personae with "Eight persons may easily play it," which becomes "ten" in subsequent editions.)[47]

Although a few exceptions do exist, outside of those by Heywood, plays printed in the sixteenth century rarely have any prefatory materials, let alone addresses to the reader. When reprinted in the seventeenth century, however, some of these plays acquire preliminaries. The 1622 edition of Shakespeare's *Othello* offers some explanation for this in "The Stationer to the Reader":

> To set forth a booke without an Epistle, were like to the old English prouerbe, A blew coat without a badge, & the Author being dead, I thought good to take that piece of works vpon mee: To commend it, I will not, for that which is good, I hope euery man will commend, without intreaty: and I am the bolder, because the Authors name is sufficient to vent his worke. Thus leauing euery one to the liberty of iudgement: I haue ventured to print this play, and leaue it to the generall-censure. Yours, Thomas Walkley[48]

Almoners traditionally wore blue coats and a badge that bore their license to beg, so in a sense, Walkley is suggesting that a book's epistle is its license to appeal for favor—certainly the strategy many epistles to readers employed. Between 1600 and 1625, epistles to readers became increasingly more conventional for printed plays. Marston's plays employ the convention; so do Dekker's. Ben Jonson turned the epistles to his readers into apologies for his critical theories, and Thomas Middleton had great fun with the convention, producing fictions as humorous as Jonson's were serious. In *The World Tost at Tennis,* the epistle from

"Simplicitie"—"to the well-wishing, well-reading vnderstander, well-vnderstanding Reader"—presents itself in response, it claims, to the printer's request to "satisfie his perusers how hee hath behaud himselfe." Simplicitie's answer is that "he was begot in Braine-ford, borne on the Bankeside of Hellicon, brought up amongst Noble, Gentle, Commons, and good Schollers of all sorts."[49] Furthermore, "he was neuer accus'd of scurrilous or obsceane language" (A4), even though Middleton's satires had been burned by the bishop of London in 1599.[50] The epistle to Middleton and Dekker's *The Roaring Girl* (1611) bids "To the Comicke, Play-readers, Venery and Laughter" and promises them "light-colour Summer stuffe . . . good to keepe you in an afternoon from dice, at home in your chambers."[51]

Addresses to readers appear to have become less the fashion in the 1630s, although some plays certainly continued the convention. Plays printed in the 1630s are more likely to have some form of a dedication instead. The epistle dedicatory to the 1633 edition of Marlowe's *Jew of Malta*, addressed to Thomas Hammon of Grayes Inne, remarks on the convention:

> So now being newly brought to the Presse, I was loath it should be published without the ornament of an Epistle; making choice of you vnto whom to deuote it; then whom . . . there is none more able to taxe Ignorance, or attribute right of merit.[52]

In its appeal for judgment, this dedicatory epistle functions in much the same way as epistles to readers. Some plays, of course, had been dedicated to particular patrons before this, but the major shift that takes place in the 1630s is the appearance of printed plays with a proliferation of dedicatory poems, probably following the practice associated with the Jonson and Shakespeare folios. The first single play that shows this practice is the 1623 edition of Webster's *Duchess of Malfi,* which contains dedicatory poems by Middleton, Rowley, and Ford.[53] The 1630 editions of plays by Ben Jonson, Richard Brome, John Ford, Philip Massinger, and James Shirley all contain several dedicatory and commemorative poems, most of which, though they may attest to the growing respectability of printed drama, thoroughly ignore the reader.[54] Readers only recover their importance after the closing of the theaters in 1642, when they become the sole public dramatic audience possible.[55]

What, then, may we conclude about the quirky few who read plays from the modest presence of epistles addressed to them? The readers we discover in the playwrights' and printers' epistles differ little from those readers Annabel Patterson and Kevin Sharpe have found reading "serious" literature: they are envisioned as intelligent and discerning, possessed of indifferent judgment, and free. Readers, as co-creators of the literary dramatic text, possessed the capacity to assure the fame of playwrights, and to ensure their perpetuity. They were also a various lot—but not so various as Heminge and Condell would have it. Often they were seen as well-educated gentlemen, occasionally as guild members, women, and men about town. They read plays as pastimes, as a pleasurable activity, but also they read for edification. For the playwrights and printers who thought of readers at all (and not all of them did), the reader of plays was someone to be delighted and taught—like the readers of any other English Renaissance literature.

## NOTES

1. William W. E. Slights, *Ben Jonson and the Art of Secrecy* (Toronto: University of Toronto Press, 1994), 6.

2. See David L. Gants, "The Printing, Proofing, and Press-Correction of Ben Jonson's Folio *Workes*," in *Re-presenting Ben Jonson: Text, History, Performance*, ed. Martin Butler (New York: St. Martin's Press, 1999), 39–58.

3. This has been especially true for the dramatic works of Shakespeare. For an excellent account of the history of the literary texts of Shakespeare's plays, see Andrew Murphy, *Shakespeare in Print: A History and Chronology of Shakespeare Publishing* (Cambridge: Cambridge University Press, 2003).

4. David Scott Kastan, *Shakespeare and the Book* (Cambridge: Cambridge University Press, 2001), 3.

5. For an analysis of the relationship between the material book and reading practices during the Interregnum, see Marta Straznicky, "Reading the Stage: Margaret Cavendish and Commonwealth Closet Drama," *Criticism* 37 (1995): 355–90. Excellent studies of the relationships between print culture and drama include Douglas A. Brooks, *From Playhouse to Printing House: Drama and Authorship in Early Modern England* (Cambridge: Cambridge University Press, 2000); Kastan, *Shakespeare and the Book*; and Joseph Loewenstein, *Jonson and Possessive Authorship* (Cambridge: Cambridge University Press, 2002). Eve Rachele Sanders, *Gender and Literacy on Stage in Early Modern England* (Cambridge: Cambridge University Press, 1998), looks at women reading and the depiction of women reading in drama but does not address reading playtexts.

6. Peter W. M. Blayney, "The Publication of Playbooks," in *A New History of Early English Drama,* ed. John D. Cox and David Scott Kastan (New York: Columbia University Press, 1997), 385–88.

7. Blayney's argument is especially effective in countering the assumptions of the New Bibliography that posited so hot a market for Shakespeare's plays that they were stolen, pirated, and otherwise illegally printed. Farmer and Lesser's article is "The Popularity of Playbooks Revisited," *Shakespeare Quarterly* 56 (2005): 1–32.

8. According to Blayney, "in the two decades before the accession of James I . . . the average number of new plays published each year was 4.8. In the next two decades it was 5.75, and in the last two decades before the theaters closed, exactly 8.0" ("Publication of Playbooks," 385). This article details the costs involved in printing and producing an edition.

9. Thomas Bodley, *The Life of Sr Thomas Bodley* (Oxford: Henrie Hall, 1647), 15.

10. Jonson, "To my Bookseller," in *The Workes of Beniamin Jonson* (London: W[illiam] Stansby, and are to be sould by Rich[ard] Meighen, 1616), 770, ll. 9–10. Heidi Brayman Hackel explains the significance of the barely sufficient skills of readers like these and the anxiety they provoked in Jonson in *Reading Material in Early Modern England: Print, Gender, and Literacy* (Cambridge: Cambridge University Press, 2004).

11. Heidi Brayman Hackel, "'Rowme' of Its Own: Printed Drama in Early Libraries," in Cox and Kastan, *New History of Early English Drama*, 113–30.

12. See Lisa Jardine and Anthony Grafton, "'Studied for Action': How Gabriel Harvey Read His Livy," *Past and Present* 129 (1990): 30–78; William H. Sherman, *John Dee: The Politics of Reading and Writing in the English Renaissance* (Amherst: University of Massachusetts Press, 1995); Eugene R. Kintgen, *Reading in Tudor England* (Pittsburgh: University of Pittsburgh Press, 1996); Kevin Sharpe, *Reading Revolutions: The Politics of Reading in Early Modern England* (New Haven: Yale University Press, 2000); Sasha Roberts, *Reading Shakespeare's Poems in Early Modern England* (London: Palgrave, 2002); Jennifer Andersen and Elizabeth Sauer, eds., *Books and Readers in Early Modern England: Material Studies* (Philadelphia: University of Pennsylvania Press, 2002); and Kevin Sharpe and Stephen Zwicker, eds., *Reading, Society, and Politics in Early Modern England* (Cambridge: Cambridge University Press, 2003).

13. Kevin Sharpe, *Reading Revolutions: The Politics of Reading in Early Modern England* (New Haven: Yale University Press, 2000).

14. Annabel Patterson, *Reading Holinshed's "Chronicles"* (Chicago: University of Chicago Press, 1994), 19.

15. Wendy Wall, *The Imprint of Gender: Authorship and Publication in the English Renaissance* (Ithaca: Cornell University Press, 1993), 176.

16. Ibid., 179.

17. Heidi Brayman Hackel discusses the relationship between prefatory materials and readers in the third chapter of *Reading Material.* Hackel contends that rather than being descriptive of their readers, prefatory materials sought to shape readers' responses to the texts. She maintains that in initial addresses, "discreet," "Christian," and "Learned" work interchangeably with "courteous," "friendly," and "docile" to fashion the "gentle" reader.

18. William Shakespeare, *The Famous Historie of Troylus and Cresseid* (London: G[eorge] Eld for R[ichard] Bonian and H[enry] Walley, 1609); Ben Jonson, *Catiline his conspiracy* (London: [William Stansby] for Walter Burre, 1611); Jonson, *Sejanus his fall* (London: G[eorge] E[ld] for Thomas Thorpe, 1605).

19. For a discussion of Jonson's relationship to his readers and the dramatic strategies this engendered, see Slights, *Ben Jonson*, esp. 6–12.

20. Wall, *Imprint of Gender*, 173, 176.

21. Ibid., 179

22. Brooks, *From Playhouse to Printing House*, 189.

23. Thomas Heywood, *The fair maid of the west* (London: [Miles Flesher] for Richard Royston, 1631), A4.

24. Thomas Heywood, *The English traveller* (London: Robert Raworth, 1633), A3.

25. Thomas Heywood, *The brazen age* (London: Nicholas Okes, 1613), A2.

26. John Lyly, *Endimion, the man in the moone* (London: J. Charlewood, for the widdowe Broome, 1591), A2.

27. Thomas Heywood, *The five prentises of London* (London: N. Okes, 1632), A2.

28. Victoria Kahn, *Rhetoric, Prudence, and Skepticism in the Renaissance* (Ithaca: Cornell University Press, 1985).

29. Sharpe, *Reading Revolutions,* 10.

30. Christopher Marlowe, *Tamburlaine the Great* (London: Richard Jhones, 1590), A2; *Tamburlaine the great* (London: Richard Johnes, 1597), A2.

31. John Marston, *The wonder of women or The tragedie of Sophonisba* (London: John Windet, and are to be sold by [W. Cotton], 1606), A2.

32. John Fletcher, *Philaster, or love lies a bleeding* (London: W[illiam] J[ones] for Richard Hawkins, 1634), A2v.

33. John Webster, *The white divel* (London: N[icholas] O[kes] for Thomas Archer, 1612), A2v; *The devils law-case* (London: A[ugustine] M[athewes] for John Grismand, 1623), A2v.

34. John Marston, *The malcontent* (London: V[alentine] S[immes] for William Aspley, 1604), A3v.

35. Jonson, *Catiline,* A3.

36. Ben Jonson, *Ben: Jonson his Volpone or The foxe* (London: [George Eld] for Thomas Thorpe, 1607), A1v.

37. Thomas Dekker, *The shomakers holiday* (London: Valentine Sims, 1600), A3.

38. Thomas Heywood, *A pleasant comedy, called A mayden-head well lost* (London: Nicholas Okes for John Jackson and Francis Church, 1634), A3.

39. Richard Brome, *The royall exchange* (London: for Henry Brome, 1661), A2.

40. *Comedies and Tragedies Written by Francis Beavmont and John Fletcher Gentlemen* (London: for Humphrey Robinson and Humphrey Moseley, 1647), A2–A2v; subsequently cited in the text.

41. For a further discussion of the Moseley preface as it pertains to women play-readers, see chapter 3.

42. *Mr. William Shakespeares comedies, histories, & tragedies* (London: Isaac Jaggard and Ed. Blount [at the charges of W. Jaggard, Ed. Blount, J. Smithweeke, and W. Aspley], 1623), A3.

43. Richard Brome, *Five new playes* (London: [Thomas Roycroft] for Humphrey Moseley, Richard Marriot, and Thomas Dring, 1653), A2.

44. Ibid., no signature.

45. Thomas Middleton, *Two new playes. Viz. More dissemblers besides women. Women beware women* (London: for Humphrey Moseley, 1657), A3, A3v.

46. John Lyly, *Sixe court comedies* (London: William Stansby for Edward Blount, 1632), A5.

47. *A most pleasant comedie of Mucedorus . . .* (London: for William Jones, 1598), A2v.

48. William Shakespeare, *The tragoedy of Othello, the Moore of Venice* (London: N[icholas] O[kes] for Thomas Walkley, 1622), A2.

49. Thomas Middleton, *A courtly masque: the devise called the world tost at tennis* (London: George Purslowe, and are to be sold by Edward Wright, 1620), A4.

50. For the circumstances surrounding this event, see Cyndia Susan Clegg, *Press Censorship in Elizabethan England* (Cambridge: Cambridge University Press, 2000), chap. 9.

51. Thomas Middleton and Thomas Dekker, *The Roaring Girle* (London: [Nicholas Okes] for Thomas Archer, 1611), A3.

52. Christopher Marlowe, *The famous tragedy of the rich Jew of Malta* (London: J[ohn] B[eale] for Nicholas Vavasour, 1633), A3r–v.

53. John Webster, *The tragedy of the Dutchesse of Malfy* (London: Nicholas Okes for John Waterson, 1623).

54. According to Blayney, "only five of the playbooks first printed in 1583–1602 contained dedications (5 percent). In 1603–1622 the number rose to twenty-two (19 percent), and in 1623–1642, after the Jonson and Shakespeare collections had helped to increase the respectability of printed plays, it soared to seventy-eight (58 percent)" ("Publication of Playbooks," 395).

55. See Straznicky, "Reading the Stage."

TWO

# Reading Printed Comedy: Edward Sharpham's *The Fleer*

LUCY MUNRO

> Onely one thing afflicts mee, to thinke that Scenes invented, meerely to be spoken, should be inforcively published to be read.
>
> John Marston, *The Malcontent* (1604)

My focus in this essay is on early-seventeenth-century readers of Edward Sharpham's *The Fleer*, a comedy first performed by the Children of the Revels at the Blackfriars theater around 1606, and printed in 1607, 1610, 1615 and 1631.[1] I look closely here at three documents that present readers or reading contexts for this play. The first is a manuscript inventory of playbooks owned by Sir John Harington, compiled around 1609 (BL Add. MS 27632), in which plays are listed by the volumes within which they were bound.[2] The second is a jest-book, *Conceits, Clinches, Flashes, and Whimzies* (1639), compiled by the poet and dramatist Robert Chamberlain, in which ten of the play's jokes are reworked. The third is a copy of the first edition of *The Fleer* (British Library 11773 c. 8), in which a seventeenth-century hand has made extensive cuts and revisions, excising around one-third of the play and several characters. The revision was carried out after Sharpham's premature death in 1608, but before the outbreak of war in 1642; it is usually dated to the 1620s or 1630s.[3] It has generally been studied as an example of theatrical revision: John Kerrigan treats it as a "non-authorial" revision, comparing it with the extant texts of Shakespeare's *King Lear*; Clifford Leech views it as the adaptation of a play for a specific performance. In what follows, however, I view the revision as one reader's response to the play and compare the reviser's attitude toward the text with that of the hypothetical reader of Harington's bound volume of plays or the compiler of *Conceits, Clinches, Flashes, and Whimzies*.

The presentation of plays as reading material posed problems for those who marketed and disseminated printed books. David Scott Kastan is probably right to argue, summing up the problems associated with an assumed relationship between text and performance, that "neither one is the effect of the other; neither reproduces, or draws upon (except rhetorically) the other's claim to authenticity. The printed play is neither a pre-theatrical text nor a post-theatrical one; it is a *non*-theatrical text."[4] The printed play is generally, however, a post-theatrical *event*, and a "rhetorical" claim to theatrical authority, presented on a title page or in a preface, may have a greater impact than Kastan implies. In printed editions of *The Fleer*, the publisher provides the reader with paratextual material aimed at presenting Sharpham's work as both a post-theatrical and a non-theatrical text. This material provides a reader of the play with a range of interpretive models, and surviving evidence suggests that readers absorbed these variant modes of reading, approaching the play in markedly different ways. The fact that contemporaneous or nearly contemporaneous readers might arrive at different conclusions concerning a text's interpretation is crucial: as Roger Chartier reminds us, "all who can read texts do not read them in the same fashion."[5] Before we look at individual readers of *The Fleer*, however, it is necessary to examine the ways in which comedy could be presented to a print audience, and to investigate in greater detail the interpretive perimeters offered to readers of the printed play.

## Reading Printed Comedy

In his poem "Against Fruition [2]" John Suckling writes:

> Women enjoy'd (where e're before t'have been)
> Are like Romances read, or sights once seen:
> Fruition's dull, and spoils the Play much more
> Than if one read or knew the plot before.[6]

The anonymous author of the preface to *The Family of Love* (1608) writes, "Plaies in this Citie are like wenches new falne to the trade, onelie desired of your neatest gallants, whiles the'are fresh: when they grow stale they must be vented by Termers and Cuntrie chapmen." In other words, "stale" plays are—like experienced prostitutes—appropriate to spectators of a lower social status; Suckling uses the same erotic trope to suggest that sexual and dramatic "play" are both marred by overfamiliarity. Similar connections between dramatic and erotic performance are drawn in Edmund Waller's "In Answer of Sir John Suckling's Verses":

> Plays and Romances read, and seen, do fall
> In our opinions, yet not seen at all:
> Whom would they please? to an Heroick tale,
> Would you not listen, least it grow stale?[7]

Suckling and Waller agree that reading a play before seeing it detracts from the pleasures of performance, and although Waller also argues that reading a play is better than not seeing it at all, reading is nonetheless characterized as the inferior experience.

Elsewhere, however, plays are identified as reading material in their own right rather than theatrical offshoots. In Harington's library, the surviving list indicates, ephemeral quarto texts were bound together in more substantial volumes. In other libraries, plays were grouped with literary or sub-literary texts: Scipio Le Squyer's catalogue, drawn up in 1632, includes playtexts—*Romeo and Juliet, A Game at Chess, Volpone, The Faithful Shepherdess,* and *The Spanish Tragedy*—in a category called "Poesy," which encompasses all kinds of classical and modern literary works.[8] Collected volumes such as Samuel Daniel's *Works* (1601) and Ben Jonson's *Workes* (1616) also arguably obviate the differences between drama and other literary genres, since both volumes contain plays and non-dramatic poetry. They therefore contribute to the naturalizing of printed plays within seventeenth-century libraries, encouraging readers such as Le Squyer to group plays with other literary genres.

As Waller and Suckling suggest, however, the status of plays as reading material was fragile. The situation is possibly even more complex when the play in print is a comedy; with its dependence on visual and verbal jokes, comedy might be an incongruous target for publishers. In prefatory material attached to *Parasitaster, or The Fawn*, John Marston instructs us, "Comedies are writ to be spoken, not read: Remember the life of these things consists in action." He has nonetheless seen his play to the publisher, and expects it to be read, telling the reader, "If any wonder why I print a Comedie, whose life rests much in the Actors voice Let such know, that it cannot auoide publishing: let it therefore stand with good excuse, that I haue been my owne setter out."[9] Although comedies may make for poor reading, they are, paradoxically, in demand on the booksellers' stalls. In light of this contradiction, how were comedies to be approached by readers?

Edward Sharpham's dedication to Robert Hayman in his second extant comedy, *Cupid's Whirligig*, demonstrates one possible strategy, emphasizing the printed comedy's capacity to raise a laugh from its reader:

> Heere lies the Childe, who was borne in mirth,
> against the strict rules of all Childe-birth:
> and to be quit, I gaue him to my friend,
> Who laught him to death, and that was his end.[10]

Printed comedy, like staged comedy, induces laughter. To present such laughter in print may, however, be problematic, since, as Henri Bergson argues, mirth is usually a social act: "Laughter appears to stand in need of an echo."[11] Laughter demands company and shared experience, something that cannot be assumed in the kind of solitary reading implied by the presence of marginalia in printed books. Reading out loud would be a different matter, and it is possible that this was considered an equally valid mode of reading. In one of the prefaces to her collected *Playes* (1662), Margaret Cavendish writes:

> Scenes must be read as if they were spoke or Acted. Indeed Comedies should be read a Mimick way, and the sound of their Voice must be accorded to the sense of the Scene; and as for Tragedies, or Tragick Scenes, they must not be read in a pueling whining Voice, but a sad serious Voice, as deploring or complaining.[12]

In Cavendish's model, writers and readers are mutually dependent—"there are as few good Readers as good Writers"—and a play should be read as if it were a performance.[13]

Bearing in mind the possibility that comedies were read aloud, we might compare the reading strategies presented in contemporaneous jest-books. Jest-books and printed plays seem to have shared a common audience; both were printed in cheap, ephemeral formats, and they are sometimes found together in early library catalogues. The collections of Edward, second Viscount Conway (1594–1665), and Frances Wolfreston (1607–1677), for instance, included plays and jest-books alongside other popular secular and religious material.[14] Both jest-books and comedies are marketed by publishers in terms of their ability to provoke mirth in readers; both genres are uncomfortably positioned on the border between orality and silence. In *Conceits, Clinches, Flashes, and Whimzies*, Chamberlain asks that the reader be "as merry in the reading as I and some other of my friends were in speaking of them"; the jest-book should be read in the same spirit in which its constituent jests were originally spoken.[15] A similar strategy is evident in Sharpham's dedication to *Cupid's Whirligig*, and it is possible that the jest-book provided a model through which a comedy could overcome its origins and find acceptance in print. If individual jests can thrive in published form, there is no reason why printed comedies, which have the added attractions of structural complexity and sustained narratives, should not succeed.

Other early modern texts suggest, however, that a play's comic reputation may depend on its success in performance. If a play has been unsuccessful in performance, is it better to market it as a non-theatrical piece? A useful comparison can be drawn with the publishers' preface in the first edition of Shakespeare's *Troilus and Cressida*, found only in its second issue, which is noticeably uneasy in its attempts to assert the comic worth of the play despite its apparent lack of stage success. Whereas the first issue asserted the stage provenance of the play, the preface to the second issue opens with the statement, "Eternall reader, you haue heere a new play, neuer stal'd with the Stage, neuer clapper-clawed with the palmes of the vulgar, and yet passing full of the palme comicall."[16] The title page statement that the play was printed "As it was acted by the Kings Maiesties | seruants at the Globe" is replaced in the second issue by a description of part of the play's plot: "Excellently expressing the beginning | of their loues, with the conceited wooing | of Pandarus Prince of Licia."[17] A theatrical claim is transformed into a literary one. The remainder of the preface is similarly poised between performance and print. "The most displeased with Playes," the publishers write, "are pleasd with his Commedies," setting up a distinction between "Playes," which are performed, and "Commedies," which are consumed in print. *Troilus and Cressida* is compared with the best of classical comedy, that is, print comedy: "It deserues such a labour, as well as the best Commedy in Terence and Plautus" (¶2v). Comedy is reconfigured as a classicized literary genre, characterized by "wit" rather than by physical clowning or, indeed, by laughter.

A slightly different relationship between comic reputation and performance can be found in the publication history of Francis Beaumont's *The Knight of the Burning Pestle* (first printed 1613). As Zachary Lesser has described, its first edition is, like *Troilus and Cressida*, marketed as a literary work, the play being described in publisher Walter Burre's dedication as "of the race of Don Quixote."[18] The second edition of 1635, however, was published in the context of successful performances "by

Her Majesties Servants | at the Private house in Drury lane," as its title page states, advertising the play as "Full of Mirth and Delight." In addition, the 1635 edition drops Burre's dedication to Robert Keysar, substituting a more standard address "To the Readers of this Comedy," in which the play is described as "a merry passage, here and there interlaced . . . with delight."[19] The successive editions of *The Knight of the Burning Pestle* therefore suggest that successful comedies could be marketed on the laughter they provoked in performance, while for unsuccessful plays of a doubtful comic status, publishers might resort to literary allusion. Both methods are, however, aimed at providing the play with an identity beyond that of the original stage performance.

## Reading *The Fleer*

The marketing of *The Fleer*, a play that seems to have been successful in the theater, is similar to that of the 1635 edition of *The Knight of the Burning Pestle*. The 1607 title page reads, "*THE* | FLEER. || As it hath beene often played in the | *Blacke-Fryers* by the Children of | the Reuells. || *Written by* Edward Sharpham *of the* | Middle Temple, Gentle- | man," emphasizing both the performance history of the play and the status of its writer.[20] On its first publication, *The Fleer* was prefaced by an address to the reader, probably written by publisher Francis Burton; this preface was retained in Nathaniel Butter's later editions. Like Sharpham in the preface to *Cupid's Whirligig*, Burton emphasizes the printed comedy's capacity to induce laughter:

> The Author is inuisible to me (viz: ith' Country) but whereabouts I cannot learne; yet I feare hee will see mee too soone, for I had of him before his departure an Epistle or Apological præmble (this being his first Minerua) directed vnto you, which should haue bin in this Page diuul'gd, and (not to ieast with you because this booke plaies that part sufficiently) I haue lost it, remembring none of the Contentes. And therfore (kind Readers) I doe presume thus to salute you; vse these Comicall discourses fauourablie and you shall haue some from the Author heereafter more worthie your fauours and affections: through a narrow window you may view a broad Field; so in this modicum you may conceiue his great desire to delight you. (A3r–v)

Representing the author as a novice,[21] Burton pushes the comic worth of the play itself and the promise of better to come. Given that he does not mention the play's success on the stage in the preface itself, its title,

"To the Reader and Hearer," may indicate that Burton, like Cavendish, thinks that comedies should be read aloud.

In his statement that *The Fleer* "comes not like a Mous-trap to inueigle your good opinions" (A3r), the publisher may also be situating the play among his other publications: *The Mous-Trap* was the title of a book of epigrams by Henry Parrott published by Burton in 1606. Searching for ways to sell the play, Burton compares it favorably with one of his own productions and places *The Fleer* in the print culture of St. Paul's Churchyard. The preface engages with the fear articulated in the preface to *The Family of Love*: that once it is divorced from the success of the stage production, a play will become "stale" and of no use to the discerning reader. One way of countering this problem is to supplement the play's theatrical origins and to suggest, either implicitly or explicitly, that it can be associated with other print genres. In the case of *The Fleer*, this genre seems to be that of print humor, such as epigrams and jests. The play is prevented from becoming stale through its capacity to provoke laughter; we might also compare Thomas Middleton's preface to *The Roaring Girl*, which promises the reader "Venery, and Laughter."[22]

Like the publisher of the second edition of *The Knight of the Burning Pestle*, Burton is able to stress both *The Fleer*'s theatrical provenance and its capacity to provoke laughter; in associating the play with popular print genres, he strengthens his case further and suggests a way in which *The Fleer* can outlive its immediate context. The play thus gains rhetorical authority from two disparate locations—theater and print shop—and is simultaneously a post-theatrical and non-theatrical text. Two different interpretive models are therefore provided to readers of *The Fleer*. They are free to focus on the title page's claim to theatrical authority, approaching the play in terms of its dramatic context, but they can easily connect the play with jest-books and print humor. These different modes of reading can be seen, I suggest, in the seventeenth-century reception of Sharpham's comedy.

## *The Fleer* Bound

Having looked at the ways in which the printed *Fleer* is presented to readers by its publisher, I now turn to the first of my documentary contexts for the play's reception. The list of plays belonging to Sir John Harington is intriguing in part because it lists plays by bound volume, demonstrating one way in which early modern drama could be encountered by a reader. Some care has been taken in the ordering of volumes. Two-part plays are bound together, such as the two parts of *Henry IV* in volume 1, and the two parts of "Queen Elis.," presumably Heywood's *I* and *II If You Know Not Me You Know Nobody*, in volume 2 (fol. 43r; Greg, 1311). Most of the volumes are generically mixed, but they often group similar plays together. For instance, volume 3, which includes *The Fleer*, lists comedies followed by tragedies:

retorn from<br>
Scourge of Symony ^.<br>
Blurt m$^{r}$: Constable.<br>
Henry the viij$^{t}$.<br>
humo$^{r}$<br>
Everie man out of his<br>
Fleyre<br>
The fawn.<br>
The Isle of gulls.<br>
Romeo and Iulyet.<br>
Sophonisba.<br>
(fol. 43r; Greg, 1311)

There may also be an occasional effort to keep plays performed by particular companies together, since *The Fleer*, *The Fawn*, and *The Isle of Gulls* were all performed by the Children of the (Queen's) Revels. If so, it has not been systematized, since even in this volume the Queen's Revels' *Sophonisba* is separated from *The Isle of Gulls* by the Chamberlain's Men's/King's Men's *Romeo and Juliet*, which is itself detached from the same company's *Every Man Out of his Humour*. *Blurt Master Constable* and "Henry the viij$^{t}$" (almost certainly Samuel Rowley's *When You See Me You Know Me*, published in 1605) were performed by the Children of Paul's and the Prince's Men, respectively. The plays are not even solely commercial theater productions, since *The Scourge of Simony* (better known as the second part of *The Return from Parnassus*) was performed at Cambridge University.

It is tempting to think that the grouping of *The Fleer* with *The Fawn* is deliberate, since Sharpham's play is closely related to Marston's. *The Fawn* was first performed by the Children of the Queen's Revels, probably during 1604, but seems to have been taken to the Children of Paul's: it was published in 1606 with the title page assertion, "AS | IT | HATH BEEN DIVERS TIMES PRE- | sented at the blacke Friars, by the Children of the | *Queenes Maiesties Reuels, and since at Powles.*" *The Fleer* seems to have been designed to fill the gap in the Queen's Revels repertory left by *The Fawn*, since it is clearly a response to the earlier work. Whereas Marston's play features a duke who disguises himself as a character called Fawn—the embodiment of courtly flattery—Sharpham's features a duke who disguises himself as a character called Fleer, the embodiment of fleering, or jeering, plain speech. Fawn leaves his dukedom to spy on his son Tiberio, trying to regulate the latter's lack of passion and steer him into an advantageous marriage. Fleer has been deposed from his dukedom, and spies on his daughters, Florida and Felecia, who are working as prostitutes in London; he acts as their pander but eventually regulates their excess of passion and steers them into advantageous marriages.[23]

The grouping of *The Fleer* with *The Fawn* in Harington's bound volume thus highlights the political valences of Sharpham's play and the importance of its disguised-ruler narrative. In addition, the reader approaches *The Fleer* in something analogous to its original performance context in the Jacobean repertory system.[24] Like a playgoer, the reader has access to a cross-section of plays performed by a variety of companies in a variety of venues, some of them new and others recently revived. He or she also has access to a neat subset of Queen's Revels plays in which issues of rule are debated, since *The Isle of Gulls* is a scandalous piece of political satire closely based on Sidney's *Arcadia*, featuring a king who absents himself from his realm and withdraws to the titular island. The interpretation of *The Fleer* available to readers of Harington's volume might therefore, in its appeal to the contexts of the Queen's Revels company and the wider theatrical milieu, be more closely aligned with the implications of the play's printed title page than its prefatory material.

## *The Fleer* in Jest

The potential reading of the play in terms of its repertory context and political narrative is contradicted by another seventeenth-century reading of the play. In 1639, ten jokes from *The Fleer* were appropriated in Robert Chamberlain's jest-book *Conceits, Clinches, Flashes, and Whimzies* (see fig. 2-1).[25] Stripping them from the narrative structure of the play, the jest-book reduces jokes to their bare constituent parts:

> One said the midwives trade of all trades was most commendable, because they lived not by the hurts of other men, as Surgeons do; nor by the falling out of friends as Lawyers do: but by the agreement betwixt party and party. (B3v)

*Conceits Clinches*

14

One aſked why a Knight tooke place of a Gentleman, it was anſwered becauſe they were Knights now a days before they were Gentlemen.

15

One ſaid the midwives trade of all trades was moſt commendable, becauſe they lived not by the hurts of other men, as Surgeons do; nor by the falling out of friends as Lawyers do: but by the agreement betwixt party and party.

One

*Flaſhes and Whimzies.*

16

One ſaid a good Client was like a ſtudy gown, that ſits in the cold himſelfe to keepe his Lawyer warme.

17

One ſaid the fees of a pander and a punie clarke are much alike, for the pander had but two pence next morning for making the bed and that was a penny a ſheet.

18

A woman was commending a boyes face, piſh quoth another give me a mans face, a

B 4 boyes

FIG. 2-1. Robert Chamberlain, *Conceits, Clinches, Flashes, and Whimzies, Newly Studied, With Some Collections but Those Never Published Before in This Kinde* (London, 1639), B3v–4r. By permission of the British Library.

The jest is a comparison of three comic "types": the midwife, the surgeon, and the lawyer. In the play, however, it appears as part of a comic set piece in which the foolish, tobacco-addicted gallant Petoune asks for advice about how to woo the elderly Fromaga, waiting gentlewoman to Florida and Felecia:

> *Ruff.* Thou shalt commend his loue to Mada[m] *Fromaga.*
> *Fl.* His loue to her? what Signior, in loue with my Ladies Antient?
> *Sp.* Why her Ancient?
> *Fl.* Because shee carries her colours for her, but tis in a box: but signior you shall haue a good match on't, though she be not rich, yet shee's an ancient woman and is able to get her liuing, by midwiferie, and I can tell yee tis not the worst trade going, considering how young and olde,

> and all doe their good wils to set them a worke: and tis a good hearing, better they gette then the Lawyers, for your mid-wiues liue by the agreement betweene partie and partie, & the falling in of louers, but the Lawyers liue by the falling out of friendes. (F3r–v)

In *The Fleer*, the joke takes some of its force from the audience's familiarity with Fromaga and the comic absurdity of Petoune's wooing her: the joke has a subject. The jest-book cannot create this specificity of character and situation within its own generic constraints, and adds instead a second point of comparison for the generalized "midwife"; it also restructures the joke's punch line so as to make the jest shorter and more snappy.

This modulation of effect is clear in some of the other appropriated jokes. The book's eighteenth jest, for instance, reads, "A woman was commending a boyes face, pish quoth another give me a mans face, a boyes face is not worth a haire" (B4v). In *The Fleer*, this joke is situated within a discussion between the sisters Susan and Nan about their suitors. Nan asks Susan whether her lover is handsome, to which Susan replies, "'Tis the person and conditions I respect, and not face, for euery Boy has a good face, and its not worth a hayre" (B4r). Although the jest-book presents the joke as part of a dialogue, it cannot capture one aspect of the joke's impact in performance, which depends in part on the fact that both Susan and Nan are being played by boy actors. Moreover, because the play was performed by a children's company, their suitors were played by boys or young men, all of whom were probably beardless.[26] The jest-book generally avoids the play's theatrical in-jokes; it does not, for instance, adopt any of the jokes that depend on Antifront's disguise as Fleer, or those created when Nan and Susan disguise themselves as pages. It also selects jokes that are free of specific political targets, focusing on perennial targets such as women and lawyers; it omits, for instance, the play's jokes about the union of Britain, which were in any case stale by the late 1630s.

D. F. McKenzie has suggested that "readers make new texts and their new meanings are a function of their new forms."[27] In compiling the jest-book, Chamberlain acts in precisely the way McKenzie describes, reworking the play's jests in a different genre and putting his text back into the marketplace for a new set of readers. He also offers an interpretive model rather different from that suggested by the ordering of John Harington's library. Whereas Harington's bound volume of plays provides a cross-section of the early Jacobean theatrical repertory, encouraging a reader to view *The Fleer* in terms of its dramatic and political context, the jest-book offers more generalized social comment and stresses the comedic punch of individual jokes.

## *The Fleer* Revised

McKenzie's formulation is also relevant to my next point of discussion, the revision of *The Fleer*, where the annotator reads the play in a particular way and in marking the printed text physically reshapes it for potential performance in its new form. The most striking feature of the revision of *The Fleer* is that the reviser seems completely unconcerned with the plot involving the disguised ruler. The whole of the first and second scenes is deleted, erasing both the discussion between Antifront and the lord regarding his political exile and disguise, and the debate between Florida and Felecia in which they try to justify their new trade as courtesans resulting from the social fall precipitated by their father's exile. The play instead opens with a scene between a would-be gentleman usher and Fromaga, with Antifront taking the gentleman usher's lines: the reviser writes "begin heare" in the top right-hand corner of the page and crosses out the first speech head ("*Gent.*"), replacing it with "*Ant.*" (B2r). Similarly, the reviser generally substitutes "Antifront" for "Fleer" in speech prefixes and entrance directions on the character's first appearance in a scene and alters dialogue accordingly (e.g., F3r; see fig. 2-2). There is no connection between the "fleering" lines given to Antifront and a malcontent persona. In the revision, Antifront is not a disguised ruler but a cynical servant (perhaps making him more reminiscent of the witty slaves of Plautus and Terence, or even *The Duchess of Malfi*'s Bosola, than his original prototypes, Fawn and Malevole). Having cut the disguised-ruler plot, the adapter seems to have had problems with the play's conclusion, and the revision has not been completely worked out; it seems unlikely that *The Fleer* was ever acted in this form.

The impression given in the redaction is that Antifront is a chameleon figure, able to pose as the slow-thinking butt of Fromaga's wit, a malcontent Italian, a sinister apothecary, or an upstanding judge. The unifying motivation of Sharpham's plot is rejected, replaced by a bewildering succession of roles that display no true "self" and a series of episodic humorous situations that give a more sporadic and localized kind of pleasure to reader or spectator. Unlike the reader of Harington's bound volume, the reviser does not associate *The Fleer* with other disguised-ruler plays.

crossing your armes, and crying aye mee! the onely way to win them, is to care little for am: when they are sad doe yee sing: when they sing and are merrie, then take your time & put am too't: if they will, so: if not, let them snick vp, if you will walke in my Lord, ile shew ye manie principles I learn't of my Mother, they may doe your lordship good.

*Pis.* Go go, I will: but O vnhappie fate,
When youth and weakenes must support our state. *Exeunt.*

*Enter Fleire one way, Sparke, Ruffell and Petoune another way.*

*Sp:* How now *Fleire?*

*Ruff:* Saue you *Fleire.*

*Flei,* Saue ye Gallants: O Signior *Petoune,* shall you and I be friendes agen?

*Sp:* Why are ye enemies?

*Fle,* No great enemies, a quarrell rose betweene vs.

*Pet;* I doe not like such quarrels, a struck mee sir, and I protest and sweare to you sir by this Trinidado, had I not taken the box on my cheeke, a had broke my Pipe.

*Sp:* Why didst not strike him agen?

*Ruff:* O no, his Father's a Iustice.

*Flei,* Nay if the Father be of the peace, I see no reason the Sonne should fight.

*Ruff* What, a Coward Signior? fye, a coward?

*Fl.* A Coward? why thats his onely vertue, for a Coward abuseth no man, but a makes him satisfaction: for if a wrōg all men, a giues al men leaue to beate him, hee's like a whetstone, he sets an edge on another, & yet a wil not cut himselfe.

*Ruff.* Come, come, we must needes haue you friendes, & thou'st doe him some good offices.

*Fl.* Who? I? with all my heart, but what i'st sir? what i'st?

*Ruff.* Thou shalt commend his loue to Madā *Fromaga.*

*Fl:* His loue to her? what Signior, in loue with my Ladies Antient?

*Sp:* Why her Ancient?

*Fl:* Because shee carries her colours for her, but tis in a

F 3 box;

Fig. 2-2. Edward Sharpham, *The Fleer* (London, 1607), F3r. By permission of the British Library.

Instead, the play is read as a collection of jests and funny situations.[28] This reading can be said to be in line with Burton's address "To the Reader," where it is characterized as "a Booke . . . to make you laugh," and with the redactions of individual jokes presented in *Conceits, Clinches, Flashes, and Whimzies*.

It appears that numerous ways of reading *The Fleer* were available to a reader of the early printed editions. One potential reading follows the lead of the play's performance context and its place in the theatrical repertory, as displayed on the printed title page. Another follows the publisher's preface, in which the play's many jests are highlighted. In our documented reading contexts, Harington's catalogue, the closest witness to the play in performance, seems to encourage the former mode of reading in its repertory-like juxtaposition of plays. The jest-book appropriation of the play in 1639 and the reviser's annotations, carried out in the late Jacobean or Caroline period, rather suggest the latter. Over time, as the play becomes "stale," it is divorced from memories of its performance, and the prefatory material, emphasizing the play's comic worth, gains a greater hold over the way in which the play is read. In the revision of *The Fleer*, however, we paradoxically find that a habit of reading encouraged by the printed text is at least potentially to be returned to the theater.

In "What Is an Editor?" Stephen Orgel argues, "If the play is a book, it's not a play."[29] As a warning against our making too easy associations between text and performance, the distinction is worth making. But if we look to the evidence of reading, it may be that as far as the readers of *The Fleer* were concerned, the playbook was sometimes a play, sometimes a book. The two categories—book and play—are extremely difficult to untangle. The printed play is treated sometimes as a non-theatrical text, aligned with the non-dramatic jest-book; but it is also, sometimes simultaneously, treated as a post-theatrical text, that is, a text which claims rhetorical authority from the success of the play in performance. The various strategies taken by Burton within the same printed edition of *The Fleer*, and those taken by the publishers of *Troilus and Cressida* and *The Knight of the Burning Pestle,* are witness to this conceptual puzzle.

It seems, therefore, that different readers could approach printed comedy in a variety of ways, depending on the contexts in which they found the play and the uses to which they intended to put it. In looking at a set of historical reading contexts for *The Fleer,* we find that the meaning of the play can indeed change along with its readers, as McKenzie suggests. We also find that readers appear in some cases to be directed by the extra-dramatic material presented in title pages and prefaces. I am not suggesting that we should add yet another category to the already crowded library of reader-response theory: the "guided reader," perhaps. We should, however, pay increased attention to the contexts in which reading takes place; we should listen to the "rhetorical" claim to authority of the printed play, whether this claim is literary, sub-literary, or theatrical in nature.

# APPENDIX

Passages from *The Fleer* (1607) adapted in *Conceits, Clinches, Flashes, and Whimzies* (1639)

| *The Fleer* | *Conceits, Clinches, Flashes, and Whimzies* |
|---|---|
| *Kni.* I care not if I goe and visite her, and carrie her a Woodcocke.<br>*Fle.* You'le goe alone sir.<br>*Kni.* I, I meane so, but how should I carrie him *Fleir?*<br>*Fle.* Vnder your Cloke sir, vnder your Cloke. (F1r) | 13<br>One asked another why hee loved woodcoke so extreamly, the other answered why not I as well as you, for I am sure you never go abroad but you carry one under your cloake. (B3r) |
| *Kni.* Why sir, I hope I am a Knight, and Knights are before Gentlemen.<br>*Fle.* What Knights before Gentlemen, say ye?<br>*Kni.* Faith I.<br>*Fle*: Thats strange, they were wont to bee Gentlemen fore they were knighted. (F2r) | 14<br>One asked why a Knight tooke place of a Gentleman, it was answered because they were Knights now a days before they were Gentlemen. (B3v) |
| *Fl.* Shee's an ancient woman, and is able to get her liuing, by midwiferie, and I can tell yee tis not the worst trade going, considering how young and olde, and all doe their good wils to set them a worke: and tis a good hearing, better they gette then the Laywers, for your mid-wiues liue by the agreement betweene partie and partie, & the falling in of louers, but the Lawyers liue by the falling out of friendes. (F3v) | 15<br>One said the midwives trade of all trades was most commendable, because they lived not by the hurts of other men, as Surgeons do; nor by the falling out of friends as Lawyers do: but by the agreement betwixt party and party. (B3v) |
| *Fl.* Why your good Client is but like your studdie gowne, sits in the colde himselfe, to keep the Lawyer warme. (F3v-F4r) | 16<br>One said a good Client was like a study gown, that sits in the cold himselfe to keepe his Lawyer warme. (B4r) |

| *The Fleer* | *Conceits, Clinches, Flashes, and Whimzies* |
|---|---|
| *Fl*. Faith my fee's are like a puny Clarkes, a penny a sheete.<br>*Sp*. How a peny a sheete?<br>*Fle*. Why, if any lie with them a whole night, I make the bed ith' morning, and for that I haue two pence, and that's a peny a sheete. (F4r) | 17<br>One said the fees of a pander and a punie clarke are much alike, for the pander had but two pence next morning for making the bed and that was a penny a sheet. (B4r) |
| *Su*. Tis the person and conditions I respect, and not face, for euery Boy has a good face, and its not worth a hayre. (B4r) | 18<br>A woman was commending a boyes face, pish quoth another give me a mans face, a boyes face is not worth a haire. (B4r-v) |
| *Fle*. Your swaggerer is but like your walking spur, a gingles much, but heele neu'r pricke. (C3r) | 19<br>One compar'd a dominering fellow to a walking Spurre, that keeps a great jingling noise but never pricks. (B4v) |
| *Fle*. Your new made Gallants lay all on the backe and spend all ath belly. (C4v) | 26<br>Those that say gallants put all upon their backs abuse them, for they spend a great deale more upon their bellies. (B5v) |
| *Piso*. Pheu, but I cannot requite it.<br>*Fle*. Why my good Lord?<br>*Piso*. Shees a common thing.<br>*Fle*. But say she may turne my Lord.<br>*Piso*. Shee has beene so much worne, shees not worth the turning now. (E1r) | 28<br>One perswaded another to marry a whore because shee was rich, telling him that perhaps she might turne, turne said the other she hath been so much worne that she is past turning. (B6r) |
| *Fel*. Whats the reason *Fleir*, the Cittizens wiues weare all Corks in their shooes?<br>*Fle*. O Madam, to keepe the custome of the Cittie, onely to bee light heeld. (D1v) | 246<br>One asked what the reason was that some women were so light-heel'd now adayes? it was answered because they did wear corke-heeled shooes. (F3v) |

## NOTES

1. Edward Sharpham, *The Fleire* (London: [Edward Allde] for F[rancis] B[urton], 1607), subsequently cited in the text; *The Fleire* (London: [Thomas Purfoot] for Nathaniel Butter, 1610); *The Fleire* (London: [Thomas Snodham] for Nathaniel Butter, 1615); *The Fleire* (London: B[ernard] A[lsop] and T[homas] F[awcet] for Nathaniel Butter, 1631). The right of the company to call itself the Children of the Queen's Revels seems to have been revoked after a political row caused by the performance of John Day's *The Isle of Gulls* in February 1606. On the title pages of the printed editions of *The Isle of Gulls* (1606), *The Fleer* (1607), and *Law Tricks* (1608), they are described as the Children of the Revels.

2. For a transcription, used throughout this chapter, see W. W. Greg, *A Bibliography of the English Printed Drama to the Restoration*, 4 vols. (London: Bibliographical Society, 1939–59), 3:1306–13. For context, see Jason Scott-Warren, *Sir John Harington and the Book as Gift* (Oxford: Oxford University Press, 2001), esp. 177–235.

3. In "Revision, Adaptation, and the Fool in *King Lear*," in *The Division of the Kingdoms: Shakespeare's Two Versions of King Lear*, ed. Gary Taylor and Michael Warren (Oxford: Clarendon Press, 1983), 191–245, John Kerrigan argues that the reviser's use of secretary hand (on C3v) and the excision of jokes about the union of Britain suggest that the revision dates "from the later Jacobean or early Caroline period" (245). See also Clifford Leech, "The Plays of Edward Sharpham: Alterations Accomplished and Projected," *Review of English Studies* 11 (1935): 69–74. Sharpham's *Cupid's Whirligig* was performed by apprentices at Oxford on December 26, 1631, and it has been suggested that the revision of *The Fleer* may be connected with this performance. See F. S. Boas, "Crosfield's Diary and the Caroline Stage," *Fortnightly Review* 123 (1925): 514–22; C. G. Petter, ed., *A Critical Old-Spelling Edition of the Works of Edward Sharpham* (New York: Garland, 1986), 213–14, 385; Kerrigan, "Revision," 198. For more recent studies of manuscript annotations in printed plays, see A. H. Tricomi, "Philip, Earl of Pembroke, and the Analogical Way of Reading Political Tragedy," *Journal of English and Germanic Philology* 85 (1986): 332–45; John Pitcher, "Samuel Daniel and the Authorities," *Medieval and Renaissance Drama in England* 10 (1998): 113–48; Tricomi, "Counting Insatiate Countesses: The Seventeenth-Century Annotations to Marston's *The Insatiate Countess*," *Huntington Library Quarterly* 64 (2002): 107–22.

4. David Scott Kastan, *Shakespeare and the Book* (Cambridge: Cambridge University Press, 2001), 8.

5. Rogert Chartier, *The Order of Books: Readers, Authors, and Libraries in Europe between the Fourteenth and Eighteenth Centuries*, trans. Lydia G. Cochrane (Stanford: Stanford University Press, 1994), 4.

6. In *Fragmenta Aurea: A Collection of all the Incomparable Peices Written By Sir John Suckling* (London: [Ruth Raworth and Thomas Walkley] for Humphrey Moseley, 1646), B2v. In *Poems Written by Mr. Ed. Waller* (London: T. W. for Humphrey Moseley, 1645), G4r, "Scenes" is substituted for "sights," strengthening the poem's critique of dramatic satiety.

7. *Poems*, G4v.

8. F. Taylor, "The Books and Manuscripts of Scipio Le Squyer, Deputy Chamberlain of the Exchequer (1620–59)," *Bulletin of the John Rylands Library* 25 (1941): 156–58, citing John Rylands Library Lat. MS 319, f. 106. Le Squyer also owned copies of *Pericles* (Yale Library copy) and *The Fleer* (Huntington Library copy), but must have lent them or given them away before the catalogue was drawn up. For *Pericles*, see T. A. Birrell, "Reading as Pastime: The Place of Light Literature in Some Gentlemen's

Libraries of the Seventeenth Century," in *Property of a Gentleman: The Formation, Organisation, and Dispersal of the Private Library, 1620–1920*, ed. Robin Myers and Michael Harris (Winchester: St. Paul's Bibliographies, 1991), 119–20. The title page of *The Fleer* with Le Squyer's signature is reproduced in Petter, *Works of Edward Sharpham*, 227. On playbooks in early modern libraries, see Heidi Brayman Hackel, "'Rowme' of Its Own: Printed Drama in Early Libraries," in *A New History of Early English Drama*, ed. John D. Cox and David Scott Kastan (New York: Columbia University Press, 1997), 113–30.

9. John Marston, *Parasitaster, or The Fawne* (London: Printed by T[homas] P[urfoot] for W[illiam] C[otton], 1606), A2v, A2r.

10. Edward Sharpham, *Cupids Whirligig* (London: Edward Allde for Arthur Johnson, 1607), [A]1r.

11. Henri Bergson, *Laughter: An Essay on the Meaning of the Comic*, trans. Cloudesley Brereton and Fred Rothwell (London: Macmillan, 1913), 5.

12. *Playes Written by the Thrice Noble, Illustrious and Excellent Princess, The Lady Marchioness of Newcastle* (London: A[lice] Warren for John Martyn, James Allestry and Tho[mas] Dicas, 1662), A6v.

13. Ibid., A6v. See Cecile M. Jagodzinski, *Privacy and Print: Reading and Writing in Seventeenth-Century England* (Charlottesville: University Press of Virginia, 1999), 106–8, and chapter 3 by Marta Straznicky in this volume.

14. See Birrell, "Reading as Pastime," 121–25; Paul Morgan, "Frances Wolfreston and 'Hor Bouks': A Seventeenth-Century Woman Book-Collector," *The Library*, ser. 6, 11 (1989): 197–219.

15. Robert Chamberlain, *Conceits, Clinches, Flashes, and Whimzies. Newly Studied, With Some Collections but Those Never Published Before in This Kinde* (London: R[ichard] Hodgkinsonne for Daniel Frere, 1639), A3r–v; subsequently cited in the text.

16. William Shakespeare, *The Famous Historie of Troylus and Cresseid* (London: G[eorge] Eld for R[ichard] Bonian and H[enry] Walley, 1609), ¶2r; subsequently cited in the text.

17. For reproductions of the two title pages, see David Bevington, ed., *Troilus and Cressida* (Walton-on-Thames: Thomas Nelson, 1998), 124–25.

18. *The Knight of the Burning Pestle* (London: [Nicholas Okes] for Walter Burre, 1613), A2v; Zachary Lesser, "Walter Burre's *The Knight of the Burning Pestle*," *English Literary Renaissance* 29 (1999): 22–43; see also Douglas A. Brooks, *From Playhouse to Printing House: Drama and Authorship in Early Modern England* (Cambridge: Cambridge University Press, 2000), 44–65.

19. *The Knight of the Burning Pestle* (London: N[icholas] O[kes] for J[ohn] S[pencer?], 1635), A3r.

20. For a detailed examination of the use of these elements on title pages, see Alan B. Farmer and Zachary Lesser, "Vile Arts: The Marketing of English Printed Drama, 1512–1660," *Research Opportunities in Renaissance Drama* 39 (2000): 77–165.

21. Although *The Fleer* seems to have been his first play, Sharpham may also have written the non-dramatic piece *The Discoverie of the Knights of the Poste* (1597). See Petter, *Works of Edward Sharpham*, 97–122.

22. Thomas Middleton, *The Roaring Girle* (London: [Nicholas Okes] for Thomas Archer, 1611), A3r.

23. The play is also indebted to Marston's earlier play *The Malcontent* (Queen's Revels, 1602–3; King's Men, ca. 1604), in which the deposed duke Altofronto disguises himself as the bad-tempered Malevole. The given name of Sharpham's duke is "Antifront."

24. For a summary of the early modern repertory system, see Roslyn Lander Knutson, "The Repertory," in *A New History of Early English Drama*, ed. John D. Cox and David Scott Kastan (New York: Columbia University Press, 1997), 461–80.

25. See the appendix to this chapter. Petter identified the connection between these two works, but lists only six of the recycled jests (*Works of Edward Sharpham*, 196–97). An eleventh jest may have been inspired by *The Fleer* but changes its punch line. In *The Fleer*, Florida says, "Me thinks they haue a strange fashion heere, they take money with their wiues, and giue money to their wenches," and Fleer replies, "And good reason too (Madam) woulde you haue a man bee troubled with a wife, as long as he liues for nothing? A giues money to his wench, to be as soone rid of her as he has done with her" (D1v). In *Conceits, Clinches, Flashes, and Whimzies* we find: "One said it was a strange fashion that we had in England to receive money with wives and give money for wenches, It was answered that in ancient time women were good and then men gave money for their wives, but now like light gold they would not passe without allowance" (B6r, [no. 27]). The fact that this jest comes between two jokes taken from *The Fleer* suggests that the book's compiler, Robert Chamberlain, found his inspiration in Sharpham's play. The jest-book also takes at least two jokes from another play, George Wilkins's *The Miseries of Enforced Marriage*, and may include other theatrical material.

26. See Will Fisher, "The Renaissance Beard: Masculinity in Early Modern England," *Renaissance Quarterly* 54 (2001): 155–87.

27. D. F. McKenzie, *Bibliography and the Sociology of Texts* (London: British Library, 1986), 20.

28. Petter builds on Alfred Harbage's suggestion that Sharpham's plays were "read as jest books and manuals of sophisticated wit" (*Shakespeare and the Rival Traditions* [New York: Macmillan, 1952], 221) to argue that they were written for the same purpose (*Works of Edward Sharpham*, 196).

29. Stephen Orgel, "What Is an Editor?" *Shakespeare Studies* 24 (1996): 23.

THREE

# Reading through the Body: Women and Printed Drama

MARTA STRAZNICKY

Humphrey Moseley's preface to his edition of Beaumont and Fletcher's plays famously identifies women as a major segment of the market for printed drama:

> Some Playes (you know) written by these Authors were heretofore Printed: I thought not convenient to mixe them with this Volume, which of it selfe is entirely New. And indeed it would have rendred the Booke so Voluminous, that Ladies and Gentlewomen would have found it scarce manageable, who in Workes of this nature must first be remembred.[1]

When Moseley made this claim in 1647 women were, indeed, avid play-readers, although the assertion that their interests have a formative influence on the design of the volume is undercut by the simple fact that the preface is addressed exclusively to "Gentlemen" readers and that they alone are projected as book buyers. The rationale for limiting the contents of the volume to previously unpublished plays seemingly has less to do with women's ability to handle a "Booke so Voluminous" than it has with the need to convince "Gentlemen" customers that the book is good value: "Besides, I considered those former Pieces had been so long printed and re-printed, that many Gentlemen were already furnished; and I would have none say, they pay twice for the same Booke." Although Moseley clearly imagines that women will read the plays, he excludes them here from the kind of commercial transaction that Jean Howard has identified as the catalyst for the empowerment of female play*goers*.[2] Women did, of course, buy printed plays, the evidence for which will be discussed here, but even an astute businessman like Moseley chooses to construct them as book handlers rather than book buyers.

In this Moseley is perfectly consistent with the tendency throughout the early modern period to associate women's reading with the body: plays kiss ladies' hands or sit on their laps; licentious women have playbooks in their bedchambers (Shakespeare reportedly "creepes into the womens closets about bed time"); other playwrights are said to "ease" and "refresh" their female patrons.[3] Interestingly, this embodiment of women play-readers is found not only in anti-feminist or satirical writings but also in texts—such as the Beaumont and Fletcher folio—that are not overtly political or regulatory in design. The work of social correction that Howard links with antitheatrical depictions of the eroticized female spectator is not, therefore, so clearly identifiable where women play-*readers* are concerned. The reason, I will argue, is that early modern printed drama could be made rhetorically *discontinuous* with the commercial theater—in constructions of its impact on social relations, its cultural and material practices, and above all its ambiguous intersection with the "public" sphere—and could therefore generate alternative discourses around theatricality, privacy, and the female body. In certain respects, and most notably where they fail, those alternative discourses rehearse the gender politics that prevented women from writing for and acting on the commercial stage; but in many instances the corporeality of women play-readers legitimizes women's pleasure in drama—as both spectators and performers—in ways that are conceptually unavailable in the context of the public playhouses.

In the context of print culture, playbooks occupy an ambiguous position: usually they are aligned with other forms of recreational literature such as ballads and prose romances, but there is also a concerted effort on the part of playwrights and publishers to elevate drama to the ranks of poetry, history, or the literature of moral instruction. This variability in the cultural status of the printed play reveals, as recent scholarship has shown, the transformation of playwrights into authors as it occurred over the course of the seventeenth century.[4] But considered simply in its variations, rather than being set in an evolutionary framework examining the (male) author, the status of the printed play reveals differences in reading protocols that are not merely gendered but gendered consistently throughout the early modern period. Robert Wilmot's early Inns of Court play *The Tragedie of Tancred and Gismund* (1591) is dedicated to both men and women and thus reveals what is at stake in such distinctions among readers. The first of four dedications is addressed to the ladies Anne Gray and Mary Peter, whose "favourable countenance"

Wilmot hopes to secure.[5] The women evidently did not attend the performance of the play, and Wilmot's repeated comments on the success and prestige of the private production have the effect of emphasizing their exclusion from the elite scholarly community (which included, on this occasion, the queen and her maids of honor) to which the playbook becomes their only means of access. Wilmot, however, draws on the play's academic auspices to make a distinction between it and the "ordinarie amorous discourses of our daies," the extremely popular prose romances that were inarguably downmarket publications.[6] Notwithstanding its being "a discourse of two lovers," the play is presented as a piece of didactic "Poetrie" which itself is set within the broader world of "humane learning." But when it comes to imagining what the women are meant to do with the play, Wilmot ultimately fails to involve them in anything like serious intellectual engagement. Instead, their "perusing of some mournfull matter" is expected only to "refresh" their wits and "ease" their weariness during the "drouping daies and tedious nights" of winter. Even better than this therapeutic reading, he suggests, would be a reenactment of the play so that Gismund's "bloudie shadow, with a little cost, may be intreated in her selfe-like person to speake to ye" (*2v). There is a powerful physical presence in this imaginary scene of play-reading, not to mention a certain nightmarish quality to the women's "ease" and "refreshment"—the "mournfull matter" of the book itself, the aura of a "gloomie day" and "louring night," the bloodstained apparition ventriloquized, for maximum effect, through a female body.

When Wilmot turns to his male readers, "the worshipfull and learned Societie, the Gentlemen Students of the Inner Temple, . . . his singular good friends, the Gentlemen of the middle Temple, . . . and to all other curteous readers," he strikes an altogether different register (*4–*4v). Drawing on a predominantly masculine nexus of values—learning, friendship, and courtesy—this preface reinscribes the playbook in a well-lit world of rational debate, intellectual history, and the pragmatics of publication. In such a context, the work degenerates from "Poetrie" to a mere "Pamphlet," its ephemeral and unscholarly nature laid bare before an academic audience that will presumably scorn the presentation of a romantic tragedy to the serious attention of readers (even if in performance it garnered praise for its "depth of conceit" and "true ornaments of poeticall Arte").[7] The preface, then, does the work of "dressing" the playtext—figured overtly as a naked female body—in the only available habit of a respectable play, the academic drama of such a "reverend & lerned" predecessor as Buchanan. In her newly chastened posture, the play becomes appropriate matter for "discreet" and "wise" readers, destined for safekeeping within "the walles of your house." But here the image of male readers engaging physically with the feminized text stops short: despite the domestic setting, there is no allusion, as there was with the ladies Peter and Gray, to the male reader's body.

This invisibility, or lack of specificity, of the male reader's engagement with the text may be explained if we turn to the last of Wilmot's preliminary pieces, "A Preface to the Queenes Maidens of Honor" (A1). Here Wilmot makes it clear that this group of female readers, some of whom would have seen the play in performance, are really the ones who are meant to engage with the play as a piece of moral instruction, for it is to them that its "lively deciphering their overthrow that suppresse not their unruely affections" is most obviously applicable (*4):

> behold here for your gaine
> Gismonds unluckie love, her fault, her wo
> And death, at last her cruell Father slaine
> Through his mishap, and though you do not see,
> Yet reade and rew their wofull Tragedie.
>
> (A)[8]

Considering that Wilmot's best-defined images of reading occasions and functions involve women, it is surprising that he nowhere addresses or even considers Elizabeth as a potential reader. Not only was she present at the performance, but she was also known as an accomplished scholar with a particular interest in Senecan drama. Interestingly, the one dedication of a play to Elizabeth, Jasper Heywood's translation of *Troas* (1559), reveals that she was perceived as a very masculine kind of play-reader, attending equally to a play's matter and its linguistic qualities, and doing so with the discipline and intellectual focus expected of any humanist scholar:

> Well understanding how greatly your highnes is delighted in the swete sappe of fine and pure writers, . . . I thought it should not be unpleasant for your grace to se some part of so excellent an author in your owne tong (the reading of whom in laten I understande delightes greatly your majesty) as also for that none may be a better judge of my doinges herein, then who best understandeth my author.[9]

That Heywood casts Elizabeth as the preeminent reader and judge of his translation is less remarkable than that he credits her with the range of skills necessary to assess its quality. Why Wilmot failed to address Elizabeth in these terms is puzzling, not least because she is said to have "princely accepted" the play in performance (*3). It is clear, though, that had he done so, the division of male and female readerships could not have been made along the lines of literary competence.

At stake, then, in Wilmot's gendering of readerships is the play's status as literature, specifically as literature of moral instruction. Taken together, his preliminaries reveal a concerted effort to distinguish between the work in hand and the publicly performed drama of "the Tragedian Tyrants of our time" (*4v). To the extent that he invokes a general female readership, Wilmot does so to strengthen the claim—made in strictly theoretical terms to his male readers—that the play is of a piece with the biblical tragedies written *for reading* by eminent humanists. At the same time, the dedication to the ladies Anne Gray and Mary Peter reveals that Wilmot continues to value performance as a means of conveying the play's didactic content, but he sanctions such a performance only within a private and explicitly female household setting. In both cases, albeit in seemingly paradoxical ways, the depiction of women as readers of the play enables Wilmot to distinguish an Inns of Court "amarous poeme" from the "scurrilous" drama of the public theater.

Within a year of the publication of *Tancred and Gismund*, Mary Sidney would follow Elizabeth in demonstrating women's capacity for serious intellectual work as readers of drama. Sidney's translation of Robert Garnier's *Antonie*, first published in 1592, was widely influential, spawning as it did a succession of verse plays on classical history that consolidated English academic drama and became the typographic model for plays by professional playwrights—Jonson, Chapman, and Webster among them—who most sought literary status for their theatrical works.[10] As an act of reading itself, Sidney's translation falls squarely within the academic humanist tradition of putting literary labor at the service of religious and political goals. And as Eve Sanders has shown, Sidney's reading of Garnier reveals an independence of critical and moral judgment that far exceeds the restraints placed on women's literacy by Tudor educational theorists.[11] It is all the more notable that when Samuel Daniel comes to dedicate his own follow-up play, *Cleopatra* (1594), to Sidney, he completely mystifies her intellectual abilities, casting her as a "starre of wonder" even while crediting her with a full-scale reformation of English literature, and subverting her anticipated criticism of his negative portrayal of Cleopatra by blithely assuming that her "sweet favouring eyes" can do nothing but passively "lighten" his "darke defects."[12] If Sidney's power as a reader nevertheless emerges in the dedication, it does so in spite of Daniel's conspicuously vague representation.[13]

The image Daniel constructs of Sidney as a play-reader is, compared with Wilmot's female readers, essentially disembodied, and even if one couldn't go so far as to say that she is thereby de-feminized, it is certainly the case that in this respect she is positioned, vis-à-vis the playbook, more in an intellectual than in a physical relation. We find a similar elision of the female reader's body in other closet plays written on Sidney's model and that also posit an explicitly female readership: Thomas Kyd's *Cornelia* (1594), dedicated to the countess of Sussex; Samuel Brandon's *Octavia* (1598), dedicated to Lady Audelay; and Elizabeth Cary's *Mariam* (1613), dedicated to her sister-in-law of the same name. Like Sidney, all three female readers are figured as unearthly or superhuman beings but are nevertheless depicted as actually reading the play being dedicated to them: the countess of Sussex is a woman of vaguely "noble and heroick dispositions" but is "well accomplished" and can be trusted to read with "true conceit and entertainement"; Lucia Audelay is a "Rare Phoenix" and "Rich treasurer, of heavens best treasuries," but reads "With honors eyes, let[ting] vertues plaints be scan'd"; and Elizabeth Cary, the author's sister-in-law, is "LUNA-like, unspotted, chast, divine," but also a real-world comfort to the author in her husband's absence and "destin'd . . . T'illumine" her second play.[14] It is not difficult to understand the cultural logic behind these dedications, for all three plays are, in both content and physical appearance, aligned with the academic drama of moral and political instruction. Given early modern conceptions of the female body as weak and corrupt, dedicating such a play to a woman, even a woman of Mary Sidney's standing, necessitated a certain voiding of physical existence.[15] What comes across, however, is the distinct sense that women were not just competent but valued readers of serious philosophical and political drama.

What, then, of stage drama? How did commercial plays—the very matter of the "Tragedian Tyrants" so depised by Wilmot—depict their female readers? The first and most obvious (though no less striking) factor to consider is the near-complete absence of women as dedicatees of printed commercial drama, despite their being by all accounts a sizable and significant portion of the theater audience.[16] Of the nearly one thousand extant printed editions of early modern commercial plays, a mere half-dozen are dedicated to women—notably Jonson's *The Alchemist* to

Mary Wroth, and the collected plays of Marston, dedicated by the publisher, William Sheares, to Elizabeth Cary.[17] It is true, certainly, that commercial plays were the least likely type of printed drama to bear a dedication at all, but even so more than one hundred editions published between 1600 and 1642 have some form of dedicatory epistle.[18] That, with the exception of one (*The Alchemist*), all the plays dedicated to women were performed at the indoor, or "private," theaters is surely no coincidence.[19] The reopening of the Blackfriars theater in 1599 began a process of fracturing commercial theatrical culture into increasingly polarized markets that were indexed, at least rhetorically, to differences in social status and education, and these were in turn constructed in terms of physiology.[20] Despite the crossover of plays, actors, and audiences between the two kinds of venue, indoor theaters were—or were said to be—catering to an upmarket clientele with clean bodies, decent manners, and a taste for aesthetic refinement, summed up by Marston in the epithet the "good gentle Audience."[21] Interestingly, the distinction between outdoor ("public") and indoor ("private") theaters emerges most clearly in the preliminaries of *printed* plays, and specifically where authors and stationers are engaged in the process of repositioning a stage play from the theater to the culture of reading.[22] Not surprisingly, then, the six dedications of such volumes to women follow the same pattern as the closet drama: except for a fleeting glimpse of one white hand that transforms the "rudenesse of a Comedy" into "innocence," these women have a strictly cerebral engagement with the play.[23] They are discriminating, learned readers capable of understanding and judging dramatic poetry and, most important, protecting it from the ignorant "brainles Momes" who are ever poised to scorn a play in print.[24]

We may be tempted to consider this depiction preferable to Wilmot's images of women reading for either mere amusement or simple moral edification, but we should also take into account that these female readers are constructions in self-consciously elite plays that are negotiating their position in theatrical and print cultures. From this point of view, dedicating a play to a woman of irreproachable "honor" and "virtue," whose purity virtually nullifies her physical existence, bolsters the fiction that the play in question, its commercial auspices notwithstanding, belongs to a "private" culture of intellectual refinement. It may be significant, then, that two of the six women readers were, or would become, published writers. William Sheares's dedication of *The Workes of Mr J. Marston* (1633) to Elizabeth Cary labors to distinguish between Marston's plays and the degenerate drama—plays with "obscene speeches," scenes "stuffe[d] . . . with ribaldry," and lines "lard[ed] . . . with scurrilous taunts and jests."[25] The corporeal terminology Sheares uses here aligns the "vile and abominable" drama with the public theaters, in comparison with which Marston's plays are (however disingenuously) said to be the epitome of moral decency. Although Sheares claims that Marston himself "abhorres such Writers," it is Elizabeth Cary who, as a woman of "rare Vertues, and endowments" and a reader who is "well acquainted with the Muses," protects the plays from attack by "that precise Sect" (Prynne must be meant in 1633) who consider all drama obscene. Strangely, Sheares either doesn't know or chooses not to mention Cary's own published play, which had appeared in 1613 and physically resembled Marston's own private theater plays.[26] Her intellectual agency in vindicating the moral and literary worth of drama is limited to reading, and the reading itself is, for Cary, uncharacteristically passive.[27]

Perhaps the most striking use of the intelligent but disembodied female reader to certify a play's literary status is Jonson's dedication of *The Alchemist* (1612) to Mary Wroth. We know from other of his commendatory writings that Jonson admired Wroth as a talented author, and they apparently read each other's work on many occasions.[28] But when he addresses her as a reader of a stage play, he clothes his admiration in terms that effectively deny her any agency as a fellow writer or, indeed, as a fellow human. The controlling trope in the dedication is that of a sacrificial offering, Wroth being the goddess at whose altar he lays his dramatic gift. Although he trusts that the play will be safe in her "judgment," that judgment is subject to a crucial qualification, "(which is a SIDNEYS)," and does not involve any of the interpretive skills he goes on to demand of his "understanding" male readers.[29] While Wroth's reading is represented as passive (if enlightened) acceptance, in the epistle to the general reader Jonson makes it clear that his writing in fact demands a specific kind of critical discrimination. There, too, we find his characteristically bitter dismissal of competing theatrical work "that tickles the Spectators" and the jointly moral and aesthetic distinction between "theirs, and mine," "theirs" being "sordide, and vile," while his is indisputably a "learned" and "skilfull" composition.[30] Interestingly, however, Jonson does not distinguish between the "rude" drama and his own in terms of theatrical and print culture, even though the former is characterized by him as featuring elements that are decidedly performative (e.g., the "Concupiscence of Jigges, and Daunces").[31]

Instead, he begins the epistle "To the Reader" with the warning that the playbook about to be purchased is not of a kind with *other* printed drama then current. Whatever his precise motives in dedicating this play to Wroth, Jonson's depiction of her as a reader thus does the work of demarcating his own literary *and* theatrical practice from that favored by "the Multitude," but without attributing to her anything more than the residual power of "her Blood" as a Sidney.[32]

Jonson's dedication of an amphitheater play to a woman is, as far as we know, unique for the early modern period, but the rhetoric of mystifying her intellectual ability and negating her body is perfectly consistent with other plays that sought to disassociate themselves from purportedly vulgar forms of theatrical practice. But as we have seen, these documents are extremely rare, amounting to fewer than twenty dedications over a fifty-year period in which nearly a thousand plays were printed. This dearth can be explained by examining the constructions of women as readers of stage plays in antitheatrical tracts, conduct books, and other socially conservative writings in which the female reader effectively embodies everything that is physically and morally dangerous about the public theater. William Prynne's *Histrio-Mastix* (1633) epitomizes this line of thought:

> The obscenity, ribaldry, amorousness, heathenishnesse, and prophanenesse of most Play-bookes, Arcadiaes, and fained Histories that are now so much in admiration, is such, that it is not lawfull for any (especially for children, youthes, or those of the female sex, who take most pleasure in them) so much as once to read them, for feare they should inflame their lusts, and draw them on to actuall lewdness, and prophaneness.[33]

Over fifty years earlier, Anthony Munday had described the ill effects of public playhouses in precisely these terms:

> Are not our eies (there) carried awaie with the pride of vanitie? Our eares abused with amorous, that is lecherous, filthie and abhominable speech? Is not our tong . . . there imploied to the blaspheming of Gods holie Name; or the commendation of that is wicked? Are not our harts through the pleasure of the flesh; the delight of the eie; and the fond motions of the mind, withdrawen from the service of the Lord, & meditation of his goodnes?[34]

Significantly, Munday offers the example of a female spectator when illustrating the moral and social damage wrought by the public playhouses:

> Some citizens wives, upon whom the Lord for ensample to others hath laide his hands, have even on their death beds with teares confessed, that they have received at those spectacles such filthie infections, as have turned their minds from chast cogitations, and made them of honest women light huswives; by them they have dishonored the vessels of holines; and brought their husbandes into contempt, their children into question, their bodies into sicknes, and their soules to the state of everlasting damnation.[35]

This perception that playgoing and play-reading can destabilize the identity of a virtuous woman also finds innumerable parallels in representations of women as readers of romance and erotic poetry; indeed, the three genres are virtually interchangeable in satirical or moralistic depictions of women's reading.[36] Sir Thomas Overbury's well-known "character" of a chambermaid includes a typically compulsive and transformative reading of romance: "She reads Greenes workes over and over, but is so carried away with *The Myrror of Knighthood*, she is many times resolv'd to run out of her selfe, and become a Ladie Errant."[37] In *The Guardian*, Philip Massinger puts just such a character on the stage: Calypso, confidante to the play's heroine, confesses to her mistress that she has not merely read but read "often" and "feelingly" such romances as *Amadis de Gaul*, *Palmerins*, and *The Mirror of Knighthood*.[38] Prynne's attack on play-reading depicts similarly compulsive and self-alienating behavior: the "frequent constant reading of Play-bookes, of other prophane lascivious amorous Poems, Histories, and discourses," is dangerous precisely because there are "no women . . . so exactly chaste, which may not easily be corrupted by them, and even inflamed into fury with strange and monstrous lusts."[39]

So common did this association of eroticism with women's reading of plays and romances become that the books themselves, housed suggestively in closets and private bedchambers, could represent a woman's sexuality. Thomas Cranley's moralistic portrayal of *Amanda, or the Reformed Whore* (1635) specifies that "amorous Pamphlets" and "many merry Comedies" sit side-by-side on the bookshelf in her chamber,[40] and in a parodic inversion of this same idea, Thomas Peyton envisions a woman "in holy Habit" reading aloud from Fletcher in her closet, abandoning her vows of chastity and being transformed into a "Votaresse" of his notoriously sensual plays.[41] In the mock-moralistic work *The Academy of Love* (1641), Shakespeare himself, like Fletcher, "creepes into the womens closets about bed time." There he is "read . . . day and night" and becomes the medium of a sexual liaison between female pupils and male tutors: as the girls "open the Booke or Tome," the men "with a Fescue in their hands . . . point to the Verse."[42] Even more explicit is Robert Baron's *Cyprian Academy,* a pastoral romance containing within its pages two bibliographically distinct plays. The work was originally circulated at Gray's Inn but, like the Beaumont and Fletcher folio, is declared in print to be "most fit for Ladies." In one of the few surviving dedications to a general female readership, the volume posits an explicitly erotic scene of reading. The book is troped as an "amorous infant" who longs "rather to be dandled upon your tender knees, then lie reclused in a dustie study."[43] This dichotomy between ladies' laps and gentlemen's studies as material settings for the book inscribes the same division between (male) academic labor and (female) leisure found in the multiple readerships addressed in *Tancred and Gismund,* a division that is further reinforced here by the stated hope that women will "converse" with the book at "that time which you spend in other divertisments." This much we have seen before, but Baron goes on with the erotic innuendo: having switched metaphors partway from the book as infant to the book as jewel, he concludes by wishing his readers "all delights, & happinesse, endlesse like the rings you weare," a continual, repetitive pleasure—euphemistically invoking (through the "ring") female orgasm—that is induced by his "quavering pencell" having achieved its climax, "the period of my paines." Interestingly, the erotic scene of reading is confirmed by a male voyeur: William Beversham, a friend of Baron's at Gray's Inn, writes in his commendatory verse, set suggestively on the facing page, that he envisions ladies "dandling" the book and wishing its pleasures were "Ring-like, without any end."[44] Their desire is specifically focused on "that hand; [that] these flowrie Pastrolls pen'd," thus reinforcing the link between the author's writing instrument and his female readers' sexual pleasure: the phallic nature of the pen could hardly be more explicit. The concurrence of this eroticized image of women readers in both the address "To the Ladies and Gentlewoemen of England" and in a commendatory poem by a male friend makes it difficult to determine whether its ideological work is socially progressive or just predictably homosocial. And to complicate matters further, Baron also writes a dedication to another male friend in which reading is decidedly incorporeal, thus reaffirming the value of the intellectual labor he so cavalierly rejects—with the image of the "dustie study"—when addressing female readers.[45]

The pornographic overtones of Baron's dedication, Peyton's commendation of Fletcher's writing, and the passage from *The Academy of Love* reveal, however, that representations of eroticized female play-readers could be exploited for *pleasure* as well as admonition, and here a distinction does occur between women's reception of plays in print and theatrical culture, specifically in the playgoing culture that developed around the public theaters. The difference hinges on the material setting of reception: whether it is social or solitary, reading as imagined in connection with women and playbooks is invariably set in private space, be it an aristocratic household as in the example of Wilmot's female readers, a (parodic) classroom as in *The Academy of Love*, or a prostitute's bedchamber as in *Amanda, or the Reformed Whore*.[46] As material commodities and as products of print culture, playbooks obviously belong at some level (often self-consciously) to the public sphere, but women's *reading* of printed drama is invariably severed from economic and political fields. In this respect, women's playgoing was imaginatively precisely the opposite. Jean Howard and others have shown that in the context of the professional theater, where access to the play occurs in a public arena and is conducted through a commercial transaction, women's playgoing unsettles traditional conceptions of social order and is therefore considered immoral. According to Howard, it is the transgressive implication of women's having paid to attend the public theaters that explains why antitheatrical writers so often urge women to be "keepers at home" and not "ramble abroad" to plays.[47] But the seemingly absolute distinction drawn here between public stage and private space admits at least one potentially unsettling activity: reading. Urging the women readers of his antitheatrical tract not to "fashion yourselves to open spectacles" but rather to "keepe at home," Stephen Gosson advises them to "passe the time with your neighboures in sober conference, or if you canne reade, let bookes bee your comforte."[48] In 1579 when Gosson wrote this epistle, the reading of plays was only just emerging as a cultural practice, so it is highly unlikely that when he sanctions "bookes" for the home he is thinking of printed drama. By 1633, however, when play-reading had become, to Prynne's dismay, a "frequent constant" recreation, the dichotomy between public and private space is redrawn with specific attention to playbooks: women who would "keep under their unchaste desires" must not only "withdraw themselves from stage-plays" but also "cast away all Play-bookes."[49]

What evidence we have of women's ownership of playbooks suggests that Prynne's alarmist conception of women's domestic play-reading was not unjustified. Frances Egerton, countess of Bridgewater (1585–1636), owned a vast private library nearly half of which can be classified as literature and history, the two genres that were always hedged about with warnings where women's reading was concerned.[50] The precise number of her plays is difficult to determine because the catalogue lists, as was customary for quarto publications, a number of volumes comprising unspecified "diverse" plays. The titles that are recorded, however, indicate that her play-reading was very broad, running from masques to closet dramas to stage plays, and that she read drama in folio, quarto, and manuscript format. She owned Jonson's collected *Workes* of 1616, his *New Inne,* and a manuscript of *The Gypsies Metamorphosed,* Fulke Greville's *Tragedy of Mustapha,* Mary Sidney's *Antonius,* a volume of plays by Shakespeare, two volumes of "diverse Playes" by unspecified playwrights, and another set of "diverse playes," these "in 5 thicke Volumes."[51] The number of plays in the collection of Elizabeth Puckering (ca. 1620–1689) is also notable: there are at least twenty quarto editions, ranging back as far as Lyly's *Campaspe* of 1591, and reflecting a special interest in the private theater of the late 1630s, which we know she personally attended.[52] Puckering also owned the second folio collections of Jonson and Shakespeare, and the Beaumont and Fletcher folio of 1647, which she appears to have acquired not (as Moseley predicted) for its being a manageable tome but for its royalist stand.[53] A third known major collection, that of Frances Wolfreston (1607–1677), is equally rich in drama and includes Chapman's *Caesar and Pompey,* Ford's *Loves Sacrifice,* Heywood's *Second Part of the Iron Age* and *The Rape of Lucrece,* Shirley's *The Grateful Servant* and *Love Will Finde Out the Way,* and Shakespeare's *Hamlet, Othello, King Lear,* and *Richard II.*[54]

That playbooks are prevalent in three of the largest private libraries known to have belonged to early modern women goes some distance to substantiating Moseley's claim that women in general were, at least by mid-century, active play-readers. But book ownership alone reveals frustratingly little about why, how, and in what contexts these plays were read. To follow through on this inquiry, we need to consider the evidence of interpretive activities that survives in such forms as marginal annotations, commonplace notebooks, letters, and diaries, an endeavor that has barely begun. Yet even the meager evidence we have to hand suggests that Prynne's suspicion that play-reading, playgoing, and performance were congruent practices is well founded. Frances Egerton's library included a manuscript (and possibly autograph) copy of Jonson's masque *The Gypsies Metamorphosed,* which appears to have been written for presentation at Burley-on-the-Hill several months before being performed at Windsor in September 1621.[55] Egerton's family had close associations with several major literary figures and had patronized an acting company in the 1590s.[56] Her mother and sisters acted in masques at court, and her children performed in Milton's *Comus.* Her ownership of an early and highly authoritative manuscript of a Jonson masque[57] can therefore be assumed to reflect her family's affiliation with masque as an elite performance genre; her bequeathing the manuscript to her son John Brackley[58] further suggests that the reading of this particular dramatic text not only commemorated a performance but, for him, would affirm familial bonds as well.

Elizabeth Puckering's ownership of playbooks can also be linked with an active interest in theater. David McKitterick has shown that the specific titles she owned are almost without exception products of the "private" theater repertory of the 1630s, which we know she patronized, and at least one savvy purveyor of printed plays—Andrew Pennycuicke—considered her a fitting reader of a Whitehall/Cockpit play when he chose to dedicate Ford and Dekker's *The Sun's Darling* to her in 1656.[59] Even more interesting is her manuscript copy of Dryden's *Indian Emperor,* which contains notations indicating that it was used in a domestic performance around the time it was being publicly staged.[60] As for Frances Wolfreston, there is evidence to suggest that her playbooks were very much in the nature of commemorative editions of performances and some reason to doubt whether she actually read them at all. Her copy of Heywood's *Second Part of the Iron Age* (1632) has a brief note approving "this and the forst part of the destruktions of troy tragides both very prity ons and good ons for that storay) and i think trower then the old history bouk."[61] It is difficult to say whether Wolfreston is comparing one "bouk" with another, but the absence of the first part of the play from her library leads John Gerritsen to suggest it is equally likely that she is basing her comment on a performance as on a reading. Her knowledge of at least one play, John Ford's *Loves Sacrifice,* seems indebted to a performance even though it is recorded on her printed copy, just below Shirley's commendatory poem "To my friend Mr. John Ford." Here she has written a detailed plot summary but has so badly misspelled the names of two characters that, as Gerritsen suggests, we are led to suspect "she saw a performance (rather than merely, as is possible, having had the play read to her) and bought this copy as a result."[62] The likelihood of Wolfreston's having bought plays to commemorate performances she had attended is heightened by the fact that the majority of the "dramatic booklets" bearing her signature were at auction "uncut and unbound, stitched as issued," which almost certainly means unread.[63]

If, then, even the evidence of book ownership points to women's active engagement with drama in performance, can this also mean that the *manner* of reading replicated at some level the experience of playgoing or, more radically still, the experience of performance itself? If, for example, Elizabeth Puckering did indeed "read" the part of Cortez in *The Indian Emperor* in an oral or a visual performance, can we infer that some women at least were reading through the body as the moralists feared? Margaret Cavendish certainly was. In a domestic setting where oral play-reading appears to have been a regular social event, Cavendish developed a conception of reading plays that bears out everything Prynne feared about the sensuality of the practice and the crossover it engenders between domestic and theatrical space.[64] In one of the prefaces to her first collection of plays, Cavendish instructs her "Noble Readers" to read them "to the nature of those several humours, or passions, as are exprest by Writing: for they must not read a Scene as they would read a Chapter; for Scenes must be read as if they were spoke or Acted." When a play is skillfully read, she continues, "the very sound of the Voice that enters through the Ears, doth present the Actions to the Eyes of the Fancy as lively as if it were really Acted."[65] Interestingly, it is Shakespeare's ability to induce just such a physical transformation in the reader that Cavendish considers to be his creative genius: "In his Tragick Vein, he Presents Passions so Naturally, and Misfortunes so Probably, as he Pierces the souls of his Readers with such a true sense and Feeling thereof, that it Forces Tears through their Eyes, and almost Perswades them, they are Really Actors, or at least Present at those Tragedies."[66] In dissolving the boundary between reading, spectatorship, and performance, Cavendish flies in the face of such handwringing moralists as Vives, who warned that women reading poetic fictions "are themselves caught into it, and seem to rise above their own intellect, and even above their own nature."[67] Cavendish hasn't the slightest anxiety about bodily corruption, nor is there—it must be said—anything necessarily erotic about her reading pleasure. In other words, Cavendish frames her reading of stage plays in terms that are both materially identical with and yet aesthetically the precise opposite of both antitheatrical polemic and prefatorial discourse.

In this as in so much else, Cavendish is unique, but her conception of play-reading as inherently performative resonates with many other accounts of women's reception of printed drama, whether they censure or approve the practice. The physical pleasure that women were thought to take in play-reading was, as I have attempted to show, both circumscribed and fostered by the material setting in which it occurred: private spaces such as closets, bedchambers, or domestic households more generally. When they are depicted actually reading a play, women are never in public.[68] This may be simply because, as a species of recreational reading, play-reading would not normally have occurred outside domestic spaces.[69] But however restrictive or obvious we may find it, the privacy of play-reading—as distinct, on the one hand, from the reading of other fictional genres such as romance and, on the other, from public playgoing—also generated a new discourse and practice of female performance that could not have materialized in any other field of early modern culture.

## NOTES

1. "The Stationer to the Readers," in *Comedies and Tragedies Written by Francis Beavmont and John Fletcher Gentlemen* (London: for Humphrey Robinson and Humphrey Moseley, 1647), A4.

2. Jean Howard, *The Stage and Social Struggle in Early Modern England* (London: Routledge, 1994), 73–92.

3. William Gager, "Nobilissimae ac Doctissime Heroine, Domine Marie Penbrochie Comitissa," in *Vlysses Redux Tragoedia Nova* (Oxford: Excudebat Iosephus Barnesius, 1592), 3; Robert Baron, "To the Ladies and Gentlewoemen of England," in *Erotopaignion Or the Cyprian Academy* (London: W[illiam] W[ilson] and are to be sold by J. Hardesty, T. Huntington, and T. Jackson, 1647), A2–2v; Thomas Cranley, *Amanda: Or, The Reformed Whore* (London: [John Norton], 1635), 32; John Johnson, *The Academy of Love* (London: for H. Blunden, 1641); Robert Wilmot, *The Tragedie of Tancred and Gismund* (London: Thomas Scarlet, and are to be solde by R. Robinson, 1591), *2.

4. On this development, see Richard Dutton, *Licensing, Censorship, and Authorship in Early Modern England: Buggeswords* (Houndsmills, Basingstoke, Hampshire: Palgrave, 2000); Alan B. Farmer and Zachary Lesser, "Vile Arts: The Marketing of English Printed Drama, 1512–1660," *Research Opportunities in Renaissance Drama* 39 (2000): 95–101; Douglas A. Brooks, *From Playhouse to Printing House: Drama and Authorship in Early Modern England* (Cambridge: Cambridge University Press, 2000); and David Scott Kastan, *Shakespeare and the Book* (Cambridge: Cambridge University Press, 2001).

5. "To the right Worshipfull and vertuous Ladies, the L. Anne Graie, & the Ladie Marie Peter," in Wilmot, *Tancred and Gismund*, *2.

6. See Arthur F. Kinney, "Marketing Fiction," in *Critical Approaches to English Prose Fiction, 1520–1640*, ed. Donald Beecher (Ottawa: Dovehouse, 1998), 45–61.

7. "To his frend R. W.," in Wilmot, *Tancred and Gismund*, *3.

8. By contrast, at the performance the maids of honor are said to have attended to the "sweetnesse of voice and livelinesse of action" (ibid., *2).

9. "To the most high and vertuouse princesse, Elyzabeth by the grace of god Queene of England, Fraunce, and Ireland defender of the faith," in *The Sixt Tragedie of . . . Lucius, Anneus, Seneca, entituled Troas*, trans. Jasper Heywood ([London: Richard Tottyll,] 1559), A2v–3. On humanist reading protocols, see Anthony Grafton and Lisa Jardine, "'Studied for Action': How Gabriel Harvey Read His Livy," *Past and Present* 129 (1990): 30–78; and William H. Sherman, "The Place of Reading in the English Renaissance: John Dee Revisited," in *The Practice and Representation of Reading in England*, ed. James Raven, Helen Small, and Naomi Tadmor (Cambridge: Cambridge University Press, 1996), 62–76.

10. Mary Sidney Herbert, trans., *A Discourse of Life and Death . . . Antonius, A Tragoedie* (London: [John Windet] for William Ponsonby, 1592). On Sidney's play and the development of a distinctive "look" for literary drama, see Marta Straznicky, "Elizabeth Cary: 'Private' Drama and Print," in *Privacy, Playreading, and Women's Closet Drama, 1550–1700* (Cambridge: Cambridge University Press, 2004), 48–66.

11. On Sidney's translation of Garnier as a transgressive act of reading, see Eve Rachele Sanders, *Gender and Literacy on Stage in Early Modern England* (Cambridge: Cambridge University Press, 1998), 92–117.

12. Samuel Daniel, "To the Right Honourable, the Lady Marie, Countesse of Pembrooke," in *Delia and Rosamond augmented. Cleopatra* (London: [James Roberts and Edward Allde] for Simon Waterson, 1594), H5–7.

13. On related representations of Sidney as a reader of poetry, see Gary F. Waller, "The Countess of Pembroke and Gendered Reading," in *The Renaissance Englishwoman in Print: Counterbalancing the Canon*, ed. Anne M. Haselkorn and Betty S. Travitsky (Amherst: University of Massachusetts Press, 1990), 331–33.

14. Thomas Kyd, "To the vertuously Noble, and rightly honoured Lady, the Countesse of Sussex," in *Cornelia* (London: James Roberts for N[icholas] L[ing] and John Busbie, 1594), a ii–ii v; Samuel Brandon, "To the right honorable, and truly vertuous Ladie, the Ladie Lucia Audelay," in *The Tragicomoedi of the vertuous Octavia* (London: [Edward Allde] for William Ponsonbye, 1598), Aii; Elizabeth Cary, "To my worthy Sister, Mistris Elizabeth Carye," in *The Tragedie of Mariam, the Faire Queene of Iewry* (London: Thomas Creede for Richard Hawkins, 1613), A1.

15. On the early modern conception of the female body as inherently corrupt, see Ian Maclean, *The Renaissance Notion of Woman: A Study in the Fortunes of Scholasticism and Medical Science in European Intellectual Life* (Cambridge: Cambridge University Press, 1980). Some representative primary documents may be found in Kate Aughterson, ed., *Renaissance Woman: Constructions of Femininity in England* (London: Routledge, 1995), 41–66.

16. On women playgoers, see Richard Levin, "Women in the Renaissance Theatre Audience," *Shakespeare Quarterly* 40 (1989): 165–74.

17. The six volumes with their respective dedications are: Ben Jonson, "To the Lady, most aequall with vertue, and her Blood: The Grace, and Glory of women. MARY LA: WROTH," in *The Alchemist* (London: Thomas Snodham for Walter Burre, 1612), A2–2v; Philip Massinger, "To the right honourable and much esteemed for her high birth, but more admired for her vertue, the Lady Katherine Stanhope," in *The Duke of Millaine* (London: B[ernard] A[lsop] for Edward Blackmore, 1623), A2; James Shirley, "To the

right honorable, the Lady Dorothie Shirley," in *Changes: or, Love in a Maze* (London: G[eorge] P[urslowe] for William Cooke, 1632), A3–3v; William Sheares, "To the right honourable, the Lady Elizabeth Carie, Viscountesse Fawkland," in *The Workes of Mr. Iohn Marston* (London: [Augustine Mathewes] for William Sheares, 1633), A3–4v; William Sampson, "To the worshipfull and most vertuous Gentlewoman Mistris Anne Willoughby," in *The Vow Breaker. Or, the Faire Maide of Clifton* (London: John Norton, to be sold by Roger Ball, 1636), A3–4; and John Ford, "To my Deservingly-honoured John Wyrley Esquire, and to the vertuous and right worthy Gentlewoman, Mrs Mary Wyrley his wife," in *The Ladies Triall* (London: E[dward] G[riffin] for Henry Shephard, 1639), A3–3v.

18. On the nature and uses of prefatory matter in early modern printed drama, see Virgil B. Heltzel, "The Dedication of Tudor and Stuart Plays," *Wiener Beiträge zur Englischen Philologie* 65 (1957): 74–86; David M. Bergeron, "Printers' and Publishers' Addresses in English Dramatic Texts, 1558–1642," *Explorations in Renaissance Culture* 27 (2001): 131–60; Paul D. Cannan, "Ben Jonson, Authorship, and the Rhetoric of English Dramatic Prefatory Criticism," *Studies in Philology* 99 (2002): 180–90; and chapter 1 by Cyndia Susan Clegg in this volume.

19. On women playgoers and the private theaters, see Michael Neill, "'Wits most accomplished Senate': The Audience of the Caroline Private Theaters," *Studies in English Literature* 18 (1978): 343–44.

20. I discuss this development in "Closet Drama," in *A Companion to Renaissance Drama*, ed. Arthur F. Kinney (Oxford: Blackwell, 2002), 317–20.

21. John Marston, *Jacke Drums Entertainment* (London: [Thomas Creede] for Richard Oliue, 1601), H3v.

22. See Zachary Lesser, "Walter Burre's *The Knight of the Burning Pestle*," *English Literary Renaissance* 29 (1999): 22–29.

23. Shirley, *Changes*, A3.

24. Sampson, "To the worshipfull and most vertuous Gentlewoman," A3v.

25. Sheares, "To . . . Lady Elizabeth Carie," A3–4v.

26. For a detailed study of the typography of Cary's play, see Straznicky, "Elizabeth Cary."

27. We know from Cary's biography and from practically every public record of her life that she was an extraordinarily active reader in terms of the quantity of her reading, the determination with which she pursued it, and the extent to which she allowed it to transform her personal and political beliefs. In this respect she was the very antithesis of the obedient female reader who emerges from early modern treatises on women's education. For an account of the biographical record that emphasizes Cary's literary activities, see Barry Weller and Margaret W. Ferguson's introduction to their edition of *The Tragedy of Mariam the Fair Queen of Jewry, with The Lady Falkland Her Life by One of Her Daughters* (Berkeley: University of California Press, 1994), 1–17; on Cary's reading, see 187–90 and passim. On the ideologies of women's education, see Margaret W. Ferguson, "A Room Not Their Own: Renaissance Women as Readers and Writers," in *The Comparative Perspective on Literature: Approaches to Theory and Practice*, ed. Clayton Koelb and Susan Noakes (Ithaca: Cornell University Press, 1988), 93–116.

28. Michael Brennan goes so far as to call Wroth Jonson's "literary collaborator." For a detailed discussion of their literary relationship, see Brennan's "Creating Female Authorship in the Early Seventeenth Century: Ben Jonson and Lady Mary Wroth," in *Women's Writing and the Circulation of Ideas: Manuscript Publication in England, 1550–1800*, ed. George L. Justice and Nathan Tinker (Cambridge: Cambridge University Press, 2002), 73–93 (quotation at 84). On Jonson's relationship with other of his

female patrons, see Lesley Mickel, "'A Learned and Manly Soul': Jonson and His Female Patrons," *Ben Jonson Journal* 6 (1999): 69–87; and Barbara Smith, *The Women of Ben Jonson's Poetry: Female Representations in the Non-dramatic Verse* (Brookfield, Vt.: Ashgate, 1995), 3–7.

29. Jonson, "To . . . MARY LA: WROTH," A2v.

30. "To the Reader," in Jonson, *The Alchemist*, A3.

31. Ibid.

32. Jonson, "To . . . MARY LA: WROTH," A2. In contrast, Jonson's dedication of *Catiline his Conspiracy* (London: [William Stansby] for Walter Burre, 1611) to William Herbert attributes to him a "great and singular faculty of judgement" which is expected to recognize in the play "a legitimate Poeme." Unlike the mystification of Wroth's work as a reader, Herbert is overtly inscribed within the learned and discriminating interpretive community Jonson delineates in the prefaces to the general readers in both *The Alchemist* and *Catiline*. On Jonson's dramatic prefaces, see Cannan, "Ben Jonson."

33. William Prynne, *Histrio-Mastix* (London: E[dward] A[llde, Augustine Mathewes, Thomas Cotes,] and W[illiam] J[ones] for Michael Sparke, 1633), 913–14. Prynne's conception of the sensual danger of play-reading recalls earlier diatribes against theatergoing such as John Northbrooke's *Treatise wherein Dicing, Dauncing, Vaine playes or Enterlude . . . are reprooved* (London: by H. Bynneman, for George Byshop, 1577): "I am persuaded that Satan hath not a more speedie way and fitter schoole to work and teach his desire, to bring men and women into his snare of concupiscence and filthie lustes of wicked whoredome, than those places and playes, and theaters are" (Jii–jii v).

34. Anthony Munday, *A second and third blast of retrait from plaies and Theaters* (London: [Henrie Denham,] 1580), cited in E. K. Chambers, *The Elizabethan Stage*, 4 vols. (Oxford: Clarendon Press, 1923), 4:210.

35. Ibid., 209.

36. On women as readers of romance, see Helen Hackett, *Women and Romance Fiction in the English Renaissance* (Cambridge: Cambridge University Press, 2000); on women as readers of erotic narrative poetry, see Sasha Roberts, *Reading Shakespeare's Poems in Early Modern England* (Houndsmills, Basingstoke, Hampshire: Palgrave Macmillan, 2003). An early albeit still influential general study is Louis B. Wright, "The Reading of Renaissance English Women," *Studies in Philology* 28 (1931): 139–56.

37. Sir Thomas Overbury, *New and Choise Characters, of seuerall Authors*, 6th ed. (London: Thomas Creede for Laurence Lisle, 1615), ¶4v.

38. Philip Massinger, *Three New Playes; viz. The Bashful Lover, Guardian, Very Woman* (London: [Thomas Newcombe] for Humphrey Moseley, 1655), H6–6v. The play was licensed in 1633 and performed at court in 1634.

39. Prynne, *Histrio-Mastix*, 923, 905. It is interesting to note that Prynne makes the same claim about "youthes" as play-readers; this could be suggestively paired with Francis Beaumont's depiction of a romance-smitten apprentice reader in *The Knight of the Burning Pestle* (London: [Nicholas Okes] for Walter Burre, 1613). In this context it seems significant that Burre is specifically concerned to dispel the impression that Beaumont's play is "of the race of Don Quixote" (A2), although he goes on to allow some interplay of dramatic and romance genres.

40. Cranley, *Amanda*, 32.

41. Thomas Peyton, "On Mr Fletchers Works," in *Comedies and Tragedies*, A5.

42. Johnson, *Academy of Love*, 96–100.

43. Baron, "To the Ladies and Gentlewoemen of England," in *The Cyprian Academy*, A2v.

44. "On his beloved friend the Authour, and his ingenious Cyprian Academy," ibid., A3.

45. In this epistle, however, the author and (male) patron come into physical contact—"your rare parts of vertue induced me to kisse your hands" (ibid., A1v)—thus heightening the likelihood that the address to women readers is part of a homosocial exchange in which the author and his male readers conjure an image of female sexual and reading pleasure only to violate the private spaces in which it occurs. Other examples of this prefatorial move are examined by Wendy Wall in *The Imprint of Gender: Authorship and Publication in the English Renaissance* (Ithaca: Cornell University Press, 1993), 169–226.

46. On women and private reading spaces, see Sasha Roberts, "Shakespeare 'creepes into the womens closets about bedtime': Women Reading in a Room of their Own," in *Renaissance Configurations: Voices/Bodies/Spaces, 1580–1690*, ed. Gordon McMullan (Houndsmills, Basingstoke, Hampshire: Macmillan, 1998), 31–39.

47. Howard, *Stage and Social Struggle*, 74–76, citing Prynne, *Histrio-Mastix*, 992–94.

48. Stephen Gosson, "To the Gentlewomen, Citizens of London," in *The Schoole of Abuse* (London: [Thomas Dawson for] Thomas Woodcocke, 1579), cited from *Markets of Bawdrie: The Dramatic Criticism of Stephen Gosson*, ed. Arthur F. Kinney (Salzburg: Institüt für Englische Sprache und Literatur, 1974), 50–51.

49. Prynne, *Histrio-Mastix,* 453.

50. For an overview of prescriptions for women's reading in the early modern period, see Jacqueline Pearson, "Women Reading, Reading Women," in *Women and Literature in Britain, 1500–1700*, ed. Helen Wilcox (Cambridge: Cambridge University Press, 1996), 80–99; and Mary Ellen Lamb, "Constructions of Women Readers," in *Teaching Tudor and Stuart Women Writers*, ed. Susanne Woods and Margaret P. Hannay (New York: MLA, 2000), 23–34.

51. For a transcription of the catalogue and a detailed discussion of Egerton's library, see Heidi Brayman Hackel, "The Countess of Bridgewater's London Library," in *Books and Readers in Early Modern England: Material Studies*, ed. Jennifer Andersen and Elizabeth Sauer (Philadelphia: University of Pennsylvania Press, 2001), 138–59; the catalogue transcription is at 147–54.

52. See David McKitterick, "Women and Their Books in Seventeenth-Century England: The Case of Elizabeth Puckering," *The Library,* ser. 7, 1 (2000): 359–80.

53. McKitterick notes that among Puckering's books is a cluster "bought mostly between the 1640s and the 1660s, notable for a commitment to contemporary poetry and other imaginative writing, much of it royalist" (ibid., 375). The Beaumont and Fletcher volume would certainly fit this profile, especially considering Moseley's own royalist sympathies. On the intersection of political values and marketing strategy in Moseley's dramatic publications, see Paulina Kewes, "'Give Me the Sociable Pocket-books . . .': Humphrey Moseley's Serial Publication of Octavo Play Collections," *Publishing History* 38 (1995): 5–21.

54. For a list of known copies of Wolfreston's books, see Paul Morgan, "Frances Wolfreston and 'Hor Bouks': A Seventeenth-Century Woman Book-Collector," *The Library*, ser. 6, 11 (1989): 211–19.

55. C. H. Herford, Percy Simpson, and Evelyn Simpson, eds., *The Gypsies Metamorphosed*, in *Ben Jonson*, vol. 7 (Oxford: Clarendon Press, 1941), 548.

56. Hackel, "The Countess of Bridgewater's Library," 140.

57. Herford and Simpson, *Ben Jonson*, 7:541.

58. Hackel, "The Countess of Bridgewater's Library," 147.

59. McKitterick, "Women and Their Books," 376–77. At the same time, she appears to have collected drama assiduously throughout the 1650s when the theaters were closed, and the volumes she acquired at this time (all published, incidentally, by Moseley) reflect more of a political than an aesthetic commitment. Cf. note 53. Pennycuicke's dedication is addressed "To the Right Honorable my very good Lady, the Lady Newton, Wife to the Worshipfull Sir Henry Newton, Knight," and is one of four variant but substantially identical dedications of this piece. Greg suggests that because it (and two others) survive in single examples only, they "may have been printed specially for presentation copies." W. W. Greg, *A Bibliography of the English Printed Drama to the Restoration*, 4 vols. (London: Bibliographical Society, 1939–59), 3:874.

60. See McKitterick, "Women and Their Books," 362; and Fredson Bowers, "The 1665 Manuscript of Dryden's *Indian Emperour*," *Studies in Philology* 48 (1951): 738–39.

61. The transcription is from John Gerritsen, "*Venus* Preserved: Some Notes on Frances Wolfreston," *English Studies: A Journal of English Language and Literature*, supp. to vol. 45 (1964): 273.

62. Ibid.

63. Ibid., 271.

64. Cavendish makes a number of references to oral play-reading which suggest that this was not an unusual activity in her household. In a dedicatory epistle to her husband, Cavendish says that "this Book of Playes" would never have been written "had not you read to me some Playes which your Lordship had writ" ("The Epistle Dedicatory," in Margaret Cavendish, *Playes* [London: A. Warren, for John Martyn, James Allestry, and Tho. Dicas, 1662], A3), and in one of her *Sociable Letters*, which is devoted to the practice of reading aloud, she writes that "I never heard any man Read Well but my Husband, and have heard him say, he never heard any man Read Well but B. J. [almost certainly Ben Jonson] and yet he hath heard many in his Time" (Cavendish, *CCXI Sociable Letters* [London: William Wilson, 1664], 362–63). On reading aloud as a sociable practice, see Roger Chartier, "Leisure and Sociability: Reading Aloud in Early Modern Europe," in *Urban Life in the Renaissance*, ed. Susan Zimmerman and Ronald Weissman (Newark: University of Delaware Press, 1989), 103–20; and Mary Ellen Lamb, "The Sociality of Margaret Hoby's Reading Practices and the Representation of Reformation Interiority," *Critical Survey* 12.2 (2000): 17–32.

65. Cavendish, untitled epistle, in *Playes*, A6v.

66. Cavendish, *Sociable Letters*, 246. Cavendish also makes it clear she has read Jonson's plays: "His Comedies that he hath published, could never be the actions of one day" (*Playes*, A4v).

67. Juan Luis Vives, *Vives and the Renascence Education of Women*, ed. Foster Watson (London: Edward Arnold, 1912), 107.

68. Even Cavendish, who has such a well-developed sense of the corporeality of play-reading, condemns theatergoing and professional acting. On Cavendish's attitude to public theater, see Straznicky, *Privacy, Playreading, and Women's Closet Drama*, 82–83.

69. For a general account of the spaces in which play-reading occurred, see Heidi Brayman Hackel, "'Rowme' of Its Own: Printed Drama in Early Libraries," in *A New History of Early English Drama*, ed. John D. Cox and David Scott Kastan (New York: Columbia University Press, 1997), 113–30. On the development of the taste for privacy in the early modern period, see Orest Ranum, "The Refuges of Intimacy," in *A History of Private Life*, vol. 3, *Passions of the Renaissance*, ed Philippe Ariès and Georges Duby (London: Belknap Press, 1989), 218–25.

FOUR

# Closet Drama and the Case of *Tyrannicall-Government Anatomized*

ELIZABETH SAUER

The channeling of performance into print and the realignment of the dramatic mode are timely subjects of inquiry in light of the scholarly interest in the book trade, publication history, and reading practices, including play-reading. The early modern theater had served in the Renaissance as a charged territory and site of affiliation, presenting opportunities for various kinds of social formation as well as critical commentary on current affairs. Stage productions in turn helped satisfy the growing hunger of early modern society for domestic news and information about affairs abroad.[1] In the Jacobean period, playwrights, including Thomas Middleton, Philip Massinger, Richard Brome, Henry Shirley, and Ben Jonson, used the stage subversively to participate in contemporary debates. In her influential discussion on this subject, Margot Heinemann observes that the critical discourse of the stage was sharpened in the public, political sphere during the following decade: "If there was an attempt by some opposition leaders to encourage use of the stage as a political medium, it seems likely that it was still continuing and indeed intensifying in the late 1630s."[2] Among the learned and scholarly works of drama of the decade which contributed to the critical discourse of the stage, one might cite two examples: Nathanael Richards's *Messalina* (1634–36), Richards being the eulogist of Middleton, and *Julia Agrippina* (1638) by Thomas May, the official historiographer of the Parliament.

An antitheatrical prejudice grew up alongside the fascination with theater culture. This antagonism against stage productions was not, however, as severe as in the 1580s.[3] The later Puritans' concerns about the social and moral dangers posed by the theaters were resolved to some degree by the establishment of more private playhouses and the greater respectability accorded to playgoing. Moreover, the possibility that the theaters might give way to reformed stages was also entertained, though William Prynne remained skeptical: "I take it for my owne part; that Christians should rather argue thus; They are onely reduceable to good, and lawfull ends, but they are not yet reduced: their abuses may bee reformed, but as yet they are not corrected: therefore *wee must take them as we finde them now*, unpurged, uncorrected; and so we must *needes avoyde them, yea, condemne them*." After praising the virtues of dramatic verse as "*usefull and commendable among Christians*, if rightly used," Prynne identifies various exemplary ancient and modern poets and playwrights, including Gregory Nazianzen and George Buchanan, who, in different centuries, deployed the drama in a manner he approved. While condemning theatrical performances, Prynne maintains it is "lawfull to compile a Poeme in nature of a Tragedie, or poeticall Dialogue, with severall acts and parts, to adde life and luster to it, especially, in case of necessitie when as truth should else be suffocated." Nazianzen is again invoked, this time as a poet who relied on the dramatic mode to advance morality. In certain cases, then, it may be "lawfull to read Playes or Comedies now and then for recreation sake"; thus, if a play's content is wholesome, it may be read, and even recited.[4]

The translation of the theater experience into the writing, printing, and reading of plays to which Prynne alludes was already enacted in the productions of the anti-court Senecan tragedies of the Sidney circle, inspired by Buchanan's anti-persecution drama. Play-reading served not only as a way of ensuring the "wholesome" consumption of dramatic works but also as an act of textual revolt and political resistance. In the mid-seventeenth century, the predominantly royalist dramatic political allegories and satires aimed to redeem the royalist cause[5] and encouraged play-reading as political engagement. Little attention, however, has been directed at anti-royalist, antiestablishment dramas, which relied on the conventions of the private-public closet drama, as well as on classical and biblical models. Such writings offered alternative venues and sites of critical participation and enabled meaningful interventions in political debates.[6]

Parliament was aware of the role that dramatic productions could perform in the formation of political and communal identities. The August 1642 *Special order . . . concerning Irregular Printing, and . . . the suppressing of all false and Scandalous Pamphlets* was followed several weeks later by the closure of the theaters (and bear gardens) as potential breeding grounds for civil unrest and sedition. Parliament issued the order of September 2, 1642, at a time of political and social upheaval, and the printed version of the ordinance appeared as part of a two-page document titled *A Declaration of the Lords and Commons . . . For the appeasing and quietting of all unlawfull Tumults and Insurrections . . . Also an Ordinance of both Houses for the suppressing of Stage-Playes*. Instability in Ireland and internal unrest in England, which is described in some detail in the first declaration, called for a period of solemnity, not mirth. The concerns about the moral content of plays remained unaddressed while the order concentrated instead on the inappropriateness of festivities during a time of crisis: "While these sad Causes and set times of Humiliation doe continue, publicke Stage-Playes shall cease, and bee forborne. Instead of which, are recommended to the People of this Land, the profitable and seasonable Considerations of Repentance, Reconciliation, and Peace with God."[7]

Parliament's closure of the theaters after the outbreak of war did indeed gratify the anti-theater lobbyists; but it was also a security measure to discourage riotous assemblies, forestall possible royalist propaganda by the court companies, and prevent the dramatizing of popular grievances. The issuing of the September 1642 ordinance was thus perhaps motivated more by politics than by morality.[8] The management of political discourse involved curtailing the activities of the theater and the playwrights. But, as we discover more explicitly in the 1648 ordinance against stage performances, spectators themselves proved to be a threat to the regime and were punished for their defiance.

Although it is true that play-like pieces had already become manifest before 1642 and that they were on occasion even performed, pamphleteers now more regularly and self-consciously moved into the space largely vacated by the playwrights and actors. *The Actors Remonstrance* rehearses the complaints of the unemployed players who lament: "We might be enforced to act our Tragedies"; "Some of our ablest Poets [must resort] to get a living by writing contemptible penny-pamphlets"; "Nay, it is to be feared, that shortly some of them . . . will be encited to enter themselves into *Martin Parkers* society, and write ballads."[9] Thus despite the measures taken to control producers and productions of the stage, drama did not die in the 1640s and 1650s; instead, theatrical forms were truncated, compressed, or mixed around, as demonstrated by Lois Potter, Nigel Smith, Dale Randall, and Susan Wiseman.[10] The politicizing of theatrical discourse and the cultural and political work performed by alternative dramatic works are, then, of central concern in the early history of the *acting* press.[11] Having passed the first ordinance against play-acting, state officials nevertheless conceded that reformed dramas might be permissible under conditions like those outlined by Prynne or in the case of government-sponsored works such as the closet drama *Tyrannicall-Government Anatomized.*[12] Parliament ordered the printing of this translation of George Buchanan's *Baptistes* by the House of Commons Committee Concerning Printing in 1642/3. It may even have allowed actual performances of plays as stately and lofty as this, but the appeal of the play resides primarily in its performance as biblical history and political dialogue. Here, then, I consider the "book of the play" as a printed prose work that serves a polemical function.

I first trace the complex received tradition of *Tyrannicall-Government Anatomized*, under the rubric of *closet drama*—printed plays designed to be read rather than (or as well as) staged—which served as vehicles for political commentary and for the formation of alternative interpretive and political communities.[13] I situate this rare example of a parliamentary-sponsored play in relation to its literary inheritance, its engagement with the cultural and political moment in which it was printed, and the reading experience it conditions. I conclude with reference to the controversial attribution of *Tyrannicall-Government* to John Milton as polemicist and author of *Samson Agonistes* (1671), a Greek tragedy not intended for the stage.[14] In the Restoration, Milton, an admirer of Buchanan's poetics and politics, established an antagonistic relationship with the theater and marketplace, which provide the immediate contexts and material communities for his 1671 volume. Moreover, he produced an antiestablishment closet drama, one that offers "an internalised, read-only, version of that collective experience" made possible by the theater.[15]

The sixteenth-century Scottish humanist, poet, and reformer George Buchanan was the most famous author of Christian tragedies in his day, and among the first writers of Senecan tragedies. Buchanan's plays imitate the structure of those of Euripides, whose *Alcestis* and *Medea* he translated into Latin. Between 1541 and 1544 he produced his first biblical tragedy, *Baptistes sive Calumnia*, a blank verse tragedy on the arrest and death of John the Baptist, which was performed in Bordeaux in the 1540s, shown in manuscript form to Daniel Rogers in 1566, and thereafter printed in 1577. The frontmatter for *Baptistes* includes Buchanan's November 1, 1576, dedication to James VI, in which he recommends the use of the stage in imitating the classics, inspiring morality, and exposing tyrants. The dedication is followed by a prologue which includes the commonplace lament about the protean nature of audiences who indiscriminately attack theatrical productions. The true judge of his play is one who applies skill and moral sense ("aestimator candidus"), Buchanan maintains, and who recognizes that he as the playwright is aspiring to a higher or purer form of literary expression in staging the tragedy of the Baptist. The thrice-repeated reference to "calumnies" in the Latin prologue links the description of the fickle audiences to the murderers of the Baptist, and thus connects the trials of the playwright (and the historical Buchanan) to those of the Baptist as martyr.[16] While originally intended for performance by Buchanan's pupils, including Montaigne, *Baptistes sive Calumnia* was interpreted as a closet drama by Stephen Gosson, among others, who claimed that the moralizing and didactic effect of Buchanan's *Baptistes* depended on its being read.[17]

Although Buchanan was not connected to the Sidney circle, his play has much in common with the members of this group.[18] Under the patronage of Sidney's sister, the countess of Pembroke, playwrights of the Sidney circle refined the conventions of the Senecan models in developing the Sidnean closet dramas. English translations of Robert Garnier's neo-Senecan tragedies provided the basis for the overtly political, anti-court texts produced by members of the circle, including Fulke Greville, Samuel Daniel, William Alexander, Samuel Brandon, and Elizabeth Cary. The classicizing dramas interrogate theories of monarchy, tyranny, and rebellion by treating the evils of absolutism and the duties and corruption of kings and royal favorites. Generic features include the trappings of Italianate Senecanism; the primacy of speech and narrative over action; long rhetorical monologues and philosophical and moral discourses; the casting of women as heroes and villains; and the inclusion of a nuntius, as well as of a chorus that speaks from a limited rather than an authoritative position. The closet drama, moreover, provides an effective medium for staging the conflicts of a social rebel. The reader's assessment of the heroic nature of this controversial figure is inevitably frustrated by the play's resistance to any conclusive judgments about the protagonist.

The appeal of *Baptistes* extends beyond its dual function as a play and readerly text. Readily lending itself to allegorization, *Baptistes* also served as political commentary, and was interpreted variously as a warning against Henry VIII's marriage to Anne Boleyn, a condemnation of

Henry for his execution of Sir Thomas More, and an admonition to James VI of Scotland (Buchanan's pupil) about the evils of tyranny, specifically his attachments to the Scottish Catholic nobility. When brought before the Lisbon Inquisition in 1550, Buchanan swore under oath that the tragedy was about Sir Thomas More, Anne Boleyn, and Henry VIII, a gesture likely designed to appease the authorities. Buchanan's explanation about the political subtext remained unknown until the publication of the Lisbon documents in the 1890s; but even when this interpretation surfaced, it failed to settle the question about the play's significance.[19] Since he had become a Protestant by the time of his trial, it is all the more curious that Buchanan now cast his protagonist as a Catholic martyr rather than the Protestant reformer he was assumed to be. Still, Buchanan's latest interpretation would have met with approval from the authorities on the continent. No evidence exists of the extent to which Buchanan's inquisitors were satisfied with his response or whether they had even read the now lost manuscript play.[20] What we do know, however, is that the status of *Baptistes* as print, its association with Buchanan as the Scottish champion of Protestantism, and its amenability to political allegorization facilitated its entry into seventeenth-century political culture and literary history.

While it is true that the English translation of *Baptistes*, *Tyrannicall-Government Anatomized*, represents a rare if not unique example of a parliamentary-sponsored play, it is misleading to suggest that the play is devoid of a literary and generic context, or that members of Parliament otherwise expressed aversion to the genre of drama. In fact, dramatic conventions were commonly featured in the printed materials produced by Parliament in managing its public relations when "coordinating printing plans with legislative strategies had become an art of politics."[21] Parliament actually produced a wide range of alternative playtexts: legal proceedings, parliamentary speeches,[22] trial accounts, pamphlets, and satires. The release of *Tyrannicall-Government Anatomized* itself followed shortly after Parliament's issuing of the first printed speeches and newsbooks. Taken together, these government-sponsored writings shifted the theater to the political stage, the courtroom, and the court of public opinion. The ensuing war of words was played out in writings with dramatic conventions and performative effects, many of which "staged debates and posed questions, bringing to print culture the dialogic genre and space of drama in which, in the end, the reader or auditor has to choose and perform."[23] As Kevin Sharpe notes, a large number of the Thomason Tracts raise questions and present arguments and cases in dramatic forms. These are the new playtexts of the seventeenth century, all of which were intended to encourage active engagement and an alternative form of play-reading. Considered in relation to this context, the appeal of *Tyrannicall-Government Anatomized* to the House of Commons is all the more apparent.

Translated into a readerly prose text, *Tyrannicall-Government Anatomized* omits the frontmatter to *Baptistes*, including Buchanan's November 1, 1576, dedication to James VI and the prologue on the protean audience. The parts into which *Tyrannicall-Government Anatomized*, unlike *Baptistes*, is divided make it more conducive to reading while also inviting an interpretation of the work as a drama. Simultaneously exposing and disguising the text's original verse form, the translator renders his intentions unclear. Peter Hume Brown, Buchanan's biographer, who interpreted *Baptistes* through the lens of *Tyrannicall-Government Anatomized*, which he attributed to Milton, claimed that the latter is "hardly a drama at all, but simply a series of dialogues which naturally end with the death of the Baptist. There is no attempt at a plot, and there is not a single dramatic incident."[24] While Brown too easily dismisses the palimpsest nature of the text as play and prose work, he is justified in observing that the dramatic effect of *Tyrannicall-Government Anatomized* is partly a function of its exchanges and its parallelisms and dialogism. Throughout the play, values such as order, dignity, and authority (*ordo, dignitas, auctoritas*) are contrasted in their true and ironic senses.[25] John thus is accused of the crimes of which his enemies are guilty. While attacking John for being "puff'd with pride / Through the madnesse of the multitude" (*TGA* 55–56; 4), Malchus himself is exposed for his arrogance by Gamaliel (*TGA* 140–44; 6). Characterized by Malchus as an upstart who undermines the old law by establishing new sects and new rites (*TGA* 88–89; 5), and identified by Herod as one who will usurp his government by turning "all upside down" (*TGA* 582; 13), John in fact declares his intent to restore order to a corrupt society: "How piously I prize the holy Rites / And ancient institutions" (*TGA* 494–95; 12), he asserts.

The play and most of its speeches center directly on the question of the law and the tools of law enforcement. In response to Gamaliel's proposal that he apply arguments, reasons, and wit to bring John to justice, Malchus retorts that "cord, sword, and fire" (*TGA* 165; 6) are the only means of taming an insurrectionist. The issue of justice, however, is most obviously explored through the exposition of the internal theater, particularly that of Herod, to which a readerly text best lends itself. The role of judge is ascribed to readers who are privy to the central irony in the play identified by Buchanan in the epistle in *Baptistes*: tyrants are tormented when they seem especially to be thriving (*B* E9; A2v). Like *Baptistes*, *Tyrannicall-Government Anatomized* dramatizes the trial or case of conscience—what William Ames in the seventeenth century defined as "a practical question concerning which the conscience may make a doubt."[26] The mode was popularized by parliamentarians and royalists alike for publishing the struggles of conscience or (mock) confessions of political opponents, thus legitimizing past or proposed acts of justice.

In *Tyrannicall-Government Anatomized*, Herod, who is portrayed more ambiguously than his various counterparts in the earlier mystery plays, is persuasive and rhetorically well versed, as indicated by his ability to speak in Senecan commonplaces; and yet he also displays his weakness in submitting to his wife and daughter. Queen Herodias shares the role of tyrant with Malchus by being more conventionally evil. The exchange that opens part two mirrors the scenario from part one. Herodias, who assumes the voice of a Machiavellian prince in challenging the king's policies, repeats Malchus's arguments, particularly about the profanation of the old law—though she concentrates on secular rather than sacred law. Herod echoes Gamaliel's retorts about the just exercise of monarchical power. Struggling with his conscience and the terms of his political authority thereafter, Herod defends his impartiality while outlining to John the accusations directed against him; although he must punish John for his crimes against the state, Herod is willing to forgive the injury committed against his own person (*TGA* 449–50; 11). Herod's leniency is, however, short-lived, as evidenced in the final soliloquy of part two, which, according to the Chorus, discloses the "hidden meaning of [the Tyrant's] mind" (*TGA* 536; 12). By part five, the queen shames Herod into keeping his promise to grant his daughter's request for the head of the Baptist. Like Nicholas Grimald's character of Herodias in *Archipropheta*, which Buchanan used as a model for the queen, Herodias in *Baptistes* and *Tyrannicall-Government Anatomized* contributes to Herod's tyranny, but Herod wrongly blames her entirely for John's execution (*B* 1257; 60; *TGA* 1349; 25). The drama does more than just expose tyranny: it treats the subject complexly, showing how the tyrant is fashioned through the rhetorical arts of intellectual persuasion; indeed, as Rebecca Bushnell notes, "the political vocabulary defining tyranny and kingship was itself a locus of ideological struggle."[27]

The publication of the translated *Baptistes* involved in turn the translation of sixteenth-century political history into seventeenth-century events. Buchanan, it seems, had been right about the ongoing relevance of the position against tyranny offered by *Baptistes* and about the play's allegorical inclinations and design, which catered to popular interpretive practices. It is intriguing, as Dale Randall observes, that "the Commons itself deemed the resuscitation, translation, and publication of a potent old play to be an appropriate and effective way of aerating serious contemporary issues for English readers, including the King."[28] Curiously the 1643 title page indicates that the translation was "Presented to the KINGS most Excellent MAJESTY by the Author," the king in this case being the son of the monarch to whom *Baptistes* was dedicated. Perhaps Parliament was identifying itself as Charles's tutor, in light of the role that Buchanan originally played for James. Read as seventeenth-century political allegory, *Tyrannicall-Government Anatomized* casts Charles as Herod, Henrietta Maria as Herod's wife, and Parliament as John himself. The tyrant and his female accomplice are now allied with Catholicism, while the protagonist is properly Protestant again. In the eighteenth century, Francis Peck develops the allegory, identifying Herod with Charles I, Herodias and her daughter with "the one character of Q. HENRIETTA MARIA," Malchus with Archbishop Laud, Gamaliel with Bishop Williams, John the Baptist with William Prynne, the nuntius as "A rumor to surmise the intended making away of PRYNNE," and the Chorus of Jews as the Chorus of English puritans (271).

Though portrayed as a prophet and not as the messiah, John plays the part of the Christ-like martyr, speaking of his heavenly mission and undergoing trial and interrogation. His responses to the authorities, particularly to Malchus at the heart of the play, are deliberately evasive (*TGA* 819–33; 15–16), and he continually defends his decision *not* to act. Surprisingly, the eventual martyrdom of John is not of great significance to the Chorus, except insofar as it urges an examination of its own condition. In response to the Nuntius's testimony of John's decapitation and his counsel not to mourn for the martyr, the Chorus exclaims, "Verily you have utter'd nought amisse, / But we whom errors and opinion draw, / Foolish by flying death with death doe meet, / The water drowning whom the fire hath spard" (*TGA* 1448–51; 27). The inevitable confrontation with death, on which the Chorus dwells at the end of the tragedy, recalls the Chorus's earlier meditation on the "dark inner parts" of the mind (*TGA* 291; 9) in which numerous wild creatures are caged.

This closet drama thus self-consciously dramatizes the individual's struggles with both political tyranny and the tyrant within.

Classical Senecan dramatic writings did make occasional appearances in Civil War and Interregnum political culture, *The Tragedy of That Famous Roman Oratour Marcus Tullius Cicero* (1651) being the best example. Printed during the Commonwealth by Richard Cotes—appointed the official printer to the City of London in 1642—the play created a mythic vocabulary for and was used to validate republicanism, according to Susan Wiseman.[29] Continuing the tradition of the Greville circle's anti-tyrant drama, *The Tragedy of . . . Cicero* comes closest of all Interregnum plays to approximating old-fashioned Senecan tragedy.[30] The poet, Laureas, assigns to the historian, Tyro, the nuntius's task of "tell[ing] . . . the Tragick story" (E3v), though the account of Cicero's demise is relegated to a dialogue interspersed with the poet's colorful commentary. Ultimately Cicero opts for death rather than the destruction of his *Philippics*—his political writing. Reporting the dismemberment of Cicero, Tyro describes the amputation of the hands "that wrote those glorious *Philippicks*," to which Laureas adds, "Those illustrious hands / Which once held up this tottering Common-wealth, / And set her on her feet, when she was falling / From her proud orbe into a gulph of Fire" (E4r). The act of writing described in *The Tragedy of . . . Cicero* is, like the composition of the tragedy itself, an act not just of textual revolt but of political engagement.

At the same time, *The Tragedy of . . . Cicero* is marked both by obscurity and by the critique and evasion of historical events. The author moves between parliamentary and monarchical rule, an ambivalence that registers as well in the diverse contemporary interpretations of the text as republican and aristocratic. In contrast to Lois Potter, who maintains that the play "clearly supports the Commonwealth," and Susan Wiseman, who highlights the play's republican sentiment and Cicero's popular early modern identification as a "positive figure of secular republicanism," Nigel Smith characterizes *Cicero* as "a fully fledged anti-republican play" concerned with Cicero's murder.[31] According to Smith, *Cicero* treats the struggles of aristocratic power in the nation, and is at once critical of the regicide and concerned to identify the benefits of republicanism as an unattainable ideal. The complexity of the play and the different critical responses that constitute its reception history underscore Dale Randall's observation that "inconstancy lies at the bottom of all the major tragic action" and of all readerly representations of that action.[32]

Perhaps the most famous defender of republicanism in the period, one whose own writings were not spared the wrath of the monarchical regime, was Milton. His contribution to the anti-tyrant discourse in both the political and literary spheres is considerable. Among his models was George Buchanan, and long before producing his readerly drama *Samson Agonistes* (if we deem it a product of the 1660s), Milton situated himself in a canon of his making that included Buchanan. In his attack in the *Second Defense* on the excesses of popular tragedy, Milton invokes Buchanan's art as a counter-cultural example: "Now, poets who deserve the name I love and cherish, and I delight in hearing them frequently. Most of them, I know, are bitterly hostile to tyrants, if I should list them from the first down to our own Buchanan."[33] Poetics and politics go hand in hand for Milton, as they did for Buchanan, who likewise enlisted the reader in his service. While play-reading specifically would be lent a sense of deficiency after the waning of humanism, and certainly after the reopening of the royalist theaters in the Restoration, Milton insisted on the revolutionary and restorative nature of this form of critical and political engagement for his like-minded readers, whom he identifies in opposition to uncultivated or "vulgar" pro-royalist theater audiences.[34]

The new regime at this time was responsible for a "sharp contraction" of the public sphere as it exerted its influence over the press and modes of cultural production. Playwrights sympathetic to royalism closed off their texts from dissent by addressing a clientele captivated by spectacle. Milton is thus uncomfortably aware that certain readers will bring their expectations of heroic drama to their experience of the poem. "How else could Milton have responded but with intense curiosity and competitiveness when a form suddenly appeared in the mid-1660s that claimed to do exactly what had preoccupied him in the 1640s and toward which he had made his own notes and plan?" Steven N. Zwicker asks in a study of *Paradise Regained* as an anti-heroic form.[35] Like *Paradise Regained*, with which it was published, *Samson Agonistes* competes as a literary work and material object in a climate where court sponsorship of the theater otherwise precluded the production of such writings. As a closet drama indebted to the classical tragedy, *Samson Agonistes* takes on the form of an oppositional drama. The interpretive community Milton hoped to cultivate distanced itself from the Caroline theater culture, which was used to secure the control of the recently restored monarchy. The readership "hypothesized" by Milton or "postulated" by *Samson Agonistes*, for example, would be familiar with the Aristotelian theory of catharsis, the philosophy of Cicero and Plutarch, the works of Seneca and Martial, and the Renaissance tragedies of Italian playwrights who follow the ancients. The best judges of *Samson Agonistes* would, moreover, be not unacquainted with the greatest Greek playwrights, Aeschylus, Sophocles, and Euripides, "the three Tragic poets unequall'd yet by any," who offer models for the design of the plot.[36] The imagined community of partisan readers constitutes "an invisible public of like-minded readers" who participate individually in the kind of collective experience that theaters in the ancient republics had made possible.[37]

The interpretive experience is heightened in the concluding scene of the poem, which offers different accounts of Samson's act of (self-) destruction and invites an examination of the tragic hero's competing motives. In this controversial scene, Milton takes us "on a roller coaster of possible truths," while setting the stage for its controversial reading history.[38] The poem develops the tension between contradictory reports of Samson acting willfully (*SA* 1643) and of being "tangl'd in the fold / Of dire necessity" (*SA* 1665–66). Manoa first raises the issue of "Self-violence" (*SA* 1584) in his inquiry about the events leading to the deaths of the Philistines and Samson. Although the Messenger declares that Samson committed the slaughter with his own hands, he responds to Manoa by identifying the cause, "At once to destroy and be destroy'd" (*SA* 1588), as "Inevitable" (*SA* 1586). Thereafter, however, the Messenger offers a more complex reading of the scene when he attempts to re-create the interior drama: Samson stood "with head a while inclin'd / And eyes fast fixt," "as one who pray'd, / Or some great matter in his mind revolv'd" (*SA* 1636–38). While Samson's death is less controversial than Charles's martyrdom, it is more so than that of John in *Tyrannicall-Government Anatomized* or than the Son's acts of self-denial in *Paradise Regained*. The interpretive uncertainty surrounding Samson's final act again foregrounds the role of critical reader as *aestimator candidus*. But both the royalist-sponsored theater and the bookshop community ultimately impede Milton's efforts at controlling the reception of his closet drama, a genre that is itself on trial.

Milton's interest in classical readers and dramatic prescriptions in composing *Samson Agonistes* is not the only satisfactory explanation for his production of a closet drama. The play exposes Milton's concern to problematize closeted performances and encourage critical reading as an alternative performance. While its lofty style and classical sources place the text out of reach of the vulgar, *Samson Agonistes* nevertheless speaks to an antiestablishment culture through its visionary politics, its redefinition of authority and heroic performance, and its competing interpretations of the final act. Characterized in this manner, *Samson Agonistes* might be said to further the tradition of *Baptistes* and its "Englished" counterpart, *Tyrannicall-Government Anatomized.* Although the attribution of *Tyrannicall-Government Anatomized* to Milton has all but been dismissed, it continues to be cited by critics of the play. More important, what this investigation of the interrelationships of all three "closet dramas" has revealed is that the literary, polemical, and political practice of play-reading adds a vital dimension to textual analysis and reception history.

## NOTES

1. On the playwright as spokesperson for the age, see F. J. Levy, "Staging the News," in *Print, Manuscript, Performance: The Changing Relations of the Media in Early Modern England,* ed. Arthur F. Marotti and Michael D. Bristol (Columbus: Ohio State University Press, 2000), 252–78. See also chapter 6 by Alan Farmer in this volume.

2. Margot Heinemann, *Puritanism and Theatre: Thomas Middleton and Opposition Drama under the Early Stuarts* (Cambridge: Cambridge University Press, 1980), 231.

3. The antitheatrical prejudice has been "greatly exaggerated." Martin Butler, *Theatre and Crisis, 1632–1642* (Cambridge: Cambridge University Press, 1984), 96–99.

4. William Prynne, *Histrio-Mastix* (London: E[dward] A[llde, Augustine Mathewes, Thomas Cotes,] and W[illiam] J[ones] for Michael Sparke, 1633), 39–40, 832, 832–33, 923.

5. See, for example, Thomas Jordan, "The Players Petition to the Long Parliament, after being long silenc'd, that they might Play again, 1642," in *A nursery of novelties in Variety of Poetry. Planted for the delightful leisures of Nobility and Ingenuity. Composed by Tho. Jordan* (London: Printed for the author [1665?]), 79–80.

6. Lois Potter observes that the question "'Was it acted?'" fails to account for the numerous works that appeared in dramatic form in the mid-century ("Closet Drama and Royalist Politics," in *The Revels History of English Drama,* gen. ed. Lois Potter, vol. 4, *1613–1660,* ed. Philip Edwards et al. [London: Methuen, 1981], 264).

7. "A Declaration of the Lords and Commons. . . For the appeasing and quietting of all unlawfull Tumults and Insurrections. . . Also an Ordinance of both Houses for the suppressing of *Stage-Playes*" (London: for John Wright, 1642).

8. Heinemann, *Puritanism and Theatre,* 239; also see Louis Wright, "The Reading of Plays during the English Revolution," *Huntington Library Bulletin* 6 (1934): 75. David Scott Kastan argues that the injunction was "a pragmatic response to the spreading public discontent and disorder in the summer of 1642" ("Performances and Playbooks: The Closing of the Theatres and the Politics of Drama," in *Reading, Society, and Politics in Early Modern England,* ed. Kevin Sharpe and Steven N. Zwicker [Cambridge: Cambridge University Press, 2003], 171).

9. *The Actors Remonstrance, or Complaint: For the Silencing of their profession* (London: for Edw. Nickson, 1643), 6, 7.

10. Lois Potter, *Secret Rites and Secret Writing: Royalist Literature, 1641–1660* (Cambridge: Cambridge University Press, 1989); Nigel Smith, *Literature and Revolution in England, 1640–1660* (New Haven: Yale University Press, 1994); Dale B. J. Randall, *Winter Fruit: English Drama, 1642–1660* (Lexington: University Press of Kentucky, 1995); Susan Wiseman, *Drama and Politics in the English Civil War* (Cambridge: Cambridge University Press, 1998).

11. [John Ford], *The Queen, or the Excellency of Her Sex: An Excellent old Play* (London: by T. N. for Thomas Heath, 1653), A3r.

12. *Tyrannicall-Government Anatomized: Or, A Discourse Concerning Evil-Councellors* (London: for John Field, 1642/3). Also see *Tyrannicall-Government Anatomized,* in *A Critical Edition of George Buchanan's Baptistes and of Its Anonymous Seventeenth-Century Translation Tyrannicall-Government Anatomized,* ed. Stephen Berkowitz (New York: Garland, 1992). In parenthetical citations to *TGA,* the first numbers refer to verses in Berkowitz's edition, the second numbers to page numbers in the original prose version of February 9, 1642/3.

13. Marta Straznicky, "Closet Drama," in *Companion to Renaissance Drama,* ed. Arthur F. Kinney (Oxford: Blackwell, 2002), 417. Straznicky's survey focuses on prerevolutionary closet drama.

14. Francis Peck first made this attribution in *New Memoirs of the Life and Poetical Works of Mr. John Milton* (London, 1740), 278. On the attribution of the translation of *Baptistes* to Milton, see Sandra Kerman, "George Buchanan and the Genre of *Samson Agonistes,*" *Language and Style* 19 (1986): 23–24; Berkowitz, *Critical Edition,* 343–46; Butler, *Theatre and Crisis,* 99; Heinemann, *Puritanism and Theatre,* 234–35; P. Hume Brown, ed., *Vernacular Writings of George Buchanan,* Scottish Text Society no. 26 (Edinburgh: Blackwood, 1891–92), 77–87.

15. Smith, *Literature and Revolution,* 92.

16. George Buchanan, *Baptistes, sive calumnia tragoedia, auctore Georgio Buchanano Scoto* (London: Excudebat Thomas Vautrollerius, typographus, 1577), 8; for variations of "calumnies," see 7, 8. See also Buchanan, *Baptistes,* in Berkowitz, *Critical Edition,* 32; 13, 40, 49. In parenthetical citations to *B,* the first numbers refer to verses in Berkowitz's edition, the second numbers to page numbers in the original version.

17. Stephen Gosson, *Playes Confuted in Five Actions,* quoted in Arthur F. Kinney, *Markets of Bawdrie: The Dramatic Criticism of Stephen Gosson* (Salzburg: Institüt für Englische Sprache und Literatur, 1974), 177–78. In accordance with Aristotle's prescriptions and deemphasis on spectacle, Gosson judges neoclassical plays to be superior because they emphasize verbal exchanges over spectacle while exposing tyranny and empowering the critical reader.

Roger Ascham and Sir Philip Sidney were also among Buchanan's admirers. Ascham, who knew Buchanan, mentions that few tragedies in his day any longer used the ancient models of Euripides, Sophocles, and Seneca or applied the rules of Aristotle and Horace. The exceptions he cites are "M. Watsons *Absalon* and Georgius Buchananus *Jepthe.*" Lily Bess Campbell, *Divine Poetry and Drama in Sixteenth-Century England* (Berkeley: University of California Press, 1959), 182. In *An Apology for Poetry,* Sidney commends Buchanan's tragedies for "justly bring[ing] foorth a divine admiration." Other contemporaries of Buchanan, notably Henry Peacham, Sir William Temple, and Gabriel Harvey, like Gosson, valued *Baptistes* particularly for the message of the dedicatory epistle rather than for the play's dramatic qualities. Sir Philip Sidney, *An Apology for Poetry*, ed. Forrest G. Robinson (Indianapolis: Bobbs-Merrill, 1970), 80; see Berkowitz, *Critical Edition*, 136–37.

18. On the response of the Sidney circle to *Baptistes* and *De Jure Regni*, see James Emerson Phillips, "George Buchanan and the Sidney Circle," *Huntington Library Quarterly* 12 (1948–49): 23–55. See also Kerman, "George Buchanan," 21–25; and Peggy Anne Samuels, "*Samson Agonistes* and Renaissance Drama" (Ph.D. diss., City University of New York, 1993); Samuels, "Fire Not Light: Milton's Simulacrum of Tragicomedy," *Milton Quarterly* 30 (1996): 1–15.

19. James M. Aitken, *The Trial of George Buchanan before the Lisbon Inquisition* (London: Oliver & Boyd, 1939), 24, 25. On the sources for *Baptistes*, see Ian D. McFarlane, *Buchanan* (London: Duckworth, 1981), 381–85; and Berkowitz, *Critical Edition*, 105–59.

20. See Berkowitz, *Critical Edition*, 113–17.

21. David Zaret, *Origins of Democratic Culture: Printing, Petitions, and the Public Sphere in Early Modern England* (Princeton: Princeton University Press, 2000), 205.

22. A. D. T. Cromartie, "The Printing of Parliamentary Speeches, November 1640–July 1642," *Historical Journal* 33 (1990): 29–30.

23. Kevin Sharpe, *Reading Revolutions: The Politics of Reading in Early Modern England* (New Haven: Yale University Press, 2000), 335.

24. Brown, *Vernacular Writings*, 121–22.

25. For *Baptistes*, see 181, 267, 416, 650, 666, 753.

26. W[illiam] Ames, *Conscience with the Power and Cases thereof* (n.p., 1639), ii. 1, quoted in Keith Thomas, "Cases of Conscience in Seventeenth-Century England," in *Public Duty and Private Conscience in Seventeenth-Century England*, ed. John Morrill, Paul Slack, and Daniel Woolf (Oxford: Clarendon Press, 1993), 34.

27. Rebecca W. Bushnell, *Tragedies of Tyrants: Political Thought and Theater in the English Renaissance* (Ithaca: Cornell University Press, 1990), 78.

28. Randall, *Winter Fruit*, 103. Susan Wiseman reads the poem as a contemporary political allegory, suggesting an identification between Herod and Charles, who were both tyrannical despite their good intentions. "In relation to other plays published in the early 1640s which were not printed at the order of the government, this play is unusual in the way it makes an alliance with a Protestant tradition of tyrannicide found in the writings of Buchanan and others" (*Drama and Politics*, 70). Read as a topical political allegory, *Tyrannicall-Government Anatomized* must have been considered by parliament as "remarkably apt," according to A. L. Harbage, *Cavalier Drama: An Historical and Critical Supplement to the Study of the Elizabethan and Restoration Stage* (1936; New York: Russell & Russell, 1964), 178.

29. *The Tragedy of That Famous Roman Oratour Marcus Tullius Cicero* (London: Richard Cotes, for John Sweeting, 1651); cited parenthetically in the text. Wiseman, *Drama and Politics*, 79; on the play generally, see Wiseman 70–80, and Randall, *Winter Fruit*, 266–73.

30. Randall, *Winter Fruit*, 273; also see John Morrill, "Charles I, Cromwell, and Cicero (A Response to Dale B. J. Randall)," *Connotations* 1.1 (1991): 97–98, 100–101.

31. Potter, *Revels History*, 4:295; Wiseman, *Drama and Politics*, 77; Smith, *Literature and Revolution*, 84.

32. Randall, *Winter Fruit*, 272.

33. John Milton, *Second Defense of the English People*, in *Complete Prose Works of John Milton*, gen. ed. Don Wolfe, 8 vols. (New Haven: Yale University Press, 1953–82), 4:592.

34. Straznicky, "Closet Drama," 427. According to Alfred Harbage, only a few closet dramas were produced in the Restoration years, and these consisted mainly of political dialogues and Latin plays (*Annals of English Drama, 975–1700*, rev. Samuel Schoen-

baum, 2nd ed. [London: Methuen, 1964], 154–201). *Samson Agonistes* belongs in neither category and thus merits special consideration as an antitheatrical and, as I argue, a politically charged text. Also see Elizabeth Sauer, "The Politics of Performance in the Inner Theatre: *Samson Agonistes* as Closet Drama," in *Milton and Heresy*, ed. Stephen B. Dobranksi and John P. Rumrich (Cambridge: Cambridge University Press, 1998), 199–215.

35. Steven Zwicker, "Milton, Dryden, and the Politics of Literary Controversy," in *Heirs of Fame: Milton and Writers of the English Renaissance*, ed. Margo Swiss and David A. Kent (Lewisburg, Pa.: Bucknell University Press, 1995), 275.

36. John Milton, *Samson Agonistes*, in *John Milton: Complete Poems and Major Prose*, ed. Merritt Hughes (New York: Odyssey Press, 1957), 550; cited parenthetically as *SA*.

37. Leah S. Marcus, *Unediting the Renaissance: Shakespeare, Marlowe, Milton* (New York: Routledge, 1996), 211.

38. Stephen B. Dobranski, *Milton, Authorship, and the Book Trade* (Cambridge: Cambridge University Press, 1999), 56. Also see Elizabeth Sauer, "Milton and Dryden on the Restoration Stage," in *Fault Lines and Controversies in the Study of Seventeenth-Century English Literature*, ed. Claude J. Summers and Ted-Larry Pebworth (Columbia: University of Missouri Press, 2002), 88–110.

PART TWO

# Play-Reading and the Book Trade

FIVE

# Typographic Nostalgia: Play-Reading, Popularity, and the Meanings of Black Letter

ZACHARY LESSER

Part of what makes a history of reading so difficult to write is that reading occurs at the intersection of the material and the immaterial, the physical and the psychical, the letter and the spirit. Here I examine this intersection in one particular type of letter: the black-letter ("gothic" or textura) typeface. Black letter is suffused with nostalgia, both in the early modern period and in our own. The typeface has long enjoyed a privileged position among scholars because it seems to provide a material key to readership, in particular to "popular" readership and "popular culture." Since the beginnings of modern bibliography in the early twentieth century, scholars have asked the black-letter typography of "cheap print" (broadside ballads, chapbooks, romances) to serve as a "social discriminant" in differentiating "high" from "low" readers.[1]

But popular reading seems never to answer our demands to reveal itself, and our quest for it is thoroughly nostalgic. Nostalgia, according to Susan Stewart, involves the search for "re-union" or authenticity in the past, but such a "narrative utopia" works "only by virtue of its partiality," its tendentious and incomplete representation of history, making any such re-union impossible. Nostalgia thus functions to reproduce itself endlessly, as the lack that incites desire is rediscovered. Nostalgic desire does not supply some present lack with the fullness of the past, but rather reproduces the desire for fullness itself: "Nostalgia is the desire for desire."[2]

We can see a similar process at work in critical interpretations of black letter and "popular culture." Typographic nostalgia imagines the popular as a unified and distinct culture, locating in some (always shifting) past the moment of a split between high and low, elite and popular. But, as Scott Shershow writes, "rival social groups . . . never really 'have' their 'own' separate and autonomous cultures but are, instead, participants in intricately interrelated fields of cultural production whose distinctions are merely self-constructed and self-proclaimed."[3] It is not simply that the boundaries between "high" and "low" are porous, nor that our archives are inevitably tainted by cultural "mediators" who represent the popular in forms at some remove from the reality of popular culture.[4] Rather, as Roger Chartier argues, the very search for popular culture relies on a series of flawed assumptions: first, "that it is possible to establish exclusive relationships between specific cultural forms and particular social groups"; second, "that the various cultures existing in a given society are sufficiently pure, homogeneous, and distinct to permit them to be characterized uniformly"; and third, "that the category of 'the people' or 'the popular' has sufficient coherence and stability to define a distinct social identity that can be used to organize cultural differences."[5]

Because these assumptions nostalgically posit a unity and an authenticity to popular culture that dissolve on closer inspection, in discussions of black-letter printing the "people" supposedly signaled as readers of this typeface slide up and down the social scale, and the moment in which the people became separated from "high" culture (or when elites "withdrew" from popular culture) slides back and forth in time. Popular culture itself can never be "discovered" because it does not exist as an autonomous entity, neither as a "system of shared meanings, attitudes, and values" nor as "the symbolic forms . . . in which they are expressed or embodied."[6] But the search continues: the study of popular culture is the desire for popular culture.

A brief review of the work on black letter reveals that this desire springs from a fundamental misconception of the workings of the "systems of linguistic and bibliographical codings" that make up books.[7] Jerome McGann and D. F. McKenzie have stressed that the material aspects of books—typeface, layout, format—are semiotic codings and therefore must be interpreted just as much as language.[8] Almost all studies of black letter, however, see the typeface merely as a direct *index* to readership, one that has seemed all the more appealing, I suspect, because of the apparently empirical quality of bibliography as compared to literary criticism.[9]

Already in R. B. McKerrow's *Introduction to Bibliography for Literary Students*, one of the earliest and most influential New Bibliographical texts, black letter was seen as a marker of popular reading and used to distinguish "high" from "low" forms of literature.[10] But it was Charles Mish's essay "Black Letter as a Social Discriminant in the Seventeenth Century" that most entrenched the notion that the typeface could serve as an index to popular culture. Noting that some romances were printed in roman type while others were printed in black letter, and perceiving that the typographic categories aligned with generic categories, Mish concluded that "there must have been two distinct groups of readers in early Stuart times, each with its own provender," and that "the chivalric romances—those designed to satisfy middle-class tastes—are set in black letter; the sentimental or heroic romances—the reading of the upper class—make use of roman type." As roman became the standard type for English books around 1590, the use of black letter became "something of a cultural retardation," indicating "the conservatism of the middle-class reading public."[11]

Mish's argument has been accepted rather uncritically, and if the phrase "cultural retardation" has perhaps been deemed too pejorative, his notion that popular reading is a residue of formerly elite taste that has "sunk" to lower social ground has persisted. In his study of prose fiction, Paul Salzman writes that "the use of this unfashionable type-face is indicative of the conservative nature of the form and its readers" and that books printed in black letter "were read by a less sophisticated public than the newly fashionable, more expensive heroic romances, printed in roman type."[12] Bernard Capp claims that John Taylor's readers "were the 'better sort,' respectable tradesmen with a sound schooling," because "his pamphlets were generally printed in roman type, not the black letter still widely used for the most popular fare."[13] Examples could be multiplied.[14]

As I have argued elsewhere, however, while the material features of books testify to the readership imagined by publishers, the readings they expected from their customers, and the marketing strategies designed to reach them, they tell us less about the actual readers of books. Examining presentational choices such as typeface, format, and the use of woodcuts or engravings helps us to understand the position of a particular book within the entire marketplace of print, and books may indeed be positioned as "low" or "high" in this market, just as they may be positioned along a host of other ideological ranges: "scholarly" or "idle," "masculine" or "feminine," "puritan" or "Armininian." But we cannot easily identify the ideological position of a book in the market with its actual readers. Books positioned as "low" (perhaps ballads or merry tales like *Adam Bell or Tom Thumb*) did not automatically or exclusively have a "low" readership, merely a readership interested, for whatever variety of reasons, in a "low" book.[15] We can no more say that such "low" books were read exclusively by poorer or less educated readers than we can say that books polemically positioned as Arminian were read exclusively by Arminians; we know that Archbishop Laud's godly accuser William Prynne, for one, had carefully read the works of Laud and his followers.[16] Similarly, we owe the very survival of many seventeenth-century ballads to the collecting efforts of such highly privileged readers as John Selden and Samuel Pepys, interested precisely in the power of such "slight" ephemera to capture what Selden called "the Complexion of the times."[17]

Much of the "conservatism" that Mish and his followers identify in fact resides not in readers' taste but in publishers' and printers' work habits. Typography was an extremely conservative medium in early modern England, and books rarely changed from black letter to roman (or vice versa) from one edition to the next.[18] The fact that black letter was "still" used in later editions of books first printed in that typeface is not surprising, nor does it indicate an unchanging or static *reading of* these texts. And merely because roman came to dominate many classes of books does not mean that black letter is a residual "cultural retardation." As Tim Harris astutely notes, arguments that seek to "identify what 'popular culture' was like" before some putative "long-term cultural change" tend to represent culture "as a static structure, or almost as a reified object." But since culture is in fact dynamic, inevitably "over time certain facets of this culture are seen to disappear," and therefore in "adopting this conceptual approach it is inevitable that this traditional culture is always going to appear to be shrinking."[19] The Mish tradition similarly identifies black letter with "traditional" culture, then notes its shrinking use after about 1590, and concludes therefore that books printed in black letter after that date form the residual culture of the "people."

But who exactly were these "people"? For Mish, they are middle-class merchants and tradesmen, since the "lower class can hardly be said to constitute a segment of the reading public."[20] For Capp, the "people" are instead those Mish defines as the "lower class," since Taylor's roman works were read by the same "respectable tradesmen" whom Mish sees as the readers of black letter. For Hyder Rollins, black-letter ballads were "written down to the level of the least intelligent reader."[21] While black letter appears to be the material index to a class of readers, the specifics of these class formations are never stable. What this instability reveals is that black letter is in fact not an *index* but a *signifier*, a sliding signifier of the "low" that depends on how the critic defines the total spectrum of readers.

A second highly influential strand of scholarship identifying black-letter type with a particular class of "low" readers derives from Keith Thomas's groundbreaking article "The Meaning of Literacy in Early Modern England."[22] Thomas cites Mish to argue that "black letter was the type for the common people; it survived into the eighteenth century in children's primers and in the ballads and romances published in chap-book form for consumption by the unsophisticated." But Thomas adds another component to this argument by claiming that black letter type was literally easier to read than roman: "Black-letter literacy . . . was a more basic skill than roman-type literacy; and it did not follow that the reader fluent in one was equally at home in the other."[23] Thomas's argument too has been picked up somewhat hastily by scholars to indicate that "readers at the lower end of literate society" were "unable to read in Roman type works they had mastered in Gothic."[24]

But Thomas in fact provides no evidence for his claim apart from the fact that books often used for learning to read—hornbooks, catechisms, psalters—were usually printed in black letter. And the claim that some readers found roman type more difficult to read seems rather unlikely. For what it's worth, twentieth-century studies of typography by cognitive psychologists have generally concluded that all typefaces in wide circulation at a given time are equally legible.[25] More important, from the late sixteenth century on, almost no books were printed entirely in black letter: virtually all black-letter books contained a roman (and italic) title page.[26] Given that the title page was the most important marketing tool at the publisher's disposal, it seems odd to suggest that black-letter books were targeted at "early" readers because that typeface was literally easier to read, when the first part of the book these readers would see—and the part designed to attract their attention and their money—was printed in a typeface supposedly difficult for them to read. Similarly, black-letter broadsides such as ballads and proclamations were almost always printed with roman headers, including the title.

Further, while stationers evidently did feel that these classes of "early reading" books required black letter, they felt exactly the same way about a category of books obviously intended not for the common reader but for a highly specialized, elite reader: almost all law books were printed in black letter. We should therefore hesitate before accepting claims that stationers "associate[d] roman type with a higher level of literacy and education than blackletter."[27] Notably, the various scholarly explanations for black-letter law book printing—that the type "confer[red] a kind of antiquarian dignity," or that it carried state authority (being also used for official proclamations), or even that it was associated, through the link between English law and Norman French, with Norman French gothic handwriting—all assert a *semiotic* explanation, seeing black letter as a signifier carrying meaning, not as a simple index to readers.[28] But law books—and, often, large chronicle histories priced beyond the means of the "common people"—are almost always considered exceptions to the rule of the "popularity" of black letter, and thus contradictory evidence is simply excluded from consideration. Faced with the totality of evidence, however, we might conclude not that law books and chronicles are the semiotic exceptions to an indexical rule, but rather that hornbooks, primers, and catechisms were likewise thought to require black letter because the typeface carried meaning.

Black letter, after all, was also known as "English letter," a name that draws the distinction with "Roman" type more clearly; "English letter" was the dominant type for vernacular books in the first century of printing in England. Given this strong association, and the conservatism of typography in general, perhaps we should not be surprised that books designed to teach the reading of the English language were printed in English letter. We should not, however, conclude with Peter Blayney that more educated readers eventually graduated to roman type, leaving black letter behind. Blayney's claim that "the basic Latin school text, Lily's *Grammar*, was therefore printed in roman" needs to be qualified.[29] Most editions of William Lily's *Short Introduction of Grammar* were bilingual (with the latter half entirely in Latin and the first half in Latin and English), and throughout the early modern period, in fact, these editions used roman (or italic) type for their Latin and black letter for their English translations and instructions (fig. 5-1).[30] The typography of Lily's textbook, then, does not signal a split in the book trade between black-letter printing for less educated and roman printing for more educated readers, as Blayney contends. Rather, the typographic distinction drawn between the two languages in the *Grammar* shows that more educated readers were still reading plenty of black letter, and it further points us toward the semiotics of black letter in the hornbooks and primers that had earlier taught them their "English letter(s)." Similarly, as late as 1659, William Somner's *Dictionarium Saxonico-Latino-Anglicum* employed roman for its Latin and black letter for its English

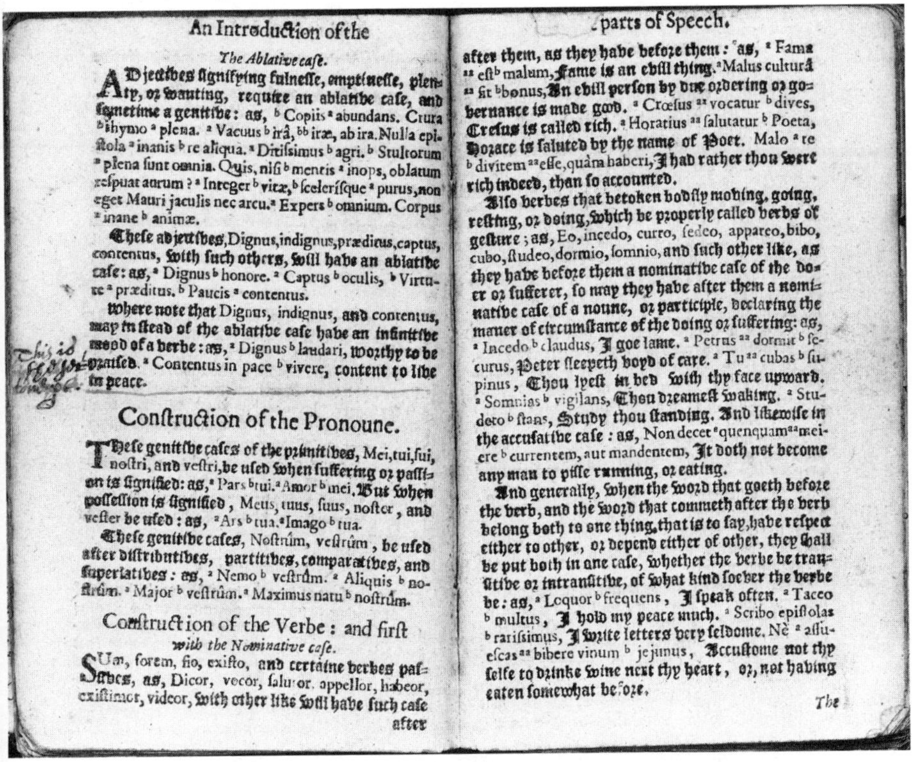

An Introduction of the

*The Ablative case.*

Adjectives signifying fulnesse, emptinesse, plenty, or wanting, require an ablative case, and sometime a genitive: as, [b] Copiis [a] abundans. Cura [b] thymo [a] plena. [a] Vacuus [b] irâ, [bb] iræ, ab ira. Nulla epistola [a] inanis [b] re aliqua. [a] Ditissimus [b] agri. [b] Stultorum [a] plena sunt omnia. Quis, nisi [b] mentis [a] inops, oblatum respuat aurum? [a] Integer [b] vitæ, [b] scelerisque [a] purus, non eget Mauri jaculis nec arcu. [a] Expers [b] omnium. Corpus [a] inane [b] animæ.

These adjectives, Dignus, indignus, prædictus, captus, contentus, with such others, will have an ablative case: as, [a] Dignus [b] honore. [a] Captus [b] oculis, [b] Virtute [a] præditus. [b] Paucis [a] contentus.

Where note that Dignus, indignus, and contentus, may in stead of the ablative case have an infinitive mood of a verbe: as, [a] Dignus [b] laudari, worthy to be praised. [a] Contentus in pace [b] vivere, content to live in peace.

Construction of the Pronoune.

These genitive cases of the primitives, Mei, tui, sui, nostri, and vestri, be used when suffering or passion is signified: as, [a] Pars [b] tui. [a] Amor [b] mei. But when possession is signified, Meus, tuus, suus, noster, and vester be used: as, [a] Ars [b] tua. [a] Imago [b] tua.

These genitive cases, Nostrûm, vestrûm, be used after distributives, partitives, comparatives, and superlatives: as, [a] Nemo [b] vestrûm. [a] Aliquis [b] nostrûm. [a] Major [b] vestrûm. [a] Maximus natu [b] nostrûm.

Construction of the Verbe: and first *with the Nominative case.*

Sum, forem, fio, existo, and certaine verbes passives, as, Dicor, vocor, salutor, appellor, habeor, existimor, videor, with other like will have such case after

parts of Speech.

after them, as they have before them: as, [a] Fama [aa] est [b] malum, Fame is an evill thing. [a] Malus culturâ [aa] fit [b] bonus, An evill person by due ordering or governance is made good. [a] Crœsus [aa] vocatur [b] dives, Cresus is called rich. [a] Horatius [aa] salutatur [b] Poeta, Horace is saluted by the name of Poet. Malo [a] te [b] divitem [aa] esse, quàm haberi, I had rather thou were rich indeed, than so accounted.

Also verbes that betoken bodily moving, going, resting, or doing, which be properly called verbs of gesture; as, Eo, incedo, curro, sedeo, appareo, bibo, cubo, studeo, dormio, somnio, and such other like, as they have before them a nominative case of the doer or sufferer, so may they have after them a nominative case of a noune, or participle, declaring the maner of circumstance of the doing or suffering: as, [a] Incedo [b] claudus, I goe lame. [a] Petrus [aa] dormit [b] securus, Peter sleepeth voyd of care. [a] Tu [aa] cubas [b] supinus, Thou lyest in bed with thy face upward. [a] Somnias [b] vigilans, Thou dreamest waking. [a] Studeo [b] stans, Study thou standing. And likewise in the accusative case: as, Non decet [a] quenquam [aa] meiere [b] currentem, aut mandentem, It doth not become any man to pisse running, or eating.

And generally, when the word that goeth before the verb, and the word that commeth after the verb belong both to one thing, that is to say, have respect either to other, or depend either of other, they shall be put both in one case, whether the verbe be transitive or intransitive, of what kind soever the verbe be: as, [a] Loquor [b] frequens, I speak often. [a] Taceo [b] multus, I hold my peace much. [a] Scribo epistolas [b] rarissimus, I write letters very seldome. Ne [a] assuescas [aa] bibere vinum [b] jejunus, Accustome not thy selfe to drinke wine next thy heart, or, not having eaten somewhat before.

The

FIG. 5-1. William Lily, *A Short Introdvction of Grammar, generally to be vsed* (London, 1633), D5v–6r. By permission of the Folger Shakespeare Library.

translations of Anglo-Saxon words (fig. 5-2). Printed at Oxford for the use of scholars, the large folio dictionary, with a Latin title page, was obviously not meant for the beginning reader. Most catechisms as well (*pace* Thomas) employed various typefaces, and they too illustrate the use of black letter as a signifier of basic English knowledge, for catechisms generally use roman for the questions and black letter for the responses demonstrating the catechumen's knowledge and acceptance of the fundamental tenets of the English church.[31]

Much of the meaning of black letter may not have been fully conscious to printers and publishers; its use in primers and hornbooks may be another example of what I have elsewhere called "typographic inevitability."[32] But the semiotics of black letter could become not just conscious but polemical in particularly charged political moments: when

M A | M A | M E

num, clientum vel vassallorum cœtus. a multitude, train or retinue of men, clients, vassals or tenants: the manred or company of homagers. ⁊ ealle hi bugon to Israhela manrædene. i. *atque omnes in Israelitarum clientelam redacti sunt.* Jos. 21. 44. Horum munus & officium *Belgis* man-schap.
Man-slaga. Homicida. a manslayer.
Man-slæge. man-slege. *ut,*
Man-sliht. (*al.* slyht.) Homicidium. man-slaughter.
Mans-long. *i. e.* manners-leng.
Man-sumnunge. *ut* amansumnunge.
Man-swara. Dejerator. a great swearer. *item* perjurium. perjury.
Man-swerian. Pejerare. to forswear.
Man-swica. Seductor, deceptor, circunventor. a seducer, a deceiver, a cheater.
Man-swora. Perjurus. a perjured person.
Man-ðeof. *Vide* man, Mannus.
Man-ðwære. Mitis, mansuetus, tame, mild.
Man-ðwærian. Mansuescere, mansuefacere. to become or wax tame or gentle: also, to make tame or gentle.
Man-ðwærnesse. Mansuetudo. mildnesse, gentlenesse, meeknesse, tamenesse.
Manunge. Admonitio, monitum, exhortatio. an admonition, a warning, an advertisement, an exhortation. *item* exactio. a levying. gafoles manung. tributi exactio.
Man-weorc. Malum, nefas. evill, naughtinesse. ad verbum, malum opus.
Man-weorðunge. Falsus cultus. false worship.
Man-wræce. Infandus, nefandus. *MS.* horrible, wicked, villanous, heinous.
Man-wyrð. Vitæ hominis æstimatio, pretium, vel valor. the price or value of a mans life or head: every man, according to his degree being rated at a certain price, according whereunto satisfaction was made to his Lord upon the killing of him. *V.* man-bot.
Mapulðorn. Acer, arbor. a maple-tree.
Mara. *L. M.* p. 3. c. 1. morbus. Incubus, Ephialtes. the night-mare. *V.* mære.
Mara. *i. e.* mære. major.

Maran-land. Terra firma, continens. the continent, the main land.
Mar-beam. Morus. the mulberry tree.
Marc. *i.* mearc.
Mare. Plus, majus, magis, amplius. more. mare ⁊ mare. *magis, magisque.* ge ða mare ge ða mætre. *tam publicus quam privatus. Bed.* Hist. li. 4. c. 25.
Margene. margne. *i. e.* morgen.
Marman- (*al.* marm- ) stan. Marmor. marble, or a marble stone.
Marne. Mane. morne, morning.
Maroaro. Moravia. the country of *Moravia.*
Marða. *ut* mærða. Mirabilia.
Martige. Martius mensis. the moneth of March.
Martyr. Martyr. a martyr.
Martyrad. martyrode. martyrode. *i.* gemartyrad.
Martyrdom. Martyrium. martyrdome.
Martyrhade. *idem.*
Marubie. Marrubium. the herb horehound.
Mare. Parula. *D.* fortasse, Parra. *Vide* colmase. quin & cogitandum de *Teutonico* meese. *i.* parus, *Gallis*, mesange.
Mase. Gurges. a swallow or deep pit in water, a gulfe, a whirlpool.
Massere. Mercator. a merchant.
Maðelan. *i. e.* mæðelan.
Maðele. Tumultuosus. tumultuous.
Maðelere. *ut* mæðelere.
Maðel-ern. *i. e.* mæðel-ern.
Maðelung. Garrulitas, verbositas. much or busie babling, pratling, talking, or speaking.
Maðmas. *i. e.* madmas.
Maðm-horda mæst. Arca *Noæ* sic dicta. *q.* gazophilaceorum præstantissimum.
Maðm-hus. *i. e.* madme-hus.
Maðm-hyrd. Thesaurarius. a treasurer.
Maðu. Cimex. a kind of stinking worme that biteth men in their beds, as fleas do: a punie, a wall-louse.
Mattuc. Bipalium. a mattock. *V.* meottoc.
Matu. Malignus. Psal. *Sax.* 34. 30. malicious, envious, spitefull, cruell, wicked.
Mapan. Secare. to cut, to mow.
Mapillan. Malle. to have liever, to will rather.
Max-wyrte. *L. M.* p. 1. capp. 36. 38. 41. it. p. 2. c. 24. quod-

dam (forte) diluti genus. woort, or new beer. *Vide* mæxwært.

M E

Me. Me. me.
Mead-sceat. *i. e.* med-sceat.
Meagolnesse. Potentia, potestas, vires, facultas. power, might. þancian drihtne mid ealre heortan meagolnesse. i. *Domino gratias agere cum omni cordis potentia.*
Meahte. Numen, potestas. power and authority. *item* potentatus. puissance, great power. *it.* auxilium. help. *it.* nutus. a beck, a nod. *V.* mæht.
Mealewe. Farina. meal.
Mealm-stan. Saxon. *Orosii* interpres, li. 4. c. 23. hit bið eac georplic þ mon hearðlic gnide þone hnes-cestan mealm-stan. æfter þam þ he þence þone seles tan hwet-stan þær on to geræcanne. *fortasse*, lapis quidam mollior.
Mealt. Brasium, byne, hordeum madefactum. malt. *Belgis*, malt, mout.
Mealwe. Malua. a mallow. wilde mealwe. malua agrestis. wild mallow. mersc-mealwe. althæa, ibiscus. marsh-mallow.
Mearc. Signum, nota, character. a signe, a note, a character, a mark. *item* terminus. a bound. Hinc Latino-barbarum *marca, marcha*, pro limite imperii. The borders between both *England* and *Scotland*, and between *England* and *Wales* are vulgarly called the *Marches.* item, memmus idem cum mancos, mancs, & mancus, de quo in Glossar. nostro.
Mearcan. mearcian. Signare, obsignare, notare. to mark, to signe, to note. *Kiliano*, marcken.
Mearcunge. Obsignatio, notatio. a signing. *item* capitulatio, in capitula, vel per capitula divisio vel distributio. a dividing by or into chapters.
Mearð. *i. e.* mearð.
Mearg. *ut* merg.
Mearh. *idem.* mearh gehæc. Isicium. a certain kind of pudding called an *Ising*, or *sausage*. mearh hæccel. *idem.* item, farcimen. a pudding made with marrow.
Mearð. Præmium. reward. *N.* perperam, ni fallor: merces scil.
Cc pro

FIG. 5-2. William Somner, *Dictionarivm Saxonico-Latino-Anglicum* (London, 1659), 2Cir. By permission of the Folger Shakespeare Library.

Archbishop Laud tried to impose a new prayer book on the Scottish church in 1637, he had the commanding folio book printed in black letter, as virtually all folio Books of (English) Common Prayer had been printed. Part of the resentment aroused by Laud's effort, part of what sparked the rioting that ultimately led to war, was the typography of the book.[33] Laud's choice of black letter was designed to extend his drive for uniformity of religious practice ("common prayer") to the Kirk, which had long been printing its own Book of Common Order in roman, the typeface of the godly Geneva Bible.[34] Black letter here emphasized not only the antiquity and authority of black-letter chronicles and state proclamations but also something of the semiotics of primers and catechisms: the "Englishness" of the typeface and of the episcopacy was the central issue in many Scottish minds.

Black letter thus carried many meanings in early modern England: state authority, antiquity, the English language, the established English church, even the foreign quality of the "stage Dutch" spoken by characters in many printed plays. And, of course, the use of black letter was also partially determined by the more mundane requirements of printers: the amount and kinds of type they stocked, the type used in other books they were simultaneously printing. We must resist the reductionism that would see only a single meaning to the typeface, which was used in a wide variety of contexts, or that would see no meaning at all in it, only an index to "popular culture." But one of the dominant meanings of black letter in this period, I am suggesting, was the powerful combination of Englishness (the "English letter") and past-ness (the "antiquated" appearance of black letter by the seventeenth century) that I call typographic nostalgia. It is this combination that allows black letter to evoke the traditional English community, and a large part of what scholars are really discovering when they perceive "popular culture" in black letter is the construction of this nostalgia in the very texts they are reading.[35]

Like most nostalgic myths, typographic nostalgia presents an image of unity, as shown by the use of the typeface in the Book of Common Prayer, catechisms, and official proclamations, all texts designed to enforce conformity. Modern critical nostalgia about black letter has often reinscribed this myth: taking their cue from Peter Burke's influential study of European popular culture, scholars often take black letter to represent the "common culture" of English people of all ranks, before the "withdrawal" of the elites from the "little tradition" they shared with the common people.[36] For example, while Tessa Watt is careful to avoid the nostalgic attempts of Mish and others to isolate "the people" and the texts that supposedly made up "their" culture, her largely revisionist account rejects "confrontational models" in favor of a broadly consensual model of culture, locating in black-letter ballads and cheap print the "common ground" of early modern English Protestantism.[37]

The danger here, as Peter Stallybrass and Allon White have argued about popular culture studies in general, is of overlooking conflict and contestation in a "simple before/after model" that almost inevitably succumbs to "an idealist or idealizing moment of apocalypse or nostalgia around the 'disappearance'" of organic culture and "real community."[38] Attention to the politics of reading can help us avoid this danger. On the one hand, certainly many black-letter texts were among the cheapest and hence most widely available in the period, and these were probably purchased, read, or listened to by a wide range of people; in this sense, we can speak of the part they played in the "common" culture of England. On the other hand, we should not assume that all people consumed these texts in the same way: a laborer who reads a black-letter ballad on a tavern wall is not reading quite the "same" text as a nobleman who transcribes the printed ballad into his manuscript commonplace book, or as Selden and Pepys, who bought and read ballads as part of a large collection.[39] If, as Fredric Jameson has argued, "a history lesson is the best cure for nostalgic pathos," then focusing our analysis on the ways in which black letter could be *read*, the meanings it carried in the full context of both the book trade and English social hierarchy, offers the best cure for typographic nostalgia.[40]

I want to suggest how such an analysis might proceed by looking at the career of one important publisher of black-letter texts in the seventeenth century, John Wright, and at his black-letter publication of one of the most successful early modern printed plays, Thomas Dekker's *The Shoemaker's Holiday*. As I have shown elsewhere, publishers in early modern England tended to specialize in the kinds of books they produced, in order to find a profitable niche within the marketplace of print.[41] Wright was no exception. By examining Wright's career from its beginning in 1605 through 1631, when he published his final edition of *Shoemaker's*, I will first show that Wright was a "popular" publisher according to three specific, but not necessarily interrelated, meanings of that term: first, most simply, his books sold well and were often reprinted; second, he employed a business strategy that emphasized the "tried and true"; and third, the books in which he specialized have traditionally (but, as I have been arguing, erroneously) been seen by critics as "for the common people." I then turn to *Shoemaker's*, arguing that the typographic nostalgia of black letter perfectly parallels the nostalgic politics of Dekker's play, and that this confluence helped not only to ensure the play's popularity but also to construct the very meaning of popularity itself.

John Wright published two of the three best-selling plays of the early modern professional stage, *Mucedorus* (fifteen editions by 1660) and *Doctor Faustus* (nine editions), in addition to *Shoemaker's* (six editions), another of the top fifteen best-sellers.[42] Among his non-dramatic books were some of the period's other best-sellers, including Philip Stubbes's *Life and Death of Katherine Stubbes* (twenty-four editions by 1640), John Dod and Robert Cleaver's *Exposition of the Ten Commandments* (eighteen editions), the anonymous *Shepherd's Kalendar* (sixteen editions), and William Perkins's *Death's Knell* (which claims sixteen editions on its title pages, though not all are extant). But, as Tessa Watt argues, "there is no straight equation between 'popularity' in numerical terms and print for the 'popular' classes," since literacy was weighted toward the high end of the social scale.[43] Further, there is no direct equation between numerical popularity and black-letter printing. While three of the four non-dramatic best-sellers mentioned here were so printed (all but Dod and Cleaver's *Exposition*), two of them were religious books, associated with black letter through its use in many editions of the Bible and the Book of Common Prayer, and the third, *The Shepherd's Kalendar*, may have used black letter for its effect of typographic nostalgia, as I suggest later. By contrast, only three of the fifteen best-selling plays were printed in black letter (all editions of *Faustus* and *Shoemaker's*, and four of six editions of *1 & 2 Edward IV*), and the overall best-seller *Mucedorus* used roman type throughout its history. Certainly for plays, then, numerical popularity did not automatically translate into black letter.

While Wright published many of the period's best-selling books, he generally did not publish all or even the majority of their editions. Wright employed a business strategy that might itself be described as "popular publishing," as he sought to acquire the rights to books that had already gone through a substantial number of editions for other publishers. Wright published 113 titles between 1605 and 1631, but *his* first editions of these books were, on average, between the second and third *overall* editions; a full 25 percent of his initial publications were already reprints. Wright published the seventh edition (of ten) of Henry Smith's popular sermon *The Trumpet of the Soul*, and the seventh (of ten) of Thomas Lupton's book of receipts, *A Thousand Notable Things*. Dod and Cleaver's *Exposition* had already gone through seventeen editions when Wright acquired the rights to it, and *The Shepherd's Kalendar* thirteen; his first edition of Perkins's *Death's Knell* was the tenth overall, and he began publishing *Katherine Stubbes* with the eleventh.

Since critics have generally expected that best-sellers, because of their very popularity, can "tell us about the values, tastes, and expectations of their mass audience," Wright will thus look like a publisher targeting the common people, the "little tradition," or the broadly consensual mainstream.[44] But he will look so *only as a side effect or epiphenomenon* of what seems to be an underlying business decision to invest in acquiring rights to profitable books rather than searching for new copy in the hope of correctly gauging the market himself. Even apart from the problems inherent in taking numerical popularity as a guide to popular culture, then, Wright's commercial strategy seems aimed not at a specific group of consumers so much as at a specific kind of book (the proven seller), and without direct evidence (always hard to come by), we cannot be sure who the actual readers of these books were. If Wright's strategy might be called "popular" because he sought out books that had already proved their worth, we must not presume that this strategy was either unique to or necessary for stationers interested in "popular culture." John Trundle, another stationer involved in the publication of cheap print, took the opposite approach from Wright, seeking out new and promising copy and selling the rights to stationers with more capital at their disposal to produce the edition.[45]

Wright has already been the subject of extensive study by Tessa Watt, who concluded that, along with his partners in the syndicate formed to produce, market, and distribute ballads in the 1620s, Wright helped to develop the trade in "penny merries" and "penny godlies" (small books of one to one and a half sheets) that formed the core of "popular" print culture in the late seventeenth century.[46] From 1605 to 1631, six in ten books published by Wright were broadsides, penny books, and short pamphlets (three and a half sheets or less), and during the same period, over 60 percent of his output was black-letter printing, an extremely high proportion for a seventeenth-century publisher. There can be no doubt that Wright was specializing in cheap print, nor that black-letter books tended to be shorter, and hence cheaper, than books printed in roman. Of Wright's black-letter books, 65 percent fall into Watt's "cheap print" category (shorter than four sheets); among his roman books, the proportion is almost exactly the reverse, with 63 percent being four sheets or longer. What is clear, then, is that, excluding official publications such as Bibles and law books, black letter was used disproportionately for short, cheap books such as ballads and "penny merries"; what is *not* clear, however, is exactly what "cheap print" tells us about "popular culture." Price has been the defining element in most studies of popular culture, and yet, as Watt herself concluded after her analysis, the idea that cheap books "were aimed at and consumed by a definable social group may be a myth."[47]

We should remember, too, that a full 40 percent of Wright's output during these years was made up of books that cannot be called "cheap print," and that these longer, more expensive books included all his plays, both those, like *Mucedorus*, printed in roman, and those, like *Faustus* and *Shoemaker's*, printed in black letter. Overall, Wright's twenty-six play editions (of ten titles) averaged almost eight sheets.[48] At least since Alfred Harbage's work in the 1940s and 1950s, there has been a persistent critical desire to categorize some plays as "popular" and others as "elite"; but if we take price to be the most important guide to popular print, we must exclude virtually *all* printed plays from popular culture.[49]

While Wright might be considered a "popular" publisher in these specific senses, and while black-letter printing was clearly an important part of his specialty, his use of black letter cannot be easily or immediately taken to mean he was targeting "popular" or "common" readers. Rather, Wright often seems to have used the typeface for the meaning it carried. His broadside ballads, like all ballads, were printed in black letter, but Wright also brought out a very similar category of book—which we might call "broadside news verses"—in roman type. Like ballads, these broadside news verses were single- or half-sheet folios with a woodcut illustration (fig. 5-3); like almost all of Wright's ballads, they went through only one edition, and Wright employed one of his usual printers (Edward Allde) for both kinds of book. Both categories must have been among the cheapest books on the market, and, like ballads, the news verses dealt with subjects accessible to people of all sorts and degrees, including the death of King James and the return of the still unmarried Prince Charles from Spain, a mourning and a celebration, respectively, in which virtually all Londoners participated in some way.

The comparison with broadside news verses should lead us toward a semiotic—rather than an economic or indexical—rationale for the typographic inevitability of the black-letter ballad. Typographic nostalgia,

Prince Charles
His
Welcome to the Court,
Or, a true Subiects loue for his happy
returne from *Spaine*.

Deluding thoughts, baniſh your triuiall feares,
No more let Brittany lament with cares:
Feare not the danger of the ſurging ſeas,
Forbeare to pray, the churliſh windes to pleaſe:
But pray and praiſe, his name that checkt the winde
Which brought our hopes according to our mind.
Let not the feare of Treaſon ſtirre your thought:
Treaſon, in treaſons net will ſoone be caught;
Danger is fled, and all your hopes ſtand faſt,
The Prouerbe's true, long lookt for came at laſt,
Long did we looke, longing thy face to ſee,
Long time, our longing could not happy be:
Long we expected for to ſee our deare,
Long did we long, yet could not get thee here,
Long time the churliſh windes did falſely blow,
Long did they ſtriue our fortunes to o'rethrow:
While the Southweſt, blew ſuch a proſperons gaile,
That caus'd a Princely minde to hoiſt vp ſaile.
Bleſt be the ſeas, whoſe waues forbore to riſe:
Bleſt be the windes, which brought our deareſt prize.
Britaine in mourning blacke, did hourely mourne,
While princely *Charles* did happily returne:
Princely thy thoughts, that durſt ſo dangerous venture
Princely thy heart, where reaſon ſtill doth enter:
Princely thy minde, who led thee on to this,
And princely waſt thou vs'd, great Britaines Bliſſe.
*Spaine* we ſhall loue thee in deſpight of hate,
Who loued that Prince, that makes vs fortunate:
The vſage of that man, is more then common,
Greater content was neuer giuen no man:
We feard, but fearleſſe, was our cauſe of feare,
*Charles* was well vſed, while he liued there:
A princely minde beares the great King of *Spaine*,
To vſe him well, and ſee him ſafe againe:
May all that vs'd him well, be vs'd as well,
May they in happineſſe eternall dwell,
May *Britaine* ſtriue, to giue that goodneſſe praiſe
That ſent our hopes, diſpairing here delayes:
Long lookt for *Charles*, tho doubleſt our delight,
Long lookt for Prince, we now attaine thy ſight.
Long haue we wiſht thy perſon for to ſee,
And now poore *Britaines* hopes appeaſed be:
Renowned *Charles*, thy ſight reioyceth more
Then all the Gold, that waſted Englands ſhore:
Gold is but droſſe, but Princely *Charles* is pure,
His name ſhall liue, his Fame ſhall ſtill indure:
The ſighes and ſobs, that came from euery breſt;
The many prayers, poore people haue expreſt
The ſad laments, for thy long abſence there,
The direfull woe occaſion of our care:
All was concluded, in this line and more,
Great *Britaines* Ioy is ſafely come to ſhore:

*Neptune* did ſtriue, to waft you ſafe to land;
The windes did ſtriue, who ſhould haue moſt cōmand:
The Seas were pleas'd, that you ſhould mildely paſſe
And laid the billowes, like to a chriſtall Glaſſe:
Our mindes were pleas'd, when we did ſee you here,
Who can more welcome be, then *Britaines* Deare?
Royall Prince *Charles*, thy heart reioyceth hearts,
Thy friends likewiſe, to their deſeru'd deſarts
That tooke ſuch care, vpon thy perſon deare,
Shall be made welcome ſince Prince *Charles* is here:
Thou ſhew'dſt thy ſelfe a Prince of noble worth,
Great *Britaines* fame, thou brauely didſt ſet forth:
The King, the Queene, nay all the Grands in *Spaine*,
May count our *Charles* a ſecond *Charlemaine*:
The louely Lady, hy-borne Princeſſe ſhe,
Thy worthy actions did reioyce to ſee.
Our Engliſh Fleete met him in royall ſort,
In *Biſcay*, and at Saint *Andreas* Port:
There did our friends make welcome our beſt friend,
Who did ſuch comforts to our wiſhes lend:
*Neptune* did gently cauſe the Billowes lye,
While Princely *Charles* with ſafetie ſailed by:
How many thouſands gaz'd vpon the winde,
In hope to haue it blow vnto their minde?
Raking of cloudes, with turning Weather-cockes;
Smoaking of chimneys; all our hopes ſtill mockes:
At laſt that power that doth command the windes
Gaue leaue to ſaile, and comfort to our mindes.
*Portſmouth* our Ioy did land within thy Port,
Thou gaueſt content, to City, Countrie, Court,
That happy Sunday, when thou there didſt land,
Shall in our hearts for a memoriall ſtand;
*Octobers* fift day ſhall remembred be,
Cauſe *Britaines* feares, that day were all ſet free:
*Gilſord* in Surry ſecondly did know
The happineſſe that heauen did beſtow.
And thirdly, *Lambeth* did expreſſe their Ioy,
Who could but loue the time, did griefe diſtroy.
*Yorke* houſe, as fourth attain'd his happy ſight,
Great *Buckingham*, thy preſence doth delight.
The hearts of people, next our ſecond Sunne,
May ioyes increaſe, for all our feares are done.
Laſtly, thy Father *Britaines* bleſſed Starre
Attaind thy ſight, which ventur'd hath ſo farre?
Long may we liue thy preſence for to ſee,
May thy ariuall to vs happy be.
May *Britaines* feares, end with this fearleſſe feare:
And may this care be our laſt cauſe of care.
May Court, and Citie, Countrie, nay may all
Ioy, that ſo great a Ioy, did vs befall:
Liue long great Prince, mayſt thou with iudgement (raigne,
That after death, thou maieſt glory attaine. FINIS.

Printed at London by *Edward Allde* for *Iohn Wright*. 1623. *Per me* William Hockham Souldiour.

FIG. 5-3. William Hockham, *Prince Charles His Welcome to the Court* (London, 1623). By permission of the Society of Antiquaries, London.

with its evocation of the traditional English community, must be a part of this rationale. While the broadside news verses were explicitly topical, clearly rooted in the historical moment of their creation, ballads seemed to originate from communal memory. For one thing, the broadside ballad was an old publishing format, dating back to the earliest days of printing in England, when virtually all vernacular printing used black-letter type.[50] More important, ballads were less an "individual creation" than "a piece of public property, known to an increasingly broad public," both "timeless" and "authorless," imagined less as the product of an authorizing pen than of their communal and repeated singing in tavern, village, and fair.[51] As Tessa Watt notes, by the sixteenth century, few broadside ballads name their authors; among John Wright's ballads, fewer than one in five contains an author attribution, while more than half of his non-ballad books, and two of his three broadside news verses, do. Overall, the titles that Wright published in roman were far more likely to attribute the work to an author than were his black-letter titles (53 percent versus 37 percent). Exactly this timeless, "common" quality of black letter creates the sense of unity and tradition so important to those black-letter books, such as the Book of Common Prayer (itself "unauthored"), which sought to *create* this unity.

Ballads epitomize cheap print, but another of Wright's black-letter books—and an early modern best-seller—must have been one of his most expensive. *The Shepherd's Kalendar*, which Wright published in 1631 even as he was building his catalogue of cheap "penny" books, ran to fifty sheets per folio and was his second-largest book during this period. What this massive folio shares with the broadside ballad, however, is a nostalgic idea of the English village community. As Natalie Zemon Davis has written of the French versions of these *calendriers des bergers*, "they appear a cross between a folklorist's recording and a pastoral, a shaped vision of the peasant world for country gentlemen and city people and a way for such readers to identify themselves with the simple wisdom of 'the great shepherd of the mountain.'"[52] Addressed to the "gentle Reader," Wright's edition offers just such timeless country wisdom, in the form of homely proverbs, religious catechisms, and numerous ballads sung by the shepherds. With its combination of the ancient, the pastoral, and the proverbial, the anonymous *Kalendar*, like the ballads, seems almost to emanate from the land itself. But its large format and length, and the Latin passages scattered throughout, indicate that its likely audience existed on a social level far above that of the shepherds represented in the book itself.[53] Black letter here functions as the typographic analogue to the nostalgic process that Raymond Williams sees at work in some versions of Renaissance pastoral: "Living tensions are excised, until there is nothing countervailing, and selected images stand as themselves: not in a living but in an enamelled world."[54]

What I want to suggest by this glance at some of John Wright's black-letter books is that the typeface itself has helped to construct our understanding of the "popular." A large part of the meaning of "popular culture" in scholarship since the late eighteenth century has been precisely this vision of the idealized and unified "organic community" combined with the very *spectacle of* the "low" or the "common" by those occupying higher positions on the social scale.[55] Black letter embodies *both* a nostalgia for a time or place devoid of contemporary conflict *and* the packaging and commodifying of "low domains" as "the object of nostalgia, longing and fascination."[56] No wonder, then, that scholars have tended to find popular culture in black-letter texts, since part of the function of black letter was to create this (imagined) popular culture and make it available for study.

By the time Wright began publishing his two successful black-letter plays—starting with Q2 *Faustus* in 1609, and then Q2 *Shoemaker's Holiday* in 1610—the typeface had already become unusual for playbooks. From 1576, when the first play from the professional theater was printed, through 1594, when the market for playbooks experienced its first rapid expansion, black letter was used in almost half of all editions of professional plays. From 1595 to 1608, however, the typeface began to disappear, used in only 12.4 percent of editions, and in no first editions after 1605. In the decade after Wright began publishing his black-letter plays (1609–19), the percentage had dropped even further to 6.9 percent. And, with the exception of Humphrey Lownes's 1613 edition of *1 & 2 Edward IV*, for the entire period that Wright was publishing *Shoemaker's* and *Faustus* (1609–31), he was the only publisher of black-letter playbooks, and his were the only plays appearing in the typeface. Even as Wright took over the publishing of these plays, they were already *belated*, their material presentation already seeming to allude nostalgically to the past. Over the course of Wright's career, the plays became the last of a dying breed.

*The Shoemaker's Holiday*, as many critics have argued, is itself a powerfully nostalgic play, and its typeface is thus ideally suited to—and a part of—its ideology. Other critics have well explicated the nostalgic sentiment of Dekker's play: its transformation of work into holiday; its erasure of conflict both within the hierarchical structure of the guild and between guild members and "strangers"; its substitution of the laboring craftsman for the capitalist merchant at the center of London economic power; its elision of Shrove Tuesday with the Elizabethan Accession Day, producing a nationalistic unity among the many strata of English society.[57] I focus here on one particular aspect of nostalgia in the play: the production of commodities, as exemplified by the shoes that, Cinderella-like, identify Jane and save her marriage with Rafe.

Before going off to the wars, Rafe gives a memento to his wife, a pair of shoes that have been "cut out by Hodge, / Stitcht by my fellow Firke, seam'd by my selfe, / Made vp and pinckt with letters for thy name" (B4v; 1.232–34).[58] The shoes that guarantee Rafe's marriage, ultimately allowing him to find his lost wife and prevent her bigamous marriage to Hammon, are the product of the unified labor of Eyre's journeymen, made not for the market but for their own purposes, not to be sold but to be given away. Most shoes in the seventeenth century, of course, were made quite differently. Long before *The Shoemaker's Holiday* was performed and printed, the medieval craft guilds had become dominated by merchants and traders—by capital—and "the members who remained craftsmen fell into a condition of dependence."[59] Opportunities for advancement within the guild structure declined—the days were long past when a craftsman like Eyre could rise to become Lord Mayor—and most artisans languished at the level of journeymen. Unlike in the play, however, such journeymen had little control over their products, working to supply their merchant employers, who were themselves working to fulfill the desires of the marketplace.

The central pair of shoes in this play about shoemakers, then, functions as part of the "nostalgic, idealized picture of the late sixteenth-century work world" that Ronda Arab sees in the play, which "depicts artisans as a cohesive social group" and "masks the considerably grimmer reality."[60] While in the play itself the shoes are an *example* of unalienated labor, for spectators and readers of the play, the shoes become merely a *souvenir* of unalienated labor, just as for Rafe and Jane they are a souvenir of their marriage. Souvenirs are paradigmatic of nostalgia: as fetishized objects, they combat absence and distance with a "myth of contact and presence," replacing "the memory of the body" with "the memory of the object."[61] Souvenirs do the work of memory for us—as Rafe tells his wife, "euerie morning when thou pull'st them on, / Remember me" (B4v; 1.236–37)—neatly packaging it to replace history with nostalgic narrative. So the shoes do their magical work: "I haue made them so," Rafe tells Jane, "That I can know them from a thousand mo" (B4v; 1.238–39), and their ability to produce memory creates the play's fairy-tale narrative, saving Jane from any of the more usual fates awaiting poor, working, masterless women.

Given their function as nostalgic souvenirs, we should not be surprised that the shoes guarantee marriage and domesticity. First classified as a disease in the seventeenth century by the Swiss doctor Johannes Hofer, "nostalgia" derives from the Greek *nostos* (a return home) and *algos* (pain); Hofer used the term to describe the homesickness of soldiers like Rafe.[62] Nostalgia is a disease of dislocation, of failed assimilation, of alienation.[63] For Rafe, this dislocation occurs in a spatial register (homesickness), as it does for Jane, who somehow goes missing in London and remains frustratingly untraceable after Rafe leaves: "we knowe not whats become of her" (E4r; 10.84–85); "I heare shee liues in London" (sig. E4v; 10.91–92); "one tolde mee hee sawe her a while agoe . . . weele ferret her out" (sig. E4v; 10.104–5). For Rafe and Jane, the shoes ensure *nostos*; they are not only Cinderella's glass slippers but also Dorothy's ruby ones. For the play's audience and readers, the shoes mediate a *temporal* alienation (nostalgia in its modern sense) that can never be overcome through actual return. They are souvenirs of an idyllic and largely imaginary guild economy before the split between capital and labor, when artisan-craftsmen were their own masters.

The playbook of *The Shoemaker's Holiday*, too, is a souvenir, and its black-letter typeface, I have been suggesting, helps to create its nostalgic effect—precisely the effect of organic unity that has been a continuing preoccupation of the study of "popular culture." The playbook even contains prefatory material that strongly resembles the publishing mainstay of John Wright and his partners: the ballad. On facing pages of the quarto, Wright had Valentine Simmes print the two songs performed in the play (A3v–A4r). Removed from their location in the performance, the songs take on the conventional appearance of a broadside ballad, usually printed in two parts side by side (fig. 5-4). And the first "three-man's song" seems oddly out of place for a play so deeply concerned with *civic* institutions, for it is a *pastoral* song, set during a traditional country Maying and complete with a "summer's queen" and a "nightingale, / The sweetest singer in all the forest's choir" (A3v; ll. 4–6). Temporal nostalgia and geographic nostalgia intersect in the pastoral.[64]

If nostalgia is a "social disease" involving "the dilution of the past in the service of making it available to social groups," at what social groups is this nostalgic souvenir aimed?[65] Who were the imagined readers of this "popular" playbook? Certainly we cannot exclude apprentices and journeymen who might have enjoyed this rosy depiction of their work and the mythic origins of "their" holiday, or master craftsmen who may have reveled in Eyre's rise to power, denied to themselves. Because of their structural position in the economy of early modern London, however, these groups tended to take a more hardheaded view of their situation, as when the artisan skinners complained of the merchant traders in their company, "Their oppression is growne to such a height that amongst some of them it is a matter disputable whether we be members of the company or not."[66] Perhaps instead, as Arab suggests, the play embodies the values of the capitalist merchants, nostalgically erasing the contemporary protest of artisans while simultaneously valorizing their labor, part of the "contradictory historical process by which work and production gained significant social value in conjunction with the development of an undervalued and underprivileged working class."[67]

There is another possibility. If on these readings *The Shoemaker's Holiday* resembles its souvenir shoes, on another reading the play might better be compared to the morris dance that Eyre's workers perform before Lord Mayor Oatley. As a traditional and "popular" country pastime here imported into the city, the morris recalls the evocation of the pastoral in the first three-man's song; indeed, this song may have been sung in conjunction with the dance.[68] Pastoral, of course, is a literary game of the elite, one that Wright played by publishing *The Shepherd's Kalendar*. On at least one occasion—New Year's Day, 1600—the *Shoemaker's* song and dance were performed before an audience far more elite than Lord Mayor Oatley: Queen Elizabeth and her court. As spectacles of "popular culture" exhibited for aesthetic appreciation by elite audiences, the shoemakers' morris and *The Shoemaker's Holiday* have a lot in common.[69] Similarly, *The Winter's Tale* presents "a dance of Shepherds and Shepherdesses," probably a morris of some kind, and follows it with a three-man's song by Autolycus, Mopsa, and Dorcas.[70] The presentation of an imagined *historical* "popular culture" in *The Shoemaker's Holiday* structurally parallels the presentation of an imagined *pastoral* "popular culture" in *The Winter's Tale* precisely because of the connection between temporal and spatial nostalgia. If the typographic nostalgia of black letter has helped to construct our understanding of "popular" print

*The first Three-mans*
Song.

O the month of May, the merry month of May,
So frolicke so gay, and so gréene, so gréene, so gréene:
O and then did I, vnto my true loue say,
Swéete Peg, thou shalt be my Summers Quéene.

Now the Nightingale, the pretty Nightingale,
The swéetest singer in all the Forrests quier:
Intreates thée sweete Peggie, to heare thy true loues tale,
Loe, yonder she sitteth, her breast against a bryer.

But O I spie the Cuckoo, the Cuckoo, the Cuckoo,
Sée where she sitteth, come away my ioy:
Come away I prithée, I do not like the Cuckoo
Should sing where my Peggie and I kisse and ioy.

O the month of May, the merry month of May,
So frolicke, so gay, and so gréene, so gréene, so gréene:
And then did I, vnto my true loue say,
Swéete Peg, thou shalt be my Summers Queene.

FIG. 5-4. Thomas Dekker, *The Shoomakers Holy-day* (London, 1610), A3v–4r. By permission of The Huntington Library, San Marino, California.

# *The ſecond Three-mans* Song.

*This is to be ſung at the latter end.*

Cold's the wind, and wet's the raine,
  Saint Hugh be our good ſpeede:
Ill is the weather that bringeth no gaine,
  Nor helpes good hearts in neede.

Trowle the boll, the iolly Nut-browne boll,
  And here kind mate to thee:
Let's ſing a dirge for Saint Hughes Soule,
  And downe it merrily.

Downe a downe, hey downe a downe.
  Hey dery, dery, down a down, Cloſe with the tenor boy:
Hoe well done, to me let come,
  Ring compaſſe gentle ioy.

Trowle the bowle, the Nut-browne bowle,
  And here kind, &c. as often as there be men to drinke.

At laſt when all haue drunke, this verſe.

Cold's the winde, and wet's the raine,
  Saint Hugh be our good ſpeed:
Ill is the weather that bringeth no gaine,
  Nor helpes good hearts in need.

through its evocation of idealized community combined with its commodification of the "popular" for nostalgic pleasure, then *The Shoemaker's Holiday* is a paradigmatic example of this process.

I have suggested three possible readings of this playbook based on its typographic nostalgia, this "social disease" serving three different social groups. As I have argued, we cannot reduce black-letter print to an index to a single group of "popular" consumers nor to a single reading based in a common, consensual culture. The nostalgic politics of the typeface, as of Dekker's play, function differently for different readers, and these politics must be read within the larger social structure of early modern England. Most studies of black letter have seen the typeface as marking off a certain class of "popular" texts as *beneath* certain readers, as designating those texts deemed *unreadable* by the elite.[71] I am suggesting that black letter could function in exactly the opposite manner: typographic nostalgia may in fact *enable* the continued elite reading of texts precisely *as popular culture*, as a kind of shoemakers' morris dance. And if nostalgia is not the fulfillment through the past of desires unfulfilled in the present but rather the endless creation of desire through the impossibility of its satisfaction, then what better strategy for marketing and selling a book—for creating the kind of popularity that publishers most highly value—than the evocation of desire in typographic nostalgia?[72]

## NOTES

1. I refer to the titles of a few of the most influential studies dealing with black letter, all of which I discuss in this chapter. Tessa Watt, *Cheap Print and Popular Piety, 1550–1640* (Cambridge: Cambridge University Press, 1991); Hyder E. Rollins, "The Black-Letter Broadside Ballad," *PMLA* 34 (1919): 258–339; Charles C. Mish, "Black Letter as a Social Discriminant in the Seventeenth Century," *PMLA* 68 (1953): 627–31.

2. Susan Stewart, *On Longing: Narratives of the Miniature, the Gigantic, the Souvenir, the Collection* (Durham: Duke University Press, 1993), 23.

3. Scott Cutler Shershow, "New Life: Cultural Studies and the Problem of the 'Popular,'" *Textual Practice* 12 (1998): 24.

4. These represent some of the most common self-critiques among historians who study popular culture, but it seems to me that, despite their important work (which has certainly influenced my thinking here), most of these critiques still retain the central nostalgic desire. See, for example, the essays in Tim Harris, ed., *Popular Culture in England, c. 1500–1850* (New York: St. Martin's, 1995); and Bob Scribner, "Is a History of Popular Culture Possible?" *History of European Ideas* 10 (1989): 175–91. The term "mediators" is Peter Burke's in *Popular Culture in Early Modern Europe* (New York: Harper, 1978), 65–77.

5. Roger Chartier, *The Cultural Uses of Print in Early Modern France*, trans. Lydia G. Cochrane (Princeton: Princeton University Press, 1987), 3.

6. This is the definition of "culture" that inaugurates Burke's study (*Popular Culture*, xi).

7. Jerome McGann, *The Textual Condition* (Princeton: Princeton University Press, 1991), 15.

8. Ibid.; D. F. McKenzie, "Typography and Meaning: The Case of William Congreve," in *Making Meaning: "Printers of the Mind" and Other Essays*, ed. Peter D. McDonald and Michael F. Suarez (Amherst: University of Massachusetts Press, 2002), 198–236.

9. The dichotomy, however, has been refused repeatedly by recent bibliographers, although the New Bibliographers, with their emphasis on scientific method, helped to establish it. See G. Thomas Tanselle, *A Rationale of Textual Criticism* (Philadelphia: University of Pennsylvania Press, 1989), 33–35; D. F. McKenzie, *Bibliography and the Sociology of Texts* (London: British Library, 1986), 14; Jerome McGann, "The Monks and the Giants: Textual and Bibliographical Studies and the Interpretation of Literary Works," in *Textual Criticism and Literary Interpretation*, ed. Jerome McGann (Chicago: University of Chicago Press, 1985), 180–99.

10. Ronald B. McKerrow, *An Introduction to Bibliography for Literary Students* (Oxford: Clarendon Press, 1927), 297: "By about 1580 the use of black letter in plays *and the higher kinds of English verse*, as well as in Latin books, had almost ceased," while "*popular prose* and ballads, however, continued to be printed in black letter until well on in the seventeenth century" (emphasis added).

11. Mish, "Black Letter," 628–29. The frequent, nearly ubiquitous claim that black letter disappeared as the standard typeface for English books in the late sixteenth century deserves further investigation and some qualification. Given that black letter was used throughout the period for some of the books printed in the largest runs and most frequently reprinted—ballads, many of the translations of the Bible, catechisms, some of the most popular devotional books, even law books (which required frequent updates and new editions)—I suspect that early modern readers were exposed to far more black letter during the seventeenth century than most scholars believe. The "disappearance" of black letter is skewed both by scholars' overreliance on first editions rather than the total book trade, and by the lower survival rate of cheap, short books, which would have been used to destruction.

12. Paul Salzman, *English Prose Fiction, 1558–1700: A Critical History* (Oxford: Clarendon Press, 1985), 265–67.

13. Bernard Capp, *The World of John Taylor the Water-Poet, 1578–1653* (Oxford: Clarendon Press, 1994), 67.

14. See, for example, John Barnard, introduction to *The Cambridge History of the Book in Britain,* vol. 4, *1557–1695*, ed. John Barnard and D. F. McKenzie, with assistance by Maureen Bell (Cambridge: Cambridge University Press, 2002), 4–5; D. R. Woolf, "Genre into Artifact: The Decline of the English Chronicle in the Sixteenth Century," *Sixteenth Century Journal* 19 (1988): 328; Barry Reay, *Popular Cultures in England, 1550–1750* (New York: Longman, 1998), 56–57; David Cressy, "Literacy in Context: Meaning and Measurement in Early Modern England," in *Consumption and the World of Goods*, ed. John Brewer and Roy Porter (New York: Routledge, 1993), 312.

15. See Zachary Lesser, *Renaissance Drama and the Politics of Publication: Readings in the English Book Trade* (Cambridge: Cambridge University Press, 2004); Alan B. Farmer and Zachary Lesser, "Vile Arts: The Marketing of English Printed Drama, 1512–1660," *Research Opportunities in Renaissance Drama* 39 (2000): 77–165.

16. See William Prynne, *Canterburies Doome* (London: John Macock for Michael Sparke, 1646).

17. "Libells," in *Table Talk of John Selden*, ed. Frederick Pollock (London: Quaritch, 1927), 72.

18. See Mark Bland, "The Appearance of the Text in Early Modern England," *TEXT* 11 (1998): 95. John Wright, the publisher whom I discuss later in this chapter, changed the typography of a book from its previous edition only three times from 1605 to 1631: twice from black letter to roman and once from roman to black letter.

19. Tim Harris, "Problematising Popular Culture," in Harris, *Popular Culture in England*, 23.

20. Mish, "Black Letter," 27 n. 1.

21. Rollins, "Black-Letter Broadside," 331. Rollins's view of the readers of ballads is a bit confused. He argues that it would be a "serious error to suppose that only the lower classes read ballads" (332), but he then distinguishes between the news ballads read by the lower classes and lyrical ballads for the "more cultivated readers," a distinction that simply relocates the divide to the aesthetic rather than the typographical realm. Elsewhere, he notes that ballads "have always interested educated men" but also claims that they were "produced solely for the common people." Hyder E. Rollins, *A Pepysian Garland: Black-Letter Broadside Ballads of the Years 1595–1639* (Cambridge: Cambridge University Press, 1922), xi–xii. Ultimately, it seems that Rollins adheres to the basic view of black letter as a key to popular readership, but qualifies this view in order better to make his polemical case that the ballads are "worthy" of study.

22. Keith Thomas, "The Meaning of Literacy in Early Modern England," in *The Written Word: Literacy in Transition*, ed. Gerd Baumann (Oxford: Clarendon Press, 1986), 97–131.

23. Ibid., 99.

24. Woolf, "Genres into Artifact," 328 n. 22. See similar claims by Reay, *Popular Cultures*, 45; Cressy, "Literacy in Context," 312; Paul J. Voss, *Elizabethan News Pamphlets: Shakespeare, Spenser, Marlowe, and the Birth of Journalism* (Pittsburgh: Duquesne University Press, 2001), 80; and (but not citing Thomas) Peter Blayney, "The Publication of Playbooks," in *A New History of Early English Drama*, ed. John D. Cox and David Scott Kastan (New York: Columbia University Press, 1997), 414; Ian Green, *Print and Protestantism in Early Modern England* (Oxford: Oxford University Press, 2000), 61, 65; Ian Green, *The Christian's ABC: Catechisms and Catechizing in England, c. 1530–1740* (Oxford: Clarendon Press, 1996), 255. Andrew Murphy follows Blayney to argue that "works aimed at those who were less educated . . . were printed in blackletter" (*Shakespeare in Print: A History and Chronology of Shakespeare Publishing* [Cambridge: Cambridge University Press, 2003], 30).

25. See Miles A. Tinker, *Legibility of Print* (Ames: Iowa State University Press, 1963), 46–54.

26. John Wright published sixty-six black-letter editions (non-broadsides) between 1605 and 1631; not a single one was printed with a black-letter title page. Ian Green offers a similar caveat, but seems to accept nonetheless that black letter was targeted at "early" readers (*Print*, 65).

27. Blayney, "Publication of Playbooks," 414.

28. Ibid.; Mish, "Black Letter," 630 n. 4; Bland, "Appearance of the Text," 93. Bland, it should be noted, does *not* fall into either of the two scholarly traditions I am outlining here; his essay is a rare exception that *reads* typefaces—black letter, roman, and italic—as bearers of semiotic meaning. For two other exceptions, see Lori Humphrey Newcomb's brief but trenchant critique of Mish in *Reading Popular Romance in Early*

*Modern England* (New York: Columbia University Press, 2002), 140; and Sabrina Alcorn Baron's fine article "Red Ink and Black Letter: Reading Early Modern Authority," in *The Reader Revealed*, ed. Sabrina Alcorn Baron, Elizabeth Walsh, and Susan Scola (Washington, D.C.: Folger Shakespeare Library, 2001), 19–30.

29. Blayney, "Publication of Playbooks," 414.

30. See Bland, "Appearance of the Text," 93.

31. Green, *Christian's ABC*, 256.

32. Zachary Lesser, "Walter Burre's *The Knight of the Burning Pestle*," *English Literary Renaissance* 29 (1999): 31.

33. See Jonquil Bevan, "Scotland," in Barnard and McKenzie, *Cambridge History of the Book*, 694. More than 80 percent of all English Books of Common Prayer printed in folio or quarto during the early Stuart period were black-letter books. For sizes of octavo or smaller, printers in the early Stuart period favored roman by almost the same margin, perhaps because black letter becomes increasingly difficult to read as the page gets smaller (and hence the proportion of black to white increases, far more so than with roman type), or perhaps because printers no longer stocked fonts of black letter in smaller sizes. The pattern is similar with Bibles, as Blayney ("Publication of Playbooks," 422 n. 66) and Green (*Print*, 60–66) both note.

34. On the connotations of biblical typeface, see Bland, "Appearance of the Text," 94.

35. I am influenced here by, and am paraphrasing, Shershow's incisive comment that "what scholars are really discovering when they piece together the scattered evidence of cultural reception and shifting aesthetic taste is a relentless effort to *construct* hierarchies which literally did not and do not exist except as they are proclaimed and deployed" ("New Life," 43).

36. See, for example, Burke's comment that "in 1500 . . . popular culture was everyone's culture. . . . By 1800, however, in most parts of Europe, the clergy, the nobility, the merchants, the professional men—and their wives—had abandoned popular culture to the lower classes, from whom they were now separated, as never before, by profound differences in world view" (*Popular Culture*, 270).

37. Watt, *Cheap Print*, 1–2, 325.

38. Peter Stallybrass and Allon White, *The Politics and Poetics of Transgression* (Ithaca: Cornell University Press, 1986), 195, 192. As Stallybrass and White point out, we should also avoid the other extreme of claiming that there was no consensus between the upper, middling, and lower sorts and no change in their relationship. See also Raymond Williams, *The Country and the City* (New York: Oxford University Press, 1973).

39. See Watt, *Cheap Print*, 17, on commonplace books, although she does not develop the point. For the theoretical argument, see Chartier, *Cultural Uses of Print*, 6–11, although he sometimes seems to replace the traditional dichotomy of high and low texts or cultural objects with a dichotomy of reading methods or ways of appropriating culture, almost equally static and reified.

40. Fredric Jameson, *Postmodernism: Or, the Cultural Logic of Late Capitalism* (Durham: Duke University Press, 1991), 156.

41. See Lesser, *Renaissance Drama*.

42. My analysis here excludes all forms of "non-professional" drama, such as masques, Lord Mayor's pageants, university drama, and closet drama. In counting total editions, I count individual play*books*, not each printing of a play*text*; if a play is reprinted in collection, therefore, I do not count this printing as a separate edition. This method gives a better indication of the demand for and the popularity of particular playbooks (the reprinting of *2 Henry IV* in the Shakespeare folio, for instance, tells us

very little about the sales of the 1600 edition). For a detailed discussion of methodologies for assessing popularity, see Alan B. Farmer and Zachary Lesser, "The Popularity of Playbooks Revisited," *Shakespeare Quarterly* 56 (2005): 1–32.

43. Watt, *Cheap Print,* 259; see also Jonathan Barry, "Literacy and Literature in Popular Culture: Reading and Writing in Historical Perspective," in Harris, *Popular Culture in England,* 74.

44. Scribner, "Is a History," 176 (discussing the problems with such an approach).

45. Gerald Johnson, "John Trundle and the Book-Trade," *Studies in Bibliography* 39 (1986): 177–99.

46. See Watt, *Cheap Print,* esp. chap. 7; Watt is building on—and providing the prehistory to—Margaret Spufford, *Small Books and Pleasant Histories: Popular Fiction and Its Readership in Seventeenth-Century England* (Athens: University of Georgia Press, 1982).

47. Watt, *Cheap Print,* 3.

48. Wright's 1611 edition of *Faustus* was technically an octavo (folded three times) printed on three sheets, but the edition is actually what W. W. Greg calls a "(4°-form) 8°," which uses "two ordinary sheets joined together by their longer edges," and thus resembles a quarto in size, shape, and the amount of type it could contain on a single page. Three sheets of quarto-form octavo are thus equivalent to six sheets of quarto, the usual form for *Faustus* before this edition. I therefore presume that the cost of paper (and thus the related cost of the entire production) for the three-sheet quarto-form octavo was basically equivalent to the six-sheet quarto. See W. W. Greg, *A Bibliography of the English Printed Drama to the Restoration,* 4 vols. (London: Bibliographical Society, 1939–59), 4:lvi.

49. Indeed, Watt excludes plays for precisely this reason (*Cheap Print,* 279).

50. For the early history, see Rollins, "Black-Letter Broadside," 258–60.

51. Watt, *Cheap Print,* 81.

52. N. Z. Davis, "Printing and the People," in *Rethinking Popular Culture: Contemporary Perspectives in Cultural Studies,* ed. Chandra Mukerji and Michael Schudson (Berkeley: University of California Press, 1991), 68.

53. *The shepherds kalender* (London: [Eliot's Court Press] for John Wright, 1631), A2r; for examples of Latin verses, see D5v–D6v.

54. Williams, *Country and the City,* 18. This is not to say that pastoral could never encode an oppositional or emergent ideology; for examples, see Lesser, *Renaissance Drama,* chap. 5. For a view of pastoral, and especially the country-house poem that is consonant with but also qualifies Williams, see Don E. Wayne, *Penshurst: The Semiotics of Place and the Poetics of History* (Madison: University of Wisconsin Press, 1984). Wayne emphasizes the "rhetorical and narrative strategies [of Jonson's country-house poetry] which, while often aimed at the resolution or containment of social contradictions, have the effect of revealing them in a new light" (130), and this revelation yields critique simultaneously with ideology.

55. For the early history of the academic study of popular culture, see Burke, *Popular Culture,* 3–10.

56. Stallybrass and White, *Politics and Poetics,* 191.

57. See L. D. Timms, "Dekker's *The Shoemaker's Holiday* and Elizabeth's Accession Day," *Notes and Queries* 32 (230), no. 1 (March 1985): 58; David Scott Kastan, "Workshop and/as Playhouse: Comedy and Commerce in *The Shoemaker's Holiday,*" *Studies in Philology* 84 (1987): 324–37; Marta Straznicky, "The End(s) of Discord in *The Shoemaker's Holiday,*" *Studies in English Literature* 36 (1996): 357–72; Ronda A. Arab, "Work, Bodies, and Gender in *The Shoemaker's Holiday,*" *Medieval and Renaissance*

*Drama in England* 13 (2001): 182–212. In its early editions, the play's title contains no apostrophe, and modern editors and critics have debated its placement; as Kastan writes, the issue in these debates has been "primarily whether the title refers to a holiday declared for the shoemakers (in which case the title is *The Shoemakers' Holiday)* or a holiday declared by Simon Eyre for all the apprentices of London (in which case the title is *The Shoemaker's Holiday*)" ("Workshop," 333). Of course, early modern readers would not have been faced with any such choice, since in the absence of strict rules of punctuation, the title can easily slide between the two meanings, allowing both to coexist and only increasing the nostalgic sense of totality without loss that the play presents.

58. Citations are to the first edition (Valentine Simmes, 1600), followed by scene and line numbers from Thomas Dekker, *The Shoemaker's Holiday*, ed. Anthony Parr, New Mermaids edition (New York: Norton, 1990); this edition does not divide the play into acts. Quotations from the modern edition will not always exactly match the original, of course, but I have provided the citation for the convenience of the reader.

59. George Unwin, *Industrial Organization in the Sixteenth and Seventeenth Centuries* (1904; reprint, New York: A. M. Kelley, 1963), 19. See also George Unwin, *The Gilds and Companies of London* (1908; reprint, London: Allen and Unwin, 1938).

60. Arab, "Work, Bodies, and Gender," 186.

61. Stewart, *On Longing*, 133.

62. For histories of nostalgia, see Jean Starobinski, "The Idea of Nostalgia," *Diogenes* 54 (1966): 81–103; Willis H. McCann, "Nostalgia: A Review of the Literature," *Psychological Bulletin* 38 (1941): 165–82. Hofer's *Dissertatio Medica de Nostalgia, oder Heimwhe* (Basel, 1688) has been translated by Carolyn Kiser Anspach in *Bulletin of the Institute of the History of Medicine* 7 (1934): 376–91.

63. See Nicholas Dames's excellent discussion in "Austen's Nostalgics," *Representations* 73 (2001): 117–43. Dames traces the de-pathologizing of nostalgia as it shifts from a spatial to a temporal register, although I suspect both forms have always been present. See also Stewart, *On Longing*, 139.

64. See Laurence Lerner, *The Uses of Nostalgia: Studies in Pastoral Poetry* (New York: Schocken, 1972), 40.

65. Stewart, *On Longing*, x; Dames, "Austen's Nostalgics," 131.

66. Quoted in Ian Archer, *The Pursuit of Stability: Social Relations in Elizabethan London* (Cambridge: Cambridge University Press, 1991), 144. In 1663 similar complaints were lodged within the Stationers' Company by printers against publishing booksellers.

67. Arab, "Work, Bodies, and Gender," 86.

68. See Parr's edition of *Shoemaker's Holiday*, 6, 57. But see also John Harmon, "The Placement of the Songs in Dekker's *The Shoemaker's Holiday*," *English Studies* 73.2 (1992): 121–23; Harmon argues for placing the song at 7.25, noting Margery's references to singing as she enters. But only two men, Hodge and Firk, are on stage at this point to sing the three-man's song, although such songs were not exclusively for three parts.

69. See also Straznicky's analysis of this performance and its possible reception in "The End(s) of Discord," 368.

70. *The Norton Shakespeare*, ed. Stephen Greenblatt et al. (New York: Norton, 1997), 4.4.167SD.

71. See, in addition to the examples previously cited, Peter Blayney's comment specifically on playbooks, "The preference for roman type suggests that the publishers of plays were aiming more at the middle class than the working class . . . they did *not* perceive them as belonging to the same market as jestbooks and ballads" ("Publication of Playbooks," 415), which implies that the few black-letter plays *were* aimed at the

working class, and, along with jest-books and ballads, would have been perceived as beneath middle-class sensibilities.

72. See Arjun Appadurai's comments on the "imagined nostalgia" of modern advertising, which "teach[es] consumers to miss things they have never lost" (*Modernity at Large: Cultural Dimensions of Globalization* [Minneapolis: University of Minnesota Press, 1996], 77). But perhaps all nostalgia is, in fact, imagined nostalgia for things we have never lost.

SIX

# Play-Reading, News-Reading, and Ben Jonson's *The Staple of News*

ALAN B. FARMER

When Ben Jonson's *The Staple of News* was first performed by the King's Men in February 1626, the audience apparently misunderstood the play's third act, the only one in which the fictional "Staple of News" is open and selling news reports.[1] According to Jonson, "the *allegory*, and purpose of the *Author*," had been "wholly mistaken," so, in preparing the play for the press in 1631, he inserted an address "To the Readers," not in the customary position among the preliminaries of the playbook, but rather within the text of the play itself. At the foot of page 36, immediately before the third act, he instructs readers how to "apprehend" his satirical representation of the news trade in order to prevent another "sinister interpretation" of his play:

> In this following *Act*, the *Office* is open'd, and shew'n to the *Prodigall*, and his *Princesse Pecunia*, wherein the *allegory*, and purpose of the *Author* hath hitherto beene wholly mistaken, and so sinister an interpretation beene made, as if the soules of most of the *Spectators* had liu'd in the eyes and eares of these ridiculous Gossips that tattle betweene the *Acts*. But hee prayes you thus to mend it. To consider the *Newes* here vented, to be none of his *Newes*, or any reasonable mans; but *Newes* made like the times *Newes*, (a weekly cheat to draw mony) and could not be fitter reprehended, then in raising this ridiculous *Office* of the *Staple*, wherein the age may see her owne folly, or hunger and thirst after publish'd pamphlets of *Newes*, set out euery Saturday, but made all at home, & no syllable of truth in them: then which there cannot be a greater disease in nature, or a fouler scorne put vpon the times. And so apprehending it, you shall doe the *Author*, and your owne iudgement a courtesie, and perceiue the tricke of alluring money to the *Office*, and there cooz'ning the people. If you haue the truth, rest quiet, and consider that
>
> *Ficta, voluptatis causa, sint proxima veris.*[2]

In seeking to convince his readership that the London news trade is ridiculous, Jonson makes a crucial allegation against news pamphlets: they are untrue. The pamphlets, which were often called corantos, purport to include accurate information on foreign military and political affairs, but in reality, Jonson argues, they are "made all at home" and contain "no syllable of truth." The rapidly expanding news trade is thus nothing more than an elaborate con game, "a weekly cheat to draw mony," in which those who sell corantos practice "the tricke of alluring money" to their shops and "there cooz'ning the people." Once readers learn to "reprehend" corantos, they, like Jonson, will see the "hunger and thirst after" news pamphlets as a ridiculous "folly" and rightly conclude that "there cannot be a greater disease in nature, or a fouler scorne put vpon the times," than the demand for these fallacious publications.[3]

Jonson further explains that, as part of his satire, he tried to make the play's news exactly "like the times *Newes*," with "no syllable of truth," and hence which no "reasonable man" would believe. But this strategy evidently failed. Jonson's theatrical audience took the play's news, "the *Newes* here vented," to be the same as "his *Newes*," and he worries that readers will make the same mistake. His address is marked with uncertainty; he does not trust readers to interpret his play correctly. He "prayes" they will do so, but ends with the concession that not all of them will: "*If* you haue the truth . . ." (emphasis added). In fact, the very presence of the address betrays Jonson's misgivings. He knows that some readers, like some playgoers before them, will read the play and inevitably misunderstand the author's "allegory and purpose."[4]

But why would Jonson be concerned that *The Staple of News* might be read for its news and not for its condemnation of the news trade? By the time the play was printed, whatever news it may once have contained was over five years old, and what was called news in 1626 would hardly have warranted that label in 1631. If the fictional reports in the third act specifically—the act preceded by Jonson's address—came too close to sensitive political events when the play was first performed, there would seem to have been little chance of that happening again five years later: the play's news was, at the very least, no longer new, if it could be thought of as news at all. Even the physical format of Jonson's play worked to disassociate it from news pamphlets. Whereas most plays were printed in the same quarto format as corantos, *The Staple of News* was the last play in a three-play, sixty-four-sheet folio collection; readers were highly unlikely to confuse it with a small pamphlet of two to three sheets.[5]

Critics of *The Staple of News* have tended to overlook the oddity of Jonson's address and his concern about the play being read for its news. In one influential analysis, news functions as an inert, even trivial concept, a "subordinate" plot element among three "abuses of language" explored in this play. It is a "fantastic product" sold by the play's news office, itself a "fantastic" business based on "organized lying": "The News Office, as portrayed here, simply caters to childish curiosity on the level of incredible but harmless gossip."[6] Never delineated are how, exactly, these lies and abuses of language function in the play's satire or what makes the Staple's news "harmless gossip." The actual news trade of Caroline London was rarely seen as harmless, even by Jonson; had it been, he would not have felt compelled to write a play attempting to show that it was a "tricke" and "a weekly cheat." That Jonson has a low opinion of the information in corantos comes across quite clearly, but his satire begins with the assumption not that these pamphlets are harmless but that they have "no syllable of truth in them," quite a different issue. Whatever modern critics may think of the news pamphlets from the 1620s and 1630s, the period's editors, publishers, and readers considered them to be of vital cultural and political importance, an importance that Jonson's play is dedicated to undermining by revealing the pamphlets' utter lack of truth.

*The Staple of News* can thus be seen as an early salvo in what John Milton, during the English Civil War, would call "the wars of Truth."[7] In these discursive conflicts, the truth was hardly a straightforward matter; it concerned issues not only of factual accuracy but also of political partisanship and religious factionalism. And while news itself could theoretically concern an almost inexhaustible range of topics,[8] Jonson's satire has a specific focus: weekly pamphlets on the Thirty Years' War. This war was followed by more readers, with greater regularity, for a longer period of time, than any war before it—because, as Jonson suggests, it was a war that polarized religious opinion in England. This religious polarization was, if not produced by, then exacerbated by the publication of corantos, which alerted readers to changes in the fortunes of Protestant and Catholic armies and therefore in the possible fate of the English church and, indeed, the fate of all Christendom. With so much at stake, there was nothing "childish" about "the times *Newes*," or about the news in Jonson's play.

Here, I first want to analyze Jonson's representation of the news trade, in which news readers are portrayed as credulous, vulgar women and news publishers as craven opportunists who seek to exploit the religious fears of their customers. I then want to situate Jonson's play in the wars of truth of the Caroline news trade, which pitted Protestants against Catholics and rival Protestant factions against one another. Jonson was concerned about the reception of his play, I argue, because it satirizes the religious politics of coranto readers, specifically Puritans, who he anticipates will want to read *The Staple of News* and whose political views he worries will be attributed to him and his play. *The Staple of News*, moreover, was not the only playbook in which the religious convictions of news readers were derided. Other plays printed during this period, by such authors as James Shirley, Philip Massinger, and Thomas Randolph, also addressed the religious politics of the news trade and likewise sided against coranto readers. By looking at the *The Staple of News* as a printed text in the book trade of 1631, rather than as a performed text in the theater of 1626, I intend to show why Jonson believed that his five-year-old play might be read for its news and, more broadly, how the politics of play-reading and news-reading were intimately connected during the reign of Charles I.[9]

## Vulgar Women Readers

*The Staple of News* takes its name from a fictional office set up in London to sell news, an idea Jonson first used his 1620/1 masque *News from the New World Discovered in the Moon*, in which a newsletter writer, the Factor, plans to "erect a Staple for newes ere long, wh[i]ther all shall be brought, and thence againe vented under the name of Staple-newes."[10] In *The Staple of News*, the Factor's scheme is realized by another character, Cymbal, the Master of the Staple, who has set up an office "to enter all the *Newes* . . . o' the time / And vent it as occasion serues" (8–9; 1.2.26–27). The office gathers its news by dispatching "four *Emissaries*"—defined as "Men imploy'd outward, that are sent abroad / To fetch in the commodity"—to "the 4. Cardinall Quarters" of London: the court, St. Paul's, the Royal Exchange, and the law courts at Westminster Hall (9; 1.2.50–51, 59). In addition, the office has "speciall friends" and "men of *Correspondence* i'the *Country*" who live "Through all the Shires o'the kingdome" and who both supply the office with news and purchase news from it (14; 1.5.17, 18, 21). Once the commodity has been "fetched in," it is "examin'd, and then registred," at which point it is "issu'd vnder the Seale of the *Office*, / As *Staple Newes*; no other newes be currant" (9; 1.2.34–36).

The term "staple" captures the multiple functions of Cymbal's office. A "staple" originally referred to a location where merchants had a monopoly on certain goods, but the term could also mean "the principal or basic food on which a community lives."[11] Much like London's wool staple, Cymbal's news staple will have "the exclusive right of purchase" of news, so anyone seeking this "staple commodity," one that Londoners seem unable to live without, must purchase it there. Previously, in the public sites patrolled by the four emissaries, news could be freely exchanged without any explicit governmental or monopolistic oversight, but the Staple will now bring these news centers under its control.[12] Cymbal's scheme is a fantasy for taming the social exchange and publication of news: information will be brought in or mailed to the office, issued as "*Staple Newes*," and then purchased by anyone who wants this highly desirable commodity.

The customers who end up visiting the Staple give some idea of Jonson's conception of news readers. Jonson's contempt for theatrical audiences is well known, but he often evinces a more favorable attitude toward the readers of his plays. In the same year that *The Staple of News* was printed, for example, he appealed to readers on the title page of *The New Inn*, asking them to vindicate the play's poor staging by the King's Men, by whom "it was neuer acted, but most negligently play'd," and its poor reception by the theatrical audience, by whom it was "more squeamishly beheld, and censured."[13] If the readers of *The New Inn* could rescue the play from its contamination on "the loathed stage" and help secure its rightful place among the works of Horace, Anacreon, and Pindar, why did readers of *The Staple of News* need to be instructed, perhaps in vain, about Jonson's "allegory and purpose"?[14] As it turns out, the play's topic—news—was the problem. It invited the wrong type of readers.

In Jonson's estimation, those who "hunger and thirst after publish'd pamphlets of *Newes*" were unlikely to read his play in order to learn to "reprehend" the news trade; rather, they would be tempted by the news promised in the play's title. Even though he believed that news pamphlets were untrue, not all play-readers, nor evidently all playgoers, saw corantos as "a weekly cheat to draw mony." The customers who visit the Staple certainly do not:

> 'Tis the house of *fame*, Sir,
> Where both the curious, and the negligent;
> The scrupulous and carelesse; wilde, and stay'd;
> The idle, and laborious; all doe meet,

> To tast the *Cornu copiæ* of her rumors,
> Which she, the mother of sport, pleaseth to scatter
> Among the vulgar: Baites, Sir, for the people!
> And they will bite like fishes.
>
> (41; 3.2.115–22)

A diverse range of customers descends on the news office—the curious, the negligent, the scrupulous, the careless, the wild, the staid, the idle, and the laborious—but all these customers share one essential trait: they are "vulgar." It is the vulgar who "bite like fishes" at the Staple's rumors and the vulgar who were commonly thought to make up the primary readers of news pamphlets. As the historian Adam Fox has written, the vulgar were understood to be "credulous and gullible in all that they heard, ever liable to misunderstand the truth of things, prone to distort them still further, hasty to judge, and quick to criticize their betters."[15] It logically follows, then, that the vulgar would seek out corantos, fail to recognize that the pamphlets have "no syllable of truth in them," and consequently fail to "apprehend" the real nature of the news trade. "The more intelligent merchants doe jeere" the "Corranto-Coiner," quipped Richard Brathwait in 1631, but "the vulgar doe admire him, holding his Novels oracular."[16] It is the vulgar, therefore, who would be tempted by a play about news and yet would have difficulty distinguishing between that play's satirical news and the news of "a reasonable man."

Among these vulgar readers, Jonson identifies one type as especially prone to gadding about in search of news. Before the Staple officially opens, a female customer arrives demanding "A *groatsworth* of any *Newes*, I care not what, / To carry downe this *Saturday*, to our *Vicar*" (13; 1.4.11–12). The Register calls her a "Butterwoman" (13; 1.4.13)—the first in a series of puns on the name of the bookseller and coranto publisher Nathaniel Butter—and she is directed to wait until news arrives from the Exchange or Paul's Churchyard, where Butter and his business partner, Nicholas Bourne, respectively, had their shops.[17] The gender of this first customer is no accident, for women are repeatedly figured in *The Staple of News* as vulgar readers with an obsessive desire for news and gossip.[18] Indeed, one of the primary ways that Jonson attempts to satirize the print news trade is by linking corantos to women readers.

When the Prologue begins the play's opening speech, four female playgoers, the Gossips, who have been lured to the Blackfriars by the promise of a play with news, interrupt his monologue and climb on stage. "Come Gossip," Gossip Mirth encourages her friend, "be not asham'd. The Play is the *Staple* of *Newes*, and you are the *Mistresse*, and *Lady* of *Tatle*, let's ha' your opinion of it" (3; Induction 2–4). Gossip Tattle soon confirms Mirth's assessment of her expertise, warning the Prologue, "Looke your *Newes* be new, and fresh, *M^r^. Prologue*, and vntainted, I shall find them else, if they be stale, or flye-blowne, quickly!" (3; Induction 25–27).[19] Later, in the third Intermean, Gossip Tattle elaborates on her interest, and that of women more generally, in news. Discussing a rumor about the infamous astrologer Dr. Lamb, she admits, "But whether it were true, or no, we Gossips are bound to beleeue it, an't be once out, and a foot: how should wee entertaine the time else, or finde our selues in fashionable discourse, for all companies, if we do not credit all, and make more of it, in the reporting?" (49; 3 Intermean 37–41). It is this type of consumer (and dispenser) of news that the Staple is designed to replace. It will restrict women's acquisition of news to its one office, depriving them of access to their independent information networks, which were located in such places as bake houses and conduits.[20] Until that happens, though, vulgar women will continue to seek out news, rumor, and gossip in the places where women congregate as well as in the pages of news pamphlets.

Cymbal is confident his news office will succeed, in fact, because of the interest of one particular woman. He plans to court Lady Pecunia, an allegorical personification of money, reasoning that, because she is a woman, she will naturally support his venture. "So soone as sh' heares of the *New Office*," Cymbal has reportedly boasted, "Shee'll come to visit it, as they all haue longings / After new sights, and motions!" (18; 1.6.57–61). With the riches of Pecunia in his possession, the Staple's financial success will be assured. So even though the news office plans to regulate the access of the vulgar to news, its financial prospects nonetheless seem bright owing to the overarching desire for news among women in general, and in one woman especially.

Jonson's representation of news customers as vulgar has often been used by critics to explain his opposition to the expanding news trade.[21] As Paul Yachnin argues, *The Staple of News* "is a satirical argument about the embeddedness of the news in the system of rank and social prestige," a system in which news functions as "a form of social currency traded illicitly by the vulgar." According to this line of argument, the expanding news trade, as well as the theater, allowed the vulgar to traffic in news that should have been restricted to those higher up in Jonson's ideal social hierarchy, which was based on "a ranked population regulated by the husbanding of political information."[22] Jonson's particular vision of a "hierarchical community" has even been called "reactionary" by D. F. McKenzie, who wrote, *The Staple of News* "too clearly shows the thoroughly reactionary nature of Jonson's political idealism," for "the popular press was a reflection of an egalitarian movement, and immensely educative in forming a new language for talking about politics."[23]

While the popular press may eventually have led to the social developments mentioned by McKenzie, Jonson's play is thoroughly immersed in the language of the seventeenth-century news trade, and its crucial language was not egalitarian politics but religious politics. When customers visit the Staple, Yachnin notes, "they are able to buy news items according to their area of interest," but these interests have never been quite specified, much less analyzed, by scholars.[24] Jonson's opinion of news readers does not explain *why* these readers—vulgar or otherwise—took such a keen interest in corantos, that is, why they wanted to read Butter and Bourne's pamphlets. So, although criticism of *The Staple of News* has perceptively noted Jonson's disdain for news readers, it has yet to offer a sufficient explanation for that disdain beyond social snobbery. In order to understand why these readers were eagerly purchasing corantos, we need to turn to the news sold by Cymbal's office.

## Religious Fears and "Newes of State"

When the Staple does open, Cymbal's plan for distributing carefully organized reports quickly falls apart, as the office degenerates into a site of feverish calls for news that are promptly satisfied by the Staple's employees. It becomes rapidly apparent, moreover, that the capaciousness of possible news topics will be dominated by one overriding concern: religion. The elaborate filing system the office had planned to use, one built partly on accuracy ("*Authenticall*, and *Apocryphall.* / Or *Newes* of doubtfull credit") and partly on seasonality ("*Newes* of the season," "*vacation newes* / *Terme-newes*, and *Christmas-newes*"), is subsumed under "*newes* o' the *faction*": "*Reformed newes, Protestant newes* / And *Pontificiall newes*" (14; 1.5.8–9, 12–15). By telescoping the range of news sold by the Staple, in which any and all vendible information is reduced almost exclusively to religious news, Jonson's play offers an incisive interpretation of the English news trade in the 1620s and 1630s, suggesting that its expansion was fueled by an interest in the religious implications of the Thirty Years' War. Modern historians now maintain that the war was not strictly religious in nature; its international alliances were informed by a mix of constitutional issues, overt factional and political interests, as well as religious ties. *The Staple of News*, however, shows that readers were looking at the war from a more limited perspective. For them, it was a war of religion. And it was a war of religion in their eyes partly because of what they were reading in corantos.[25]

The first reports retailed by the Staple hinge on the division between "*Protestant newes* / And *Pontificiall newes.*" When Lady Pecunia and Pennyboy Junior arrive at the office, he begins by calling for "Any, any kind [of news.] / So it be *newes*, the newest that thou hast" (39; 3.2.18–19), a request that echoes the Butterwoman's earlier desire for "any *Newes.*" But he immediately narrows his request to "Some *newes* of *State*, for a *Princesse*" (39; 3.2.20), the type of news booksellers were selling to anyone who would pay a few pence for a coranto.

He and his princess are treated to a litany of reports on "*newes* of *State*," all of which focus on Catholic powers in the Thirty Years' War. They are told that the king of Spain, Philip IV, has been chosen pope and Holy Roman Emperor (39; 3.2.21–22); that the real Holy Roman Emperor, Ferdinand II, now "trailes a pike" in General Tilly's army (39; 3.2.23–24);[26] that General Spinola "is made *Generall* of the *Iesuits*" (39; 3.2.26–27);[27] that the union of the papacy and the Holy Roman Empire in the person of the Spanish king is a sign of the coming Fifth Monarchy and hence of the Apocalypse.[28] According to copies of letters from Maximilian I, duke of Bavaria and founder of the Catholic League, this concentration of religious and political power in a single Catholic ruler has "bin long the ayme / Of the house of *Austria*" (39; 3.2.27–33). Also recounted are the latest inventions of the Jesuits, "The onely Enginers of *Christendome*" (39; 3.2.39). They have constructed a device that will raise Spinola to the moon, where he can spy on Protestant forces (39; 3.2.35–43), and the "Cooke to the Society," Mutio Vitelleschi, has created powdered eggs with yolks of "wilde fire" that can destroy cities (39; 3.2.44–52).[29] In addition, following his earlier invention of the telescope, Galileo has recently created a "burning *Glasse*" that will "fire any *Fleet* that's out at *Sea*" through the use of "*Mooneshine*" (39; 3.2.52–55).[30]

In these reports, the Staple groups leaders in the continental war together based on a common religious identity—here, Catholic—rather than a common state or national identity. The scene's humor depends on how familiar the audience was with the events and personalities of the Thirty Years' War, which newsbook readers surely were, but Jonson's method of parody involves more than simply tickling the fancy of readers by referring to famous generals and princes. Rather, Jonson uses these references with a particular purpose in mind: to represent how the vulgar read corantos. The Staple's reports are meant to intensify the possible repercussions of the war's progress, highlighting Protestants' anxieties about the conflict and their eschatological fears of a renewed Catholic dominion over all of Europe. As Ian Atherton remarks, "for many, the main way to read the news was to seek the divine hand that lay behind human actions" and to look for "the working of God's providence," an interpretative framework ridiculed by Jonson's play.[31]

The reaction of Pennyboy Junior to this series of Catholic news reports shows their intended effect. He exclaims that these recent events "will beget strange turnes in *Christendome*!" (39; 3.2.25), a term that nicely captures the political realities of the war and, more important, its overarching religious significance. These "strange turnes" could be quite alarming. Jesuitical inventions would give Catholic armies a decisive military advantage, which could hasten the ultimate defeat of all of Protestant Europe, including England. The consolidation of ecclesiastical and political power in the king of Spain not only represents a grave military threat but may also signify the imminent approach of the Apocalypse. Such reports are designed to provoke fear in their readers, and if they somehow do not, the Staple will relate stories that are even more troubling.[32]

A bit later in the scene, Pennyboy Junior expresses relief after learning that "*Cornelius-Son*," the Dutch engineer Cornelius Drebble, has countered certain Jesuit inventions by constructing an "inuisible *Eele* / To swimme the hauen at *Dunkerke*, and sinke all / The shipping there" (40; 3.2.59–62).[33] These "*Eele*-boats" reassuringly "lye before *Queen-Hyth*" protecting England from a Spanish invasion. But not content to let Pennyboy Junior's fears subside, Fitton tries to provoke new ones:

*Fit[ton].* But what if *Spinola* haue a new *Proiect*:
To bring an army ouer in corke-shooes,
And land them, here, at *Harwich?* all his horse
Are shod with corke, and fourscore pieces of ordinance,
Mounted vpon cork-carriages, with bladders,
Instead of wheeles to runne the passage ouer
At a spring-tide.
*P. Iv[nior].* Is't true?
*Fit[ton].* As true as the rest.
(40; 3.2.84, 87–93)

In Fitton's imaginative account, Spinola's project begins as a hypothetical possibility—"what if *Spinola* haue . . ."—but midway through the report, he implies that preparations are already under way: "all his horse / *Are* shod" (emphasis added). Strict factual accuracy matters less to the Staple than instilling fear in its customers, fear that compels gulls like Pennyboy Junior to purchase, and purchase repeatedly, the Staple's reports so they can learn the latest on the war. Fitton's speculative account also shows that the war was not merely a continental affair. Its progress gave rise to real worries that, for instance, the hated Spanish might invade England.[34] Jonson's parody thus suggests two different points about news-reading: first, people read corantos because of fear—fear that is both political and religious—which news publishers purposefully attempt to inflame; second, to those who understand the real nature of the news trade, these reports are about as credible as an army invading in "corke-shooes." Any "reasonable man" would know they are untrue.

Jonson's parody extends beyond the action of the play and is furthered by the typographical appearance of act 3. Two pages after his address to readers warning them against misreading the play's news, Jonson adds a series of marginal notes, twenty-four in all, that call attention to the play's fictitious reports. Previous assessments of the play's notes have generally been unkind, calling them "trite and trifling" because they "simply restate the action or the dialogue."[35] More recently, critical opinion of the notes has improved, claiming that they attempt to develop the "literary appearance" of the play and help readers better "visualize stage action."[36] What these judgments miss, however, is the distinctive character of the notes in the central Staple scene. These notes, it turns out, are an ingenious part of Jonson's satire.[37]

The scene's marginal notes begin by imitating "publish'd pamphlets of *Newes*," but then, like the Staple's reports, they turn exaggeratedly parodic. The first notes read "*Newes from* Rome"; "*Newes of the* Emperor *and* Tilly"; "*Newes of* Spinola"; "*The fifth* Monarchy, *vniting the* Ecclesiasticke *and* Secular *power*"; "*a plot of the house of* Austria"; "*More of* Spinola" (39). These "news notes" recall the phrasing of newsbook title pages and replicate the rubrics under which individual reports were printed. Coranto title pages typically advertised a combination of news from particular regions ("The Continuation of our Weekly Avisoes from forraine parts, containing many particulars of *Germany*, *France*, the *Low-Countries*, and other parts of Christendome") and news of specific generals and princes ("newes of the Prince of *Oranges* and *Spinolaes* last

40 *The* STAPLE *of* NEVVES.

*The Holanders Eele.*

CLA. Yes, Sir, they write here, one *Cornelius-Son*,
Hath made the *Hollanders* an inuisible *Eele*,
To swimme the hauen at *Dunkirke*, and sinke all
The shipping there. P. IV. Why ha'not you this, *Thom?*
CYM. Because he keeps the *Pontificiall* side.

Peny-boy *will haue him change sides:*

P. IV. How, change sides, *Thom*. 'Twas neuer in my thought
To put thee vp against our selues. Come downe,
Quickly. CYM. Why, Sir? P. IV. I venter'd not my mony
Vpon those termes: If he may change; why so.
I'll ha'him keepe his owne side, sure. FIT. Why, let him,
'Tis but writing so much ouer againe.
P. IV. For that I'll beare the charge: There's two Pieces, (Sir.
FIT. Come, do not stick with the gentleman. CYM. I'l take none
And yet he shall ha'the place. P. IV. They shall be ten, then,

*though hee pay for it.*

Vp, *Thom*: and th'*Office* shall take 'hem. Keep your side, *Thom*.
Know your owne side, doe not forsake your side, *Thom*.
CYM. Read. THO. They write here one *Cornelius-Son*,
Hath made the *Hollanders* an inuisible *Eele*,
To swimme the Hauen at *Dunkirke*, and sinke all
The shipping there. P. IV. But how is't done? CYM. I'll shew you Sir.
It is an *Automa*, runnes vnder water,
With a snug nose, and has a nimble taile
Made like an *auger*, with which taile she wrigles
Betwixt the coasts of a Ship, and sinkes it streight.
P. IV. Whence ha'you this *newes*. FIT. From a right hand I assure (you,
The *Eele*-boats here, that lye before *Queen-Hyth*,
Came out of *Holland*. P. IV. A most braue deuice,
To murder their flat bottomes. FIT. I doe grant you:

Spinola's *new proiect: an army in cork-shooes.*

But what if *Spinola* haue a new *Proiect*:
To bring an army ouer in corke-shooes,
And land them, here, at *Harwich?* all his horse
Are shod with corke, and fourescore pieces of ordinance,
Mounted vpon cork-carriages, with bladders,
In stead of wheeles to runne the passage ouer
At a spring-tide. P. IV. Is't true? FIT. As true as the rest.
P. IV. He'll neuer leaue his engines: I would heare now
Some curious *newes*. CYM. As what? P. IV. *Magick*, or *Alchimy*
Or flying i'the ayre, I care not what.
CLA. They write from *LibtZig* (reuerence to your eares)

*Extraction of farts*

The Art of drawing farts out of dead bodies,
Is by the *Brotherhood* of the *Rosie Crosse*,
Produc'd vnto perfection, in so sweet
And rich a *tincture*---FIT. As there is no *Princesse*,
But may perfume her chamber with th'*extraction*.
P. IV. There's for you, *Princesse*. P. CA. What, a fart for her?
P. IV. I meane the *spirit*. P. CA. Beware how she resents it.

*The perpetuall Motion.*

P. IV. And what hast thou, *Thom?* THO. The perpetuall Motion,
Is

FIG. 6-1. Ben Jonson, *The Staple of News* (London, 1631), 40. By permission of The Huntington Library, San Marino, California.

designes"; "diverse particulars concerning *Monsieur Tilly* his preparation and strength to oppose the said King of *Sweden.*")[38] Within corantos, discrete news items were normally introduced by rubrics that specified the origin and date of the report, such as "*From Prague the* 16 *of Ianuary*" or "*From* Leypsich *the* 31. *of May.*"[39] These initial notes, therefore, function as rather straightforward imitations of what readers could find in corantos. They also help readers locate the play's news more easily, and, like the Staple's news of state, they emphasize the ominous religious implications of the war.

But after the first few, the notes begin to enter the realm of the absurd: "*His* Egges" (i.e., Spinola's); "Galileo's *study*"; "*The burning glass, by Moon-shine*"; "*The Hollanders Eele*"; "Spinola's *new proiect: an army in cork-shooes*"; "*Extraction of farts*" (39–40; see fig. 6-1). In marginalia like these, Jonson ridicules the news in corantos and the gullibility of readers who believe such manifest falsehoods. While the first notes, like the Staple's first reports, are designed to capture the interest of readers with a string of distressing Catholic bulletins, the later ones reinforce the mounting foolishness of the Staple's wares. They point Jonson's readers to such topics as "The Art of drawing farts out of dead bodies," which has been perfected "by the *Brotherhood* of the *Rosie Crosse*" for use as perfume (40–41; 3.2.95, 98–99). Rather than inciting fear, such notes and reports are meant to come across as preposterously false. But not all readers were as certain as Jonson that coranto reports were ridiculous and untrue. And, of course, as Jonson's address to readers reveals, not all readers would be sure to recognize the parody behind the play's fictional reports.

## "The Truth"

Jonson considered news readers to be less reasonable in their evaluation of corantos than he himself was, and not simply because they were vulgar women. Readers were likely to gauge the truth of news reports using different interpretive standards than he did, standards that usually resulted from different views of religious truth. The effects of these differences rippled throughout the print news trade. For religion not only motivated the reading of news pamphlets but also divided the news trade into opposing sides.

The news of state initially read to Pecunia and Pennyboy Junior is all from "the Pontificiall side," prompting the young suitor to ask, "Ha'you no *Newes* against him [Spinola], on the contrary?" (39; 3.2.58). The clerk

Nathaniel, who until now has been silent, begins to supply him with reports on the Dutch "*Eele*-boats," but Pennyboy Junior interrupts him, asking why the other clerk, his former barber, Thomas, is not reading the Protestant news:

> *Cym[bal].* Because he keeps the *Pontificiall* side.
> *P. Iv[nior].* How, change sides, *Thom.* 'Twas never in my thought
> To put thee vp against our selues.
>
> (40; 3.2.63–65)

As Cymbal explains, the Staple divides its clerks according to "sides," with Thomas reading Catholic news and Nathaniel Protestant news. Objecting to this arrangement, Pennyboy Junior demands that his former barber read the news of "our selues" and persuades the Staple managers to let Thomas and Nathaniel switch sides. He finishes by admonishing Thomas: "Keep your side, *Thom.* / Know your owne side, doe not forsake your side, *Thom*" (40; 3.2.73–74). Pennyboy Junior's rebuke not only spells out which side he thinks a good Englishman ought to make his "owne," but it also reveals that more is at stake in the issue of "sides" than the working arrangements of two clerks. In Jonson's satirical portrait, sides lie at the heart of the news trade, and they divide everything from sources and readers to the very idea of "the truth."

Like the news sold by the Staple, the news in corantos was often organized, and occasionally advertised, according to its sides. The title page for the Butter and Bourne coranto of June 10, 1631, separates its news into two halves. It first lists Protestant news: "THE Powerfull and provident proceeding of the King of *Sweden* in *Germanie* . . ." and "The preparation of the Protestant Princes to resist the Vsurpation and tyrannie of the Emperor, and to give ayde and assistance to the King of *Sweden*." It then turns to Catholic news, signaling the transition with the italic note "*On the Other-side*": "The great and formidable Preparation of the Emperour and the Popish League, to resist the said K. of *Sweden*, and the poore oppressed Protestants," plus "The late vndertakings of the Prince of ORENGE in *Flaunders* and else-where . . ." (see fig. 6-2).[40] Although it prints news of both sides, the title page leaves no doubt about which side its publishers support. Backed by providence, Gustavus Adolphus and the Protestant princes have come together to resist the tyranny of the Emperor Ferdinand II and to liberate "the poore oppressed Protestants." The partisanship on this title page, moreover, is part of a larger trend. Most reports in corantos came from Protestant sources; according to Folke Dahl, 60 to 70 percent were "verbal translations" of items in Dutch pamphlets, usually from Amsterdam, a hotbed of international Protestantism. Whatever mistakes may have found their way into news pamphlets, these errors were not the result, as Jonson believed, of corantos being "made all at home."[41]

The publishers of corantos relied so heavily on Dutch sources both because they themselves supported the Protestant cause and because they assumed their customers did too. The title pages of corantos, complained one satirist, "euery week besmeare / Each publike post, and Church dore" around London, a standard advertising practice in the city, but one also informed by Butter and Bourne's conviction that their readers preferred news of powerful Protestants triumphing over tyrannous Catholics.[42] And some readers clearly did. One reader, for example, wrote next to reports of Protestant victories in a 1626 coranto, "good yf true."[43] In a similar vein, Donald Lupton commented in 1632, "If they write good Newes of our side, it is seldome true; but if it be bad, it's always almost too true."[44] The Suffolk clergyman John Rous recorded in his diary on October 6, 1629, news of "a sermon unprinted, lately preached at Whitehall before the King," which claimed that Puritans also preferred news of "our side": "What newes? Every man askes what newes? Every man's religion is knowne by his newes; the Puritan talkes of Bethlehem Gabor, &c."[45] Three years later, when Gustavus Adolphus was winning battle after battle, John Pory reported that "a minister in St. Mary's at Oxford prayed, very lately, it would please God to inspire the Courantiers with the spirit of truth, that we might know when to pray and where to praise."[46] These readers, like the corantos, divided news into religious sides, and, like the corantos, they plainly desired "good Newes" of the Protestant side.

The comments of these readers also suggest that news involved two different ways of assessing "the truth": factual accuracy and perspective, or what Thomas Schröder has called "an empirically verifiable representation of reality" and "objectivity, balance, and impartiality."[47] Even if corantos relayed accurate reports that were "empirically verifiable," they were still open to the charge of not printing "the truth" if they seemed to lack "objectivity." Indeed, the perspective of corantos—what they chose to report and emphasize, and what they chose *not* to report and emphasize—mattered as much as, if not more than, empirical accuracy. Not surprisingly, corantos were often attacked on both fronts; their reports were criticized because they contained factual errors and because they were insufficiently balanced between Protestant and Catholic news.

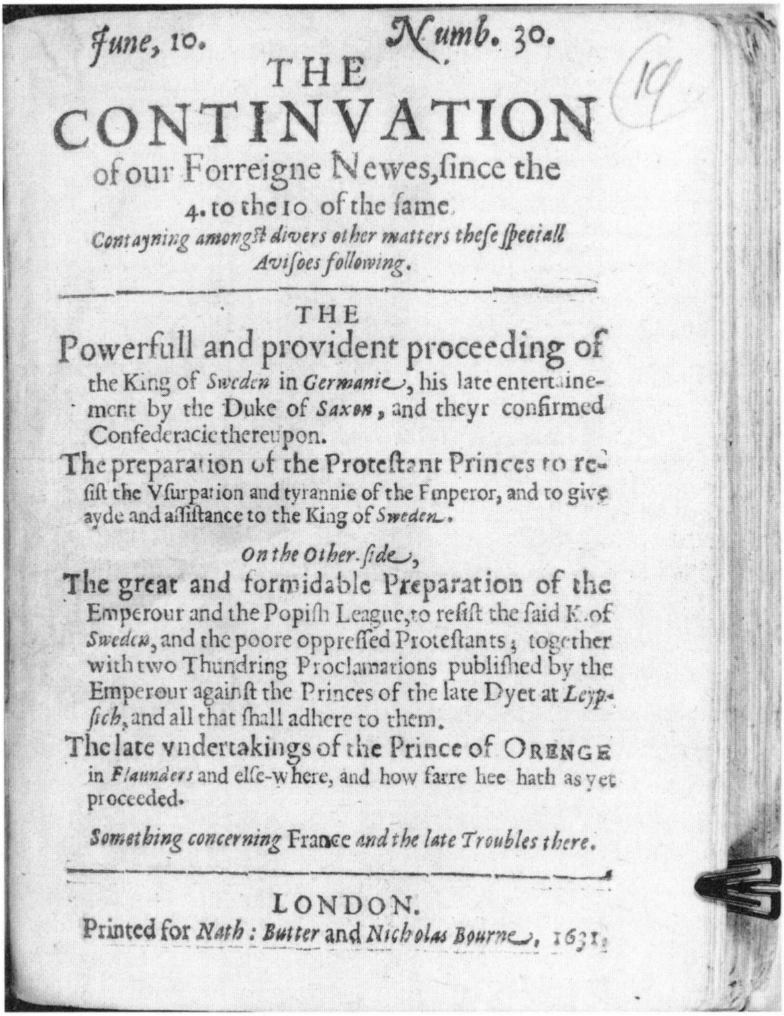

June, 10. Numb. 30.

THE CONTINVATION of our Forreigne Newes, since the 4. to the 10 of the same.

*Contayning amongst divers other matters these speciall Avisoes following.*

THE Powerfull and provident proceeding of the King of *Sweden* in *Germanie*, his late entertainement by the Duke of *Saxon*, and theyr confirmed Confederacie thereupon.

The preparation of the Protestant Princes to resist the Vsurpation and tyrannie of the Emperor, and to give ayde and assistance to the King of *Sweden*.

*On the Other-side,*

The great and formidable Preparation of the Emperour and the Popish League, to resist the said K. of *Sweden*, and the poore oppressed Protestants; together with two Thundring Proclamations published by the Emperour against the Princes of the late Dyet at *Leypsich*, and all that shall adhere to them.

The late vndertakings of the Prince of ORENGE in *Flaunders* and else-where, and how farre hee hath as yet proceeded.

*Something concerning* France *and the late Troubles there.*

LONDON.
Printed for *Nath: Butter* and *Nicholas Bourne*, 1631.

FIG. 6-2. *The Continvation of our Forreigne Newes* (June 10, 1631) (London, 1631), Burney 5*.(19) title page. By permission of the British Library.

When readers doubted the empirical accuracy of corantos, they often claimed that the pamphlets' news reports had been invented by writers living in London, not fighting on the continent. In comments that recall Jonson's address to readers, Lupton wrote that corantos "haue as many Leyes as Lines," lies invented by their authors' "owne idel braine, or busie fancies, vpon the blockes in *Paules*, or in their Chambers." "They haue vsed this trade so long," he continues, "that now euery one can say, its euen as true as a *Currantoe*, meaning that it's all false."[48] In James Shirley's *The School of Compliment*, the character Gasparo voices a similar theory on the composition of corantos. He describes "newes-makers" as younger brothers who pass themselves off as soldiers in the European wars but whose "valour is inuisible": they "will write you a battell in any part of *Europe* at an houres warning, and yet neuer set foot out of a Tauerne."[49] Like Jonson, both of these writers accuse corantos of printing inaccurate information, but they attribute these errors to the pamphlets' method of composition—they were "inuented" by young men writing in taverns—not to religious partiality.[50] Other readers, though, distrusted corantos precisely because of the pamphlets' religious bias.

Both the Oxford minister at St. Mary's who prayed that the "Courtantiers" would be inspired with the truth and the anonymous 1626 reader who hoped for Protestant victories were aware that errors made their way into corantos, but they do not appear to have reflexively distrusted these pamphlets nor to have doubted that accurate information could be found in them. These readers shared the same Protestant perspective as corantos, though, and so were willing to overlook such errors. The sermon noted by John Rous, however, made a somewhat different argument, one that suggests why readers like the Oxford minister and Jonson may have reacted so differently to corantos.[51]

The author of this sermon, Thomas Lushington, claimed that perceptions of factual accuracy were determined by religious belief, not empirical facts. Writing in 1624, Lushington maintained that Protestants spread Protestant reports while Catholics spread Catholic reports, and both believed the news of their own side. As a result, "by their *News* ye may know their *Religion*, and by their *Religion* fore-know their *News*":

> This week the *Spanish Match* goes forward, and *Bethleem Gabors* Troups are broken; and the next Week *Bethleem Gabors* Troups goe forward, and the *Spanish Match* is broken. The *Catholique* is of the *Spanish match*, and the *Protestant* of restoring the *Palatinate*; and each Party think that the safety of the *Church* and success of *religion* depends upon the event of one or other, and therefore they cross and counter-tell each others News.[52]

Like Jonson's vulgar readers, Lushington's Catholic and Protestant newsmongers take a keen interest in the news because of its implications for "the safety of the *Church* and success of *religion*." The newsmongers on each side follow the same events, but they hope for different outcomes.

As a result, the two sides "cross and counter-tell each others News," calling into question the other side's information and arguing for the truth of their own. Or, as the editor of the April 20, 1624, coranto explained, people have a "variety of humors, and write to their friends as they are affected in disposition, so as the Papist will haue it one way, and the Protestant would haue it another way." Although this editor believes "there is but one truth," he acknowledges that religion determines how people understand this "truth" and therefore what type of news they believe to be true.[53]

The link between religion and truth was especially strong because, in the minds of most early modern readers, the truth originated in the evangelical Gospel, the "good news" of Christianity.[54] In Paul's first epistle to Timothy, the apostle defines the foundation of truth as "the house of God, which is the Church of the liuing God, the pillar and ground of the trueth."[55] Or, as John Eliot described the nature of truth in a speech before the 1629 House of Commons, "the Gospel is that truth which from all antiquity is derived, that pure truth which admits no mixture or corruption, that truth in which this kingdom has been happy through a long and rare prosperity."[56] In a similar manner, Anthony White maintained in his joint 1628 sermons *Truth Purchast* and *Error Abandon'd* that "the truth . . . will be knowen by her antiquity and lastingnesse, because it is the offspring of him *that was, and is, and is to come.*" White ended his sermons with a prayer reiterating the ultimate source of truth: "O lord, by thy word and spirit guide vs all here present, by thy sonne, who is the truth."[57] Truth, by definition, was grounded in religion.

News of the Thirty Years' War was part of this religious framework for understanding "the truth," for true news of the war was seen as "the offspring of him *that was, and is, and is to come.*" And if news readers were nervous about their ability to discern the truth in contemporary news accounts, a sermon by Samuel Kenrick in 1627 would have assured them that religious truth would indeed help them overcome this obstacle. The truth, wrote Kenrick, "soone distinguishes the good from the bad; the right from the wrong," and, we might add, accurate from inaccurate news.[58] When it came to the reports in corantos, it was the religious perspectives of readers, according to Lushington, that exerted the most influence over what they took to be true. Catholics and Protestants circulated—and believed—news they wanted to be true, not news they knew to be true: "The news goes not as things are in themselves, but as mens fancies are fashioned, as some lust to report, and others to believe." Consequently, "the same relation shall goe for true or false, according to the key wherein mens minds are tuned; but chiefly as they stand diverse in Religion."[59] Judgments of factual accuracy—what "things are in themselves"—thus emerge as the products of religious perspective, "the key wherein mens minds are tuned." People's fancies govern what they believe, and their fancies are in turn governed by where they "stand" in religion. In this environment without a uniform standard of truth, the result, says Lushington, is that "false news follows true at the heels, and oftentimes outstrips it," a conclusion that Jonson's play would seem to endorse.[60]

And if the religious convictions of readers influenced how they read and responded to news publications, then there was every reason to think that *The Staple of News* itself could be subject to that same critical process. Jonson maintains that corantos "have no syllable of truth," and he ends his address by asking his readers, "If you have the truth. . . ." In the news trade, though, there was no one truth. The news arrived in conflicting reports and was filtered through differing religious perspectives. By claiming that corantos are "made all at home" with the goal of "cooz'ning the people," Jonson seems to align himself with "reasonable" readers like the satirist A. H. (probably Abraham Holland), who claimed that Bourne and Butter's "weekely Newes" was "compos'd in Pauls, / By some *Decaied Captaine*, or those *Rooks*, / Whose hungry braines compile prodigious *Books*."[61] But Jonson's criticisms of the news trade also echo those voiced by Catholics, who considered corantos to be propagandistic Protestant publications filled with lies.[62] Was Jonson's representation of the news trade in his play consistent with a "reasonable mans" opinion of corantos, or was it perhaps also the product of a different religious viewpoint? And would his readers lack "the truth" because they did not "apprehend" the factual inaccuracies in news pamphlets, or because they did not share the same religious perspective as Jonson and his play?

Critics have usually discounted the possibility of Jonson's satire being motivated by religion, arguing instead—when the play's religious dimensions have been acknowledged at all—that "the political and religious sympathies of *The Staple of News* are typically vague and insubstantial," or that the play uses news from "written and real-life source materials . . . not as purposeful interventions in the political sphere but rather as exploitative retailing of the news."[63] But in the play's satire, news readers are represented not simply as vulgar women, but as vulgar Puritans with strong pro-Dutch and anti-Spanish views. Rather than being "vague and insubstantial," the play's political and religious sympathies are firmly opposed to the views commonly associated with Puritan news readers, and firmly on the side of the English crown and its policies in 1631.

In the five years separating the play's performance and publication, England experienced two significant political changes: its foreign policy shifted in favor of Spain, and its religious settlement shifted in favor of a more ceremonial form of worship sometimes characterized as "crypto-Catholic." These changes aggravated tensions within English Protestantism, and as a consequence, the staunch Protestantism of corantos increasingly came to be seen as a source of religious discord. While early in 1626 their Protestant bias and that of their readers seemed consistent with the foreign policy of the English government, that was no longer the case in 1631, when corantos and news readers were widely assumed to possess a religious outlook in conflict with that of the English government. "The truth" was divided not only by the different perspectives of Protestants and Catholics but also by the different perspectives of two "Reformed" factions often labeled "Arminian" and "Puritan."[64] And rather than avoid this conflict within English Protestantism, *The Staple of News* stresses some of the very issues that were causing factures in the nation's religious culture.

## Puritan News

Before opening its doors to additional customers besides Pennyboy Junior and Lady Pecunia, the Register of the Staple says he expects a heterogeneous clientele to visit their "house of *fame*" where "all doe meet." But the customers who do show up are predominately Puritans. The first customer is "a she *Anabaptist*" named Dopper, who asks for "*Newes* / O'the *Saints* at *Amsterdam*" (41; 3.2.151, 123–24). Thomas, the clerk responsible for Protestant reports, fulfills her request with news that the "Saints" shortly expect the "Prophet *Baal*," who will "calculate a *time*, and halfe a *time*, / And the whole *time*, according to *Naometry*" (41; 3.2.126–29), an arcane allusion to the prediction of future apocalyptic events, including the overthrow of the Catholic Church and Islam.[65] Dopper next purchases a more expensive piece of "godly" news from Constantinople, which claims that "the *grand Signior*," the sultan of Turkey, Mustapha II, "Is certainly turn'd Christian" and plans to visit

Amsterdam "to cleare / The controuersie 'twixt the *Pope* and him, / Which is the *Antichrist*" (41; 3.2.141–46). In these accounts, Jonson's method of parody remains similar to that in the scenes with Pennyboy Junior: ridiculous bits of information are combined with sensationalistic speculations about the eschatological consequences of the war. Dopper is firmly on the side of the Protestants, but her purchases reveal the complicated national and religious politics of this side of the news trade.

Grateful for news of the Saints, Dopper blesses the emissary to the Royal Exchange, the Dutchman Hans Buz, plus "his whole *Family*, with the *Nation*." The Staple's Register has a much different reaction, grumbling in an aside, "Yes, for *Amboyna*, and the Iustice there!" (41; 3.2.149–50). While Dopper enthusiastically identifies with the Protestant Dutch, the Register remembers the ten Englishmen who were tortured and executed by Dutch soldiers in February 1623 for conspiring to seize the castle of Amboyna in the Moluccas.[66] The Amboyna massacre remained a source of Anglo-Dutch antagonism throughout the 1620s and 1630s, in fact, well into the later seventeenth century.[67] John Pory, in a newsletter from April 1631, claimed that two English captains fighting in the continental war killed seventeen Hollanders in retribution for Amboyna; three of the slaughtered Dutchmen had apparently boasted of participating in the 1623 murders.[68] Despite the Amboyna massacre, however, Anglo-Dutch relations were particularly strong when *The Staple of News* was performed in 1626, as England and the United Provinces were still committed to an offensive alliance against Spain which they had signed a year earlier.[69] By 1631, though, England's foreign policy had reversed itself, swinging over to the side of Spain.

England and Spain had ended their hostilities with the Treaty of Madrid late in 1630, and for the rest of Charles I's Personal Rule, peace would be the hallmark of English foreign policy, effectively turning the nation into "a non-combatant satellite of Spain."[70] England also emerged as a vital player in the Spanish wartime economy, minting Spanish silver in London, lowering custom rates for Spanish goods, and helping preserve the safety of ships carrying supplies to the Spanish Netherlands.[71] As the Venetian ambassador commented in April 1631, "there is no doubt that they aim here at giving an advantage to the Spaniards in everything possible," both to facilitate trade with Spain and "to injure the Dutch, whom they envy for their prosperity and consider excessively haughty."[72] This reversal placed Dopper's support for the Saints in Amsterdam directly at odds with England's new foreign policy.

Dopper's interest in the identity of Antichrist, furthermore, was an issue English religious authorities were trying to prevent the public from discussing. As part of their ecclesiastical program, the newly ascendant English Arminians established the goal of fostering less divisive relations between the Church of England and the Church of Rome, and so they sought to limit strident attacks on the pope and Catholicism, especially in print.[73] Doing so, however, required overturning a central element in the "Protestant consensus" that had existed since the Elizabethan church: the identification of the pope as Antichrist.[74] To counter this entrenched theological view, Arminians like Richard Montagu "stressed the obscurity" of identifying Antichrist, refusing to claim that either the pope or "the Turke," the two traditional candidates, was the true Antichrist. Nevertheless, Puritans like Dopper continued to interpret the world through an eschatological framework that used "pope" and "Antichrist" almost as interchangeable terms.[75]

Support for the Protestant Dutch and confidence in the identity of the pope as Antichrist had originally been consistent with the policies of Charles I early in his reign—when England entered into an alliance with the Dutch against Spain, and before the Arminians had emerged as the dominant faction in the Caroline church. But these issues were acting to exacerbate political and religious tensions by 1631, and between the performance and printing of *The Staple of News*, it had become noticeably more difficult for Puritans like Dopper to know, keep, and not forsake their "own side." The contours of the English government's "side" had shifted, both politically and religiously, and by holding the same views that they had in 1626, Puritans gradually found themselves on the wrong side of the English government.

The customer who follows Dopper into the Staple, the cook Lickfinger, exhibits other classic features of Puritan news readers, especially in his vocal opposition to Catholic Spain. After preaching a mock sermon on his plans for a mission to convert Indian cannibals in America—a project with distinctly Puritan overtones[76]—he proceeds to ask the Staple employees for, and to supply them with, an impressive variety of news items: "*Court-newes*" (42; 3.2.185), "*Newes* o the *Stage*" (42; 3.2.198), news of the recently deceased actor William Rowley (43; 3.2.205–6), "news of *Gondomar*" (43; 3.2.207), "Something of *Bethlem Gabor*" (44; 3.2.285), "A little of the *Duke* of *Bauier*" (45; 3.2.294), and news "o'the *Pageants*" (45; 3.2.298). Lickfinger's appetite furthers the play's identification of Puritans as ravenous consumers of news, and the Staple works hard to supply him with reports that match his stereotypically anti-Spanish convictions.[77] Lickfinger purchases a report on Marco Antonio de Dominis, archbishop of Spalato, who is said to have rewarded, rather than sought revenge on, the King's Men for their satire of him in Thomas Middleton's *A Game at Chess*.[78] He also buys a report on the punishment of the count of Gondomar, Diego Sarmiento d'Acuña, who, because he used Middleton's play for "cleaning his *posterior's*," was afflicted with "A second *Fistula*, / Or an *excoriation* (at the least)," news that causes Lickfinger to exclaim joyfully, "Iustice! Iustice!" (43; 3.2.207–11).[79]

Lickfinger's loathing of these Spanish agents throws into stark relief the disjunction between England's pro-Spanish foreign policy and the anti-Spanish outlook of Puritan news readers. And if Jonson's assessment of Butter and Bourne's readers was correct, they were likely to hold views similar to Dopper's and Lickfinger's and, consequently, to balk at the play's send-up of the news of their side. Whatever Jonson's actual opinion of *A Game at Chess*, the Staple's "news of the stage" does not deride his "poor English play," as has often been maintained.[80] It does ridicule anti-Spanish Puritans who believe the Staple's news of de Dominis's stupidity and Gondomar's persistent posterior problems. Both Dopper and Lickfinger fit the type of news reader who would have applauded Middleton's political satire in 1624, and yet felt alienated by the crown's recent religious and foreign policies in 1631, when England seemed more than ever aligned with Catholic Spain and indifferent, if not hostile, to the Protestant Dutch. The "truth" embraced by Puritan news readers was the target of Jonson's satire, not Middleton's play. It is this truth that informs the contrast between "the *Newes* here vented" and Jonson's "*Newes*, or any reasonable mans." While it has been suggested that "the audience's error consisted in mistaking Jonson's satiric news bulletins for the 'straight dope' of the corantos,"[81] it seems more likely that the play's original spectators mistakenly conflated, not fake news and real news, but the Puritan politics of the Staple's news with Jonson's own political views. This is almost surely the interpretive error his address to readers was meant to forestall.

## Plays "made like the times *Newes*"

The religious politics of *The Staple of News* suggest that a new way is needed for thinking about why Jonson's play might have been read for its news and, more generally, about the relationship between news and drama in Caroline England. Previous criticism of Jonson's play has stressed not its focus on religious politics but its profusion of topical references. The play is immersed in personalities and events familiar to readers of news pamphlets—Spain, the Dutch, de Dominis, Gondomar, Nathaniel Butter, *A Game at Chess*, the King's Men, William Rowley, Ferdinand II, Pope Urban VIII, Spinola, Galileo, the duke of Bavaria, Bethlen Gabor—making it "as topical as any play Jonson wrote."[82] But although these references help establish the play's connection to the news trade, some of them would have been decidedly out of date in 1631. Gondomar, Spinola, and de Dominis had all died, while *A Game at Chess* had been a theatrical sensation a full seven years earlier. With news pamphlets appearing weekly, topical references would tend to age quickly, making these, in the words of Gossip Tattle, "stale" and "flye-blowne."

Despite these outdated references, Jonson assumed another sinister interpretation of his play was still possible, and indeed probable. What would have allowed the play to be read for its news, therefore, was unlikely to have been its "flye-blowne" allusions but rather its argument about the religious politics of news-reading. In 1631, the news trade was still built on the same religious divisions as it had been in 1626; it was still peddling "*Reformed newes, Protestant newes,* / And *Pontificiall newes,*" and still fanning the flames of Puritan interest in the Thirty Years' War. But the English government had turned away from the Dutch and toward the Spanish, away from Calvinist reformation and toward Arminian ceremonialism, and away from the politics of Puritan news readers and toward the politics of Jonson's play. Even if its topical references were no longer quite as resonant, the play's representation of religious politics and England's foreign policy was still controversial five years after it had been staged at the Blackfriars.

The connection of Jonson's play to news of the Thirty Years' War is obvious—his play supplies what its title promises—but many other plays printed in the 1630s were also taking sides in the news trade's wars of truth. Thomas Randolph's witty Cambridge University comedy *Aristippus*, which went through four editions in 1630 and 1631, is organized around two characters, a student and a Puritan wild man, who are both searching for Aristippus, an Arminian philosopher; it ends with the wild man renouncing his Dutch heresy and converting to Arminianism.[83] Other plays printed around the time of *The Staple of News*—such as Beaumont and Fletcher's *Cupid's Revenge* (1630, 1635), Shirley's *The Grateful Servant* (1630, 1637), and Massinger's *The Renegado* (1630)—

also support the crown's religious policies by extolling the power of religious rites, neglecting to condemn Catholic characters and rituals, and showing English Puritans as a political threat.[84] In contrast, "Puritan" plays like Thomas Drue's *The Duchess of Suffolk* (1631), Thomas Heywood's *1 & 2 If You Know Not Me, You Know Nobody* (1632, 1633, 1639), and Samuel Rowley's *When You See Me, You Know Me* (1632), valorize England's Protestant history and its struggles against the antichristian forces of Roman Catholicism.[85] *The Staple of News* was not the only play staging or printing the news during the reign of Charles I. Other plays were too, and they also contained what Jonson called fictions close to the truth ("*Ficta sint proxima veris*")—or, if not "the truth," at least one of the truths dividing news readers and play-readers in England.

## NOTES

I thank David Scott Kastan, Jean Howard, Zachary Lesser, Julie Crawford, Tiffany Alkan, and Adam Zucker for their insightful comments on earlier drafts of this essay.

1. Following the conventions of "old-style" dating, the play's title page advertises its performance as "IN THE YEARE, 1625." On the date of the first performance of the *The Staple of News*, see Devra Kifer, "*The Staple of News*: Jonson's Festive Comedy," *Studies in English Literature* 12 (1972): 329–44; Anthony Parr, ed., introduction to *The Staple of News*, Revels Plays (Manchester: Manchester University Press, 1988), 49–50.

2. Ben Jonson, *The Staple of Newes* (London: Printed by I[ohn] B[eale] for Robert Allot, 1631), 36. All quotations are cited by page from the 1631 edition, but I have also given the corresponding line numbers from Anthony Parr's Revels edition. I have reversed the address's use of italics and roman fonts. Jonson frequently used versions of this Horatian tag, from *Ars Poetica* (338), which he translates in the second prologue of *Epicoene* as "*Poet* never credit gain'd / By writing truths, but things (like truths) well fain'd" (London: Printed by William Stansby, sold by Iohn Browne, 1620), B1v. Other versions of the tag appear in the Prologue for the Court in *The Staple of News*, on the title page of *The Devil Is an Ass* (London: Printed by I[ohn] B[eale] for Robert Allot, 1631), and in *Discoveries* (London: Printed for Richard Meighen [and Thomas Walkley], 1640), 2351–54.

3. On metaphors of infection to describe news culture, see Ian Atherton, "'The Itch grown a Disease': Manuscript Transmission of News in the Seventeenth Century," in *News, Newspapers, and Society in Early Modern Britain*, ed. Joad Raymond (London: Frank Cass, 1999), 39, 56–58; Mitchell Stephens, *A History of News: From the Drum to the Satellite* (New York: Viking, 1988), 13–20; Thomas Schröder, "The Origins of the German Press," in *The Politics of Information in Early Modern Europe*, ed. Brendan Dooley and Sabrina A. Baron (New York: Routledge, 2001), 137–38.

4. See Stuart Sherman, who also notes the anxiety in Jonson's address ("Eyes and Ears, News and Plays: The Argument of Ben Jonson's *Staple*," in Dooley and Baron, *The Politics of Information*, 34–38).

5. *The Staple of News* comprises the last nineteen sheets of the folio collection, which was probably printed in the fall of 1631. Although it may not have been released for sale until around 1640, Jonson and the play's publisher, Robert Allot, clearly expected it to arrive in London bookshops in 1631. On the complicated circumstances of the folio's printing and non-publication, see William P. Williams, "Chetwin, Crooke, and the Jonson Folios," *Studies in Bibliography* 30 (1977): 75–95; W. W. Greg, *A Bibliography of the English Printed Drama to the Restoration*, 4 vols. (London: Bibliographical Society, 1939–59), 3:1075–76; C. H. Herford and Percy and Evelyn Simpson, eds., *Ben Jonson*, 11 vols. (Oxford: Clarendon, 1925–52), 1:211, 9:85–86. On the length of corantos, see Folke Dahl, *A Bibliography of English Corantos and Periodical Newsbooks 1620–1642* (London: Bibliographical Society, 1952).

6. Richard Levin, "*The Staple of News*, The Society of Jeerers, and Canters' College," *Philological Quarterly* 44 (1965): 446–48. For similar views, see Ton Hoenselaars, "Rumour, News and Commerce in Ben Jonson's *The Staple of News*," in *Rumeurs et nouvelles au temps de la Renaissance*, ed. M. T. Jones-Davies (Paris: Klincksieck, 1997): 143–65.

7. John Milton, "Areopagitica," in *The Complete Prose Works of John Milton*, ed. Ernest Sirluck, 7 vols. (New Haven: Yale University Press, 1959), 2:562.

8. See the long list of "new news" that Democritus Junior "hears every day" in Robert Burton, *The Anatomy of Melancholy*, ed. Thomas C. Faulkner, Nicolas K. Kiessling, and Rhonda L. Blair (Oxford: Clarendon, 1989), 4–5.

9. For a trenchant argument on the importance of attending to plays at their moment of publication, as well as their moment of performance, see Zachary Lesser, *Renaissance Drama and the Politics of Publication: Readings in the English Book Trade* (Cambridge: Cambridge University Press, 2004).

10. *News from the New World Discovered in the Moon*, in Jonson's *Works* (London: Printed [by John Beale, John Dawson 2, Bernard Alsop, Thomas Harper, and Thomas Fawcet] for Richard Meighen [Thomas Walkley and Robert Allot,] 1641), 40; *Ben Jonson: The Complete Masques*, ed. Stephen Orgel (New Haven: Yale University Press, 1969), ll. 41–43.

11. *Oxford English Dictionary*, 2nd ed., s.v. "staple." See also Karen Newman, "Engendering the News," *Elizabethan Theatre*, vol. 14, ed. A. L. Magnusson and C. E. McGee (Toronto: P. D. Meany, 1996), 52.

12. Alastair Bellany, *The Politics of Court Scandal in Early Modern England: News Culture and the Overbury Affair, 1603–1660* (Cambridge: Cambridge University Press, 2002), 80–81.

13. Ben Jonson, *The New Inne* (London: Thomas Harper for Thomas Alchorne, 1631).

14. Ben Jonson, "Ode to himselfe," ibid., H1v–H2v.

15. Adam Fox, *Oral and Literate Culture in England, 1500–1700* (Oxford: Clarendon, 2000), 339.

16. Richard Brathwait, *Whimzies: or, a New Cast of Characters* (London: Printed by F[elix] K[ingston,] sold by Ambrose Rithirdon, 1631), B6r.

17. Bourne's shop was located at the south entrance of the Royal Exchange and Butter's at St. Austin's gate in Paul's Churchyard; see A. W. Pollard and G. R. Redgrave, eds., *Short-Title Catalogue of Books Printed in England, Scotland, and Ireland and of English Books Printed Abroad, 1475–1640*, 2nd ed., rev. W. A. Jackson, F. S. Ferguson, and Katharine F. Pantzer, 3 vols. (London: Bibliographical Society, 1976–91), 3:27, 33 (hereafter *STC*). For other puns on the names of Butter and Bourne, see Joad Raymond, *Pamphlets and Pamphleteering in Early Modern Britain* (Cambridge: Cambridge Uni-

versity Press, 2003), 134. For short biographies of these booksellers, see Leona Rostenberg, "Nathaniel Butter and Nicholas Bourne, First 'Masters of the Staple,'" *The Library*, 3rd ser., 12 (1957): 23–33.

18. For evidence of actual women readers of seventeenth-century news, see Joad Raymond, *The Invention of the Newspaper: English Newsbooks, 1641–1649* (Oxford: Clarendon, 1996), 241–42, 250–51; Atherton, "'The Itch grown a Disease,'" 49–50; Marcus Nevitt, "Women in the Business of Revolutionary News: Elizabeth Alkin, 'Parliament Joan,' and the Commonwealth Newsbook," in Raymond, *News, Newspapers*, 84–108.

19. I have reversed the use of italics and roman fonts in the Induction and the Intermeans.

20. Jonson's aversion to female gossips can be seen as part of his general antipathy to women's voices; see Pamela Allen Brown, *Better a Shrew Than a Sheep: Women, Drama, and the Culture of Jest in Early Modern England* (Ithaca: Cornell University Press, 2003), chap. 2. But see also D. F. McKenzie, who rightly points to the impressive critical abilities of Gossip Mirth ("'The Staple of News' and the Late Plays," *Making Meaning: "Printers of the Mind" and Other Essays*, ed. Peter D. McDonald and Michael F. Suarez [Amherst: University of Massachusetts Press, 2002], 175–76).

21. Paul Yachnin, "The House of Fame," in Anthony B. Dawson and Paul Yachnin, *The Culture of Playgoing in Shakespeare's England: A Collaborative Debate* (Cambridge: Cambridge University Press, 2001), 182–207; Don E. Wayne, "'Pox on Your Distinction!': Humanist Reformation and Deformations of the Everyday in *The Staple of News*," in *Renaissance Culture and the Everyday*, ed. Patricia Fumerton and Simon Hunt (Philadelphia: University of Pennsylvania Press, 1999), 67–91; Sherman, "Eyes and Ears, News and Plays"; McKenzie, "'The Staple of News' and the Late Plays."

22. Yachnin, "The House of Fame," 193, 196, 192. On the social fears occasioned by the widespread availability of news in the 1620s and 1630s, see also Atherton, "'The Itch grown a Disease,'" 49–51; Joad Raymond, "Irrational, Impractical and Unprofitable: Reading the News in Seventeenth-Century Britain," in *Reading, Society and Politics in Early Modern England*, ed. Kevin Sharpe and Steven N. Zwicker (Cambridge: Cambridge University Press, 2003), 189; F. J. Levy, "The Decorum of News," in *News, Newspapers*, 12–38; David Zaret, *Origins of Democratic Culture: Printing, Petitions, and the Public Sphere in Early Modern England* (Princeton: Princeton University Press, 2000).

23. McKenzie, "'The Staple of News' and the Late Plays," 192, 193.

24. Yachnin, "The House of Fame," 193.

25. Michael Colin Frearson, "The English Corantos of the 1620s" (Ph.D. diss., Cambridge University, 1993), chap. 3; Anthony Milton, *Catholic and Reformed: The Roman and Protestant Churches in English Political Thought, 1600–1640* (Cambridge: Cambridge University Press, 1995), 503–15; Robert Bireley, "The Thirty Years' War as Germany's Religious War," in *Krieg und Politik 1618–1648: Europäische Probleme und Perspektiven*, ed. Konrad Repgen and Elisabeth Müller-Luckner (Munich: Oldenbourg, 1988), 85–86. On the political realities of the war, see Brennan C. Pursell, *The Winter King: Frederick V of the Palatinate and the Coming of the Thirty Years' War* (Aldershot: Ashgate, 2003); Geoffrey Parker, ed., *The Thirty Years' War*, 2nd ed. (New York: Routledge, 1997); C. V. Wedgwood, *The Thirty Years War* (London: Jonathan Cape, 1938).

26. Jean 't Serclaes, count of Tilly, was commander of the Catholic League army from 1610 to 1632; Parr, *Staple of News*, 158; Parker, *The Thirty Years' War*.

27. Ambrogio Spinola was an Italian general who served Spain from 1605 to 1630, most of that time as the commander of the Army of Flanders; Parr, *Staple of News*, 91; J. H. Elliott, *The Count-Duke of Olivares: Statesman in an Age of Decline* (New Haven: Yale University Press, 1986); Parker, *The Thirty Years' War*.

28. As Parr notes, "the Fifth Monarchy" refers to Daniel's prophecy (2:44) of Christ's kingdom on earth (*Staple of News*, 158). All corantos are cited by their number in Dahl's bibliography, their *STC* number, and their date. The coranto from March 6, 1624 (Dahl 140; *STC* 18507.143) warned readers of an impending alliance of "the Pope, the Emperour, and the King of *Spaine*," who plan "to runne (as it were) one course for their owne glories, and increase of dominion" (quoted in Parr, *Staple of News*, 157).

29. Vitelleschi was superior general of the Society of Jesus from 1615 to 1645; Parr, *Staple of News*, 160; Robert Bireley, *Religion and Politics in the Age of Counterreformation: Emperor Ferdinand II, William Lamoraimi, S.J., and the Formation of Imperial Policy* (Chapel Hill: University of North Carolina Press, 1981).

30. News of Galileo's telescope was widely reported in publications across Europe; see Stephens, *A History of News*, 173–74, 175; Adrian Johns, *The Nature of the Book: Print and Knowledge in the Making* (Chicago: University of Chicago Press, 1998), 20–26.

31. Atherton, "'The Itch grown a Disease,'" 45; see also Raymond, "Irrational, Impractical and Unprofitable," 202–3.

32. See Sara Pearl, "Sounding to Present Occasions: Jonson's Masques of 1620–5," in *The Court Masque*, ed. David Lindley (Manchester: Manchester University Press, 1984), 73–74.

33. In 1621 Drebbel invented an underwater vessel that sailed from Westminster to Greenwich (Parr, *Staple of News*, 161).

34. In late 1625 ten thousand men were stationed at Harwich on the Essex coast out of concern over an invasion by Spinola (Parr, *Staple of News*, 163). On fears of Habsburg power and invasions of England, see Jonathan Scott, *England's Troubles: Seventeenth-Century English Political Instability in European Context* (Cambridge: Cambridge University Press, 2000), 27–30, 57; Barbara Donagan, "Halcyon Days and the Literature of War: England's Military Education before 1642," *Past & Present* 147 (1995): 74–78; Milton, *Catholic and Reformed*, 42–46; Conrad Russell, *Parliaments and English Politics, 1621–1629* (Oxford: Clarendon, 1979), 8, 73, 326; Martin Breslow, *A Mirror of England: English Puritan Views of Foreign Nations, 1618–1640* (Cambridge: Harvard University Press, 1970), chap. 3.

35. William Gifford, ed., *The Works of Ben Jonson*, quoted in Herford and Simpson, *Ben Jonson*, 6:151; Devra Kifer, ed., introduction to *The Staple of News*, Regents Renaissance Drama, gen. ed. Cyrus Hoy (Lincoln: University of Nebraska Press, 1975), xxiii.

36. Parr, introduction to *The Staple of News*, 6; Anne Barton, *Ben Jonson, Dramatist* (Cambridge: Cambridge University Press, 1984), 254.

37. See also Raymond, who has argued for the distinctive nature of these marginal notes and connected them to the later development of news headlines (*Pamphlets and Pamphleteering*, 142–44).

38. Dahl 226 (April 18, 1631; *STC* 18507.211); Dahl 121 (July 22, 1623; *STC* 18507.120); Dahl 224 (March 14, 1631; *STC* 18507.209).

39. Dahl 223 (February 18, 1631; *STC* 18507.208), B2v; Dahl 231 (June 25, 1631; *STC* 18507.218), A3r. On the derivation of these rubrics from sixteenth-century Venetian manuscript gazettes, see Stephens, *A History of News*, 151–55.

40. *STC* 18507.217 (June 10, 1631; not in Dahl).

41. Folke Dahl, "Amsterdam—Cradle of English Newspapers," *The Library*, 5th ser., 4 (1950): 173. Dahl notes, however, that English corantos were "no apish imitations of the Dutch." Rather, Butter and Bourne's editors typically mixed and matched reports from several Dutch pamphlets and from pamphlets published elsewhere in Europe.

42. A[braham] H[olland], "A Continved Inqvisition against *Paper-Persecutors*," in *A Scovrge for Paper-Persecutors* (London: Printed for H[enry] H[olland] and G[eorge] G[ibbs], 1625), A4r.

43. Dahl 184 (August 24, 1626; *STC* 18507.181); for a partial transcription of this marginalia, see Dahl, *Bibliography*, 149.

44. Donald Lupton, *London and the Covntrey Carbonadoed and Quartred into seuerall Characters* (London: Nicholas Okes, 1632), 143.

45. *Diary of Francis Rous*, ed. Mary Anne Everett Green, Camden Society, o.s. 66 (1856), 44. For an amusing description of Bethlen Gabor, prince of Transylvania, see Wedgwood, *The Thirty Years War*, 94–95.

46. Pory to Robert Greville, Lord Brooke, October 25, 1632, in William S. Powell, *John Pory 1572–1636: The Life and Letters of a Man of Many Parts* (Chapel Hill: University of North Carolina Press, 1977), microfiche supplement, 312.

47. Schröder, "The Origins of the German Press," 141–42. See also Daniel Woolf, "News, History and the Construction of the Present," in Dooley and Baron, *The Politics of Information*, 102–3; Atherton, "'The Itch grown a Disease,'" 46–48.

48. Lupton, *London and the Covntrey Carbonadoed*, 140, 142.

49. James Shirley, *The Schoole of Complement* (London: Printed by E[dward] A[llde] for Francis Constable, 1631), B2v–B3r; see also John Fletcher, *The Faire Maid of the Inne*, in *Comedies and Tragedies Written by Francis Beavmont and John Fletcher Gentlemen* (London: for Humphrey Robinson and Humphrey Moseley, 1647), 7F4v.

50. But see also F. J. Levy, who states that there is not "any reason to doubt the accuracy of the reporting" in corantos: "I do not wish to argue that everything reported in a coranto was necessarily true, merely that the level of accuracy was no lower than might be found in any group of letters reporting news from abroad" ("Staging the News," in *Print, Manuscript, and Performance: The Changing Relations of the Media in Early Modern England*, ed. Arthur F. Marotti and Michael D. Bristol [Columbus: Ohio State University Press, 2000], 267).

51. Rous's news of this sermon was not entirely accurate: the sermon had been preached by Thomas Lushington in 1624, not 1629, and it had been preached in Oxford, not "at Whitehall before the King"; it was unprinted, though, and would remain so until 1659. F. J. Levy, "How Information Spread among the Gentry, 1550–1640," *Journal of British Studies* 21 (1982): 24; Raymond, *Pamphlets and Pamphleteering*, 146–48.

52. Thomas Lushington [Robert Jones D.D., pseud.], "The Repetition Sermon," in *The Resurrection Rescued from the Souldiers Calumnies* (London: Printed for Richard Lownds, 1659), B1v–B2r.

53. Dahl 144 (April 20, 1624; *STC* 18507.147), B1v.

54. Both "evangelical" and "gospel" are etymologically derived from "good tidings" and "good news." As Lushington preached, "The *Christian* news, the talke of the *faithful* is spent in *Euangelio*, in hearing and telling some good news of their *Saviour*." *Oxford English Dictionary*, s.v. "evangely," "gospel"; Lushington, "The Repetition Sermon," B2r–v.

55. 1 Timothy 3:15; *The Holy Bible* (London: Robert Barker, 1611; *STC* 2216), U3r.

56. Quoted in Samuel R. Gardiner, *History of England from the Accession of James I to the Outbreak of the Civil War, 1603–1642*, 10 vols. (1883–84; reprint, New York: AMS, 1965), 7:37.

57. Anthony White, *Truth and Error Discovered in Two Sermons in St Maries in Oxford* (Oxford: Printed by Iohn Lichfield for Henry Curteyne, 1628), 23, 59.

58. Samuel Kenrick, *The Tell-Troth's Reqvitall, Or, Truth's Recompence* (London: Printed by Miles Flesher for Robert Mylbourne, 1627), 22.

59. Lushington, "The Repetition Sermon," B1v.

60. Ibid., B2r.

61. H[olland], "A Continved Inqvisition," A3v–A4r.

62. See, for example, Dahl 166 (March 29, 1625; *STC* 18507.164).

63. Julie Sanders, *Ben Jonson's Theatrical Republics* (New York: St. Martin's, 1998), 142; Yachnin, "The House of Fame," 191.

64. The terms "Puritan" and "Arminian" have been the subjects of rigorous scholarly debate, which has shown that both were terms of abuse deployed as polemical insults and not as precise classifications of contrasting religious identities. My point in using them is not to imply that there was any sort of doctrinal or political uniformity among the members of each group, nor to suggest that any specific individual can or could always be identified as a member of one or the other. Rather I am interested in the use of these terms as broad polemical categories to describe different ecclesiastical factions, factions that Peter Lake has argued were associated with "two rival conspiracy theories": "By the end of the 1620s, there were two structurally similar but mutually exclusive conspiracy theories, both of which purported to explain the political difficulties of the period. The one was centered on a populist Puritan plot to undermine monarchy, the other on the popish plot to overthrow English religion and law." Peter Lake, "Anti-popery: The Structure of a Prejudice," in *Conflict in Early Stuart England: Studies in Religion and Politics, 1603–1642*, ed. Richard Cust and Ann Hughes (London: Longman, 1989), 72–106, quotation at 91. On "Arminian" as a term of abuse, see Richard Montagu, *Appello Caesarem* (London: Printed [by Humphrey Lownes] for Matthew Lownes, 1625), esp. 10–13; Margo Todd, "'All One with Tom Thumb': Arminianism, Popery and the Story of the Reformation in Early Stuart Cambridge," *Church History* 64 (1995): 563–79, esp. 578; Scott, *England's Troubles*, 125–26; Nicholas Tyacke, *Anti-Calvinists: The Rise of English Arminianism c. 1590–1640* (Oxford: Clarendon, 1987), 127; Milton, *Catholic and Reformed*, 77–85, 406–7, 447. Much more has been written on the term "Puritan," but see especially Patrick Collinson, "A Comment: Concerning the Name Puritan," *Journal of Ecclesiastical History* 31 (1980): 483–88; Peter Lake, "Puritan Identities," *Journal of Ecclesiastical History* 35 (1984): 112–23; Kristin Poole, *Radical Religion from Shakespeare to Milton: Figures of Nonconformity in Early Modern England* (Cambridge: Cambridge University Press, 2000).

65. This prediction was detailed in an unpublished treatise by the German mystic Simon Studion; see Parr, *Staple of News*, 166–67; Frances Yates, *The Rosicrucian Enlightenment*, 2nd ed. (1972; reprint, London: Routledge, 2001), 46–48.

66. News of the massacre did not reach England until May 1624. For contemporary reactions, see the ballad *Newes out of East India: of the cruell usage of our English merchants at Amboyna* (London: Printed for F[rancis] Coules, 1630); *The Diary of Walter Yonge, Esq.*, ed. George Roberts, Camden Society, o.s. 41 (1848), 75; *The Letters of John Chamberlain*, ed. Norman Egbert McClure, 2 vols. (Philadelphia: American Philosophical Society, 1939), 2:562–63, 569–70, 601–2.

67. *Calendar of State Papers Venetian, 1629–32* (hereafter *CSPV*), 248, 256, 344, 395, 553, 578; Breslow, *A Mirror of England*, 85–90; Kevin Sharpe, *The Personal Rule of Charles I* (New Haven: Yale University Press, 1992), 77–78, 514; Steven C. A. Pincus, "From Butterboxes to Wooden Shoes: The Shift in English Popular Sentiment from Anti-Dutch to Anti-French in the 1670s," *Historical Journal* 38 (1995): 333–61.

68. Pory to Thomas Puckering, April 21, 1631, in Powell, *John Pory*, microfiche supplement, 156.

69. Parker, *Thirty Years' War*, 69; Jonathan I. Israel, *Dutch Republic and the Hispanic World, 1606–1661* (Oxford: Clarendon, 1982), 114–17; Simon Adams, "Spain or the Netherlands? The Dilemmas of Early Stuart Foreign Policy," in *Before the English Civil War*, ed. Howard Tomlinson (London: Macmillan, 1983), 79–101; Russell, *Parliaments and English Politics*, 260–66; Roger Lockyer, *Buckingham: The Life and Political Career of George Villiers, First Duke of Buckingham, 1592–1628* (New York: Longman, 1981), 277–85, 299, 316–17.

70. L. J. Reeve, *Charles I and the Road to Personal Rule* (Cambridge: Cambridge University Press, 1989), 256; Sharpe, *Personal Rule*, 65–104; Caroline M. Hibbard, *Charles I and the Popish Plot* (Chapel Hill: University of North Carolina Press, 1981), 19–37. In 1631, Charles I was even weighing the possibility of joining Spain in a military operation against the Dutch; see L. J. Reeve, "Quiroga's Paper of 1631: A Missing Link in Anglo-Spanish Diplomacy during the Thirty Years War," *English Historical Review* 101 (1986): 913–26; Reeve, *Charles I*, 268–74; Gardiner, *History of England*, 7:176–78.

71. J. S. Kepler, "Fiscal Aspects of the English Carrying Trade during the Thirty Years War," *Economic History Review*, 2nd ser., 25 (1972): 261–83, esp. 264–65; Harland Taylor, "Trade, Neutrality, and the 'English Road,' 1630–1648," *Economic History Review*, 2nd. ser., 25 (1972): 236–60, esp. 239–40, 252–60; Reeve, *Charles I*, 207, 256; Sharpe, *Personal Rule*, 91–92, 525.

72. Giovanni Soranzo to the Doge and Senate, April 11, 1631, in *CSPV, 1629–32*, 493.

73. This policy was designed, in part, to prevent conversions to, and encourage conversions from, Catholicism; see Milton, *Catholic and Reformed*, 48–50, 64–65, 77–85. On the resulting suppression of Puritan opinions in print, see Anthony Milton, "Licensing, Censorship, and Religious Orthodoxy in Early Stuart England," *Historical Journal* 41 (1998): 625–51; Cyndia Susan Clegg, *Press Censorship in Jacobean England* (Cambridge: Cambridge University Press, 2002), 197–223; Tyacke, *Anti-Calvinists*, 182–84. On the rise of English Arminians more generally, see Tyacke, *Anti-Calvinists*; Sheila Lambert, "Richard Montagu, Arminianism and Censorship," *Past and Present* 124 (1989): 36–68.

74. Peter Lake, "The Significance of the Elizabethan Identification of the Pope as Antichrist," *Journal of Ecclesiastical History* 31 (1980): 176.

75. Richard Montagu, *A Gagg for the New Gospell? No: A New Gagg for an Old Goose* (London: Printed by Thomas Snodham for Matthew Lownes and William Barret, 1624), 74–75; Milton, *Catholic and Reformed*, 93–127, 139; Bernard Capp, "The Political Dimension of Apocalyptic Thought," in *The Apocalypse in English Renaissance Thought and Literature: Patterns, Antecedents, and Repercussions* (Ithaca: Cornell University Press, 1984), 101–9; Christopher Hill, *Antichrist in Seventeenth-Century England* (New York: Oxford University Press, 1971), 1–40, 181–82.

76. On Puritan emigration to America, see David Cressy, *Coming Over: Migration and Communication between England and New England in the Seventeenth Century* (Cambridge: Cambridge University Press, 1987), 74–106, esp. 86; Tom Webster, *Godly Clergy in Early Stuart England: The Caroline Puritan Movement, c.1620–1643* (Cambridge: Cambridge University Press, 1997), 271–85; Sharpe, *Personal Rule*, 751–57.

77. Lickfinger's insatiable hunger for news and food, moreover, distinguishes him as a particular type of Puritan, one commonly associated with outsized, grotesque appetites; see Poole, *Radical Religion from Shakespeare to Milton*.

78. On de Dominis in England, see W. B. Patterson, *King James VI and I and the Reunion of Christendom* (Cambridge: Cambridge University Press, 1997), chap. 7.

79. "Excoriation," from the Latin *excoriāre*, "to strip off the hide"; *Oxford English Dictionary*, s.v. "excoriate." On Gondomar in 1620s London, see Thomas Cogswell,

*The Blessed Revolution: English Politics and the Coming of War, 1621–1624* (Cambridge: Cambridge University Press, 1989), esp. 15–19, 302–6.

80. Parr, *Staple of News*, 172; Yachnin, "The House of Fame," 192; Hoenselaars, "Rumour, News and Commerce," 151. The piece of evidence most frequently cited as proof of Jonson's contempt for *A Game at Chess* comes from "Conversations with Drummond," in which Jonson refers to Middleton as "a base fellow": "Markham was not of the number of the Faithfull .j. Poets and but a base fellow that such were Day and Midleton" (10.168; quoted in Herford and Simpson, *Ben Jonson*, 1:137). But see Julie Sanders, who correctly notes that "the tone of the [*Game at Chess*] episode is sympathetic towards the 'poor' suppressed play and rather more anti-Gondomar in its focus" (*Ben Jonson's Theatrical Republics*, 141–42).

81. Sherman, "Eyes and Ears," 35.

82. Newman, "Engendering the News," 59; Yachnin, "The House of Fame," 193–97; Sherman, "Eyes and Ears," 37–38; L. C. Knights, *Drama and Society in the Age of Jonson* (London: Chatton & Windus, 1937), 219–20.

83. *Aristippus* was always printed with the playlet *The Conceited Pedlar*, and in addition to the four editions of 1630 and 1631, two further editions of this playbook came out in 1635. No other playbook published before 1660 went through as many editions in the first two years, nor as many in the first six years, after its first printing as Randolph's did. For an illuminating discussion of Arminianism and *Aristippus*, see Nicholas Tyacke, "Arminianism and English Culture," in *Aspects of English Protestantism, c. 1530–1700* (Manchester: Manchester University Press, 2001), 236–37.

84. On the religious politics of *The Renegado*, see Benedict S. Robinson, "The 'Turks,' Caroline Politics, and Philip Massinger's *The Renegado*," in *Localizing Caroline Drama*, ed. Alan B. Farmer and Adam Zucker (Palgrave, forthcoming).

85. See Martin Butler, *Theatre and Crisis, 1632–1642* (Cambridge: Cambridge University Press, 1984), 198–201.

SEVEN

# Genres, Early Modern Theatrical Title Pages, and the Authority of Print

PETER BEREK

When Heminge and Condell prepared the 1623 Shakespeare folio, they did not follow the example of Ben Jonson's 1616 collection and call their volume Shakespeare's "works" or deck the volume with a sculptural title page.[1] Instead, apparently as an alternative assurance of the weightiness of their enterprise, they announced "Mr. William Shakespeare his Comedies, Histories, and Tragedies." Mockers of Jonson said that what others called "plays" he called "works." The Shakespeare folio uses generic terms as though to efface the troubling pun. Genre seems especially powerful in the 1623 folio; the classificatory terms provide the principle of organization for the volume, even though the headings of individual plays are sometimes at odds with their placement in the printed book. How powerful the words "comedy" and "tragedy" are we see again in the 1647 Beaumont and Fletcher folio, where the phrase "Comedies and Tragedies" is given the largest type and the highest place on the title page of the volume.[2]

We take for granted the inevitability of "comedy," "tragedy," and "history" both as ways of classifying early modern plays and as descriptive terms on title pages. We do so despite our knowledge that such terms are used in ways that seem inconsistent. (Famously, and not atypically, the title page of *Cambyses* [1570] describes the play as "A lamentable tragedy mixed ful of pleasant mirth," while the running title calls the play a comedy.)[3] We do so despite the notorious lack of fit between early modern writings about genre—whether Sidney or Puttenham or Italian critics or Ben Jonson—and the actualities of plays distinguished by generic terms. And we do so despite such inconvenient facts as the description "Comedies and Tragedies" heading a Beaumont and Fletcher folio whose organization has nothing to do with genre, few of whose plays fall tidily into either category—and, indeed, many of whose plays are by neither Beaumont nor Fletcher.

Such inconsistencies, I believe, suggest that part of the work done by generic terms on title pages has relatively little to do with the shape of a plot or with literary meaning. Terms such as "comedy" and "tragedy" help printers and booksellers find a market for their wares.[4] Tracing changes in the ways such terms appear on title pages can enrich our understanding of how the market for books develops, and of how what began as scripts for the popular art of playing on stages gradually takes on the status of what we would today call "literature." One theme of this chapter is the way title pages use generic terms to make plays appear to be of lasting importance. But the movement of plays into print has consequences as well for ideas about theatricality and the use of theater as a metaphor. At the end I offer some examples of how "tragedy," used in the mid-sixteenth century to associate a Protestant martyrdom with the *de casibus* tradition, becomes by the mid-seventeenth century a means of lending theatrical glory to royalist heroes. Generic terms, once a way of helping create a market for printed plays, turn into a metaphorical resource for texts of other kinds.

Generic categories belong more to the "aftermarket" of plays in print than to their initial appearance on stage. To be sure, generic terms appear very early in licensing documents for the professional theater. In 1574 the Earl of Leicester's Men are licensed to perform "Commedies, Tragedies, Enterludes, stage playes."[5] In the same year the Common Council of the City of London, in banning stage plays, says that there shall be "no playe, Comodye, Tragidye, enterlude, nor publycke shewe."[6] But documents such as these seem to be engaging in the lawyerly activity of making sure they use sufficient words to permit or prohibit the activity they have in mind. We can tell from the documents that people who talked about stage plays sometimes referred to the plays by these terms, but not much about how the terms differed from one another. This terminology remains quite consistent; when the Lord Chamberlain's Men receive their patent as the King's Men in 1603, they are authorized "freely to use and exercise the Arte and faculty of playinge Comedies, Tragedies, histories, Enterludes, moralls, pastoralls, Stage-plaies and Suche others like as theie have alreadie studied or hereafter shall use or studie."[7] Although it is tempting to see the addition of "histories" to the list as a response to the particular repertory of Shakespeare's company, exactly the same list, except for some changes in spelling, appears when the former Admiral's Men are re-licensed as the Prince's Men in 1606.[8] Similar phrases appear when in 1637 the Lord Chamberlain prohibits printers from printing plays without the permission of the acting companies that own them.[9]

Philip Henslowe's diary, however, suggests that generic categories were not very important in his practical theatrical life. When he inventories the playbooks owned by the Admiral's Men, none of the titles has a generic designation. Only a very small number of the plays whose performances or acquisition he lists are referred to by terms such as "comedy" or "tragedy." Even though Henslowe's companies performed plays about such figures as Henry V, "Richard Crookback," Cardinal Wolsey, and Henry VIII, the term "history" appears only once, for "The French History" in 1602. The few appearances of "comedy" are in titles such as "Comedy of Jeronimo" (1591; the play also appears without the generic designation), "The Venetian Comedy" (1594), and "Comedy of Humours" (1597). The term "tragedy" first appears in 1595 in the title "The World's Tragedy" (a play also apparently called "The New World's Tragedy"); "the tragedie of ffocasse" (Phocas) has two performances in May 1596. Given the relatively small proportion of Elizabethan plays that can be called "domestic tragedies," their prominence among Henslowe's plays with generic designation is notable. And Henslowe is more likely to designate a play by genre in an entry describing a transaction with authors than in an entry for a performance.[10] I am not arguing that actors and their audiences never thought about genre; sometimes generic terms appear in prologues, perhaps most notably in *A Warning for Fair Women*, a domestic tragedy played by the Chamberlain's Men printed in 1599, where Comedy, History, and Tragedy debate over who has the right to control the play about to be presented.[11] But it nonetheless appears to be the case that generic terms are strongly associated with the culture of print, not performance.[12]

To determine how generic categories were used in marketing printed plays, title pages are our best evidence. In this chapter I approach title pages in two ways. First, I concentrate exclusively on plays. Using data from W. W. Greg's *Bibliography of the English Printed Drama,* I look for changes over time in the kind of information that appears on the title pages of editions of individual plays performed by professional actors, whether boys or men.[13] In doing so I show that before 1600, it was common for plays to have some form of generic designation on the title page, but usually in complex language that evades summary under the tidy categories of the Shakespeare folio. In the first decade of the seventeenth century, the proportion of plays designated by generic terms drops. But by the 1620s, the proportions rise substantially, and the range of generic terms used becomes much simpler. In a subsequent section of the chapter, I raise a different question: Can we perceive changes in the way terms such as "comedy," "tragedy," and "history" are used on title pages in books of all kinds, not just books of plays? Here I use the on-line *English Short Title Catalogue* as my source of data. From this analysis, we can see how generic terms such as "tragedy," often used in the sixteenth century with little sense of theatrical provenance, by the middle of the seventeenth century show the impact of the Elizabethan and Jacobean theater. Both segments of my analysis support the emerging critical consensus that the growing importance of print helps shape a culture's understanding of the nature of plays and the nature of authorship.[14]

Title pages functioned as a form of what we would call advertising: they tried to persuade potential customers to buy a book. By examining title pages and seeing how they change over time, we can draw some inferences about what printers thought would make plays attractive to potential purchasers. Printers' names needed to appear to assert legal rights; booksellers' names and locations told where the volume could be purchased. Other, more discretionary information presumably served for marketing. How does the use of generic categories compare to the use of other promotable features of plays, such as the name of the theater where they had been performed, the name of the acting company, or the name of the playwright? Understandably, playwrights' names have received much attention. James P. Saeger and Christopher Fassler, using a database including only plays for the professional theater, show that as the seventeenth century proceeds, plays are less likely to be identified by acting company alone and increasingly likely to be identified by the name of an author, sometimes along with that of a company.[15] Alan B. Farmer and Zachary Lesser refine the work of Saeger and Fassler by analyzing changes over time in the listing of author's name, authorial titles implying social status, acting company, and theatrical venue. (Hypothesizing a correlation with social status, they also address whether or not Latin appears on the title page, though they find those results uninformative.) Unlike Saeger and Fassler, Farmer and Lesser analyze all plays, not just plays performed by professional actors. They show that the percentage of plays for professional actors that indicate an acting company stayed relatively constant (at about 60 percent) from the opening of the Theater in 1576 through the 1640s. The percentage of plays specifying a theater grew steadily from zero before 1596 to about 60 percent in the 1640s; the percentage listing author rose at a similar rate from below 40 percent in the 1570s and 1580s to over 80 percent at the end of the period.[16] Jeffrey Masten uses the increasing frequency of authorial attribution on title pages to argue for a change in "the discourses of authority," and asserts that the theatrical provenance of plays becomes less important and the printed book more important.[17] For Masten, Jonson's 1616 *Workes* and the 1623 Shakespeare folio both evidence and help shape the changes he chronicles. Finally, in *From Playhouse to Printing House,* Douglas Brooks offers a series of case studies of the ways in which printing practices help construct the idea of authorship.[18] Brooks rightly treats the Jonson, Shakespeare, and Beaumont and Fletcher collections as landmarks in the process.

All these writers share an interest in the material evidence for cultural phenomena. But the phenomenon that interests them more than any other is the construction of the idea of authorship in the context of the construction of the bourgeois subject. Their work is exciting and by and large persuasive. But the classifying of plays by kind also warrants attention. This classification emerges in parallel with the construction of authorship as playtexts gradually assume the status of "works." Issues of generic classification may be different, however, for plays performed by professional actors than they are for closet drama or for masques, entertainments, or other non-professional performances. Unlike closet drama, professional plays do not start out with an expectation of being read.[19] And no one would expect masques and entertainments to be designated by terms such as "tragedy" or "comedy." Thus, I have used Saeger and Fassler's convenient classification to identify the professional plays on Greg's list. I also eliminate from my counts plays that appear in collections. These volumes, I believe, make different assumptions about printed plays and their audiences than do single-play editions. Single plays, usually printed in quarto, are much less expensive than folio editions, and much less likely to be provided with the bookish appurtenances of dedications and prefatory poems. At least in the early years of the seventeenth century, single-play volumes arguably are more closely allied with theatrical performance than with the reading public.[20] Moreover, collections usually are very different from quartos with respect to title pages, and thus should not be included in a census of title-page information. If we eliminate collections from the list of professional plays, we are left with 401 titles. Beginning in the 1580s, the first decade in which professional plays reach print, table 1 shows by decade both the number and percentage of plays with generic designations.

TABLE 1. All professional plays, excluding collections

| Decade | # plays printed | # title pages indicating genre | % title pages indicating genre |
|---|---|---|---|
| 1581–1590 | 9 | 8 | 89% |
| 1591–1600 | 64 | 46 | 72 |
| 1601–1610 | 81 | 39 | 48 |
| 1611–1620 | 35 | 22 | 63 |
| 1621–1630 | 22 | 18 | 82 |
| 1631–1640 | 117 | 88 | 75 |
| 1641–1650 | 15 | 13 | 87 |
| 1651–1660 | 57 | 54 | 95 |
| Total | 401 | 288 | 72 |

*Note:* Chi square value (degrees of freedom = 7, $N$ = 401) is 44.7; $p < .0001$. This indicates a statistically significant change over time in the rate of use of generic terms.

Do these numbers tell a story? They suggest that in the 1580s and 1590s, designation by genre is common (89 percent and 72 percent). Then there is a sharp decline to 48 percent between 1601 and 1610, followed by an increased frequency of such designations beginning between 1611 and 1620 (63 percent). Generic designations are significantly less frequent in the first two decades of the seventeenth century than they were earlier, and become much more common as we get closer to 1660 and the Restoration.

Periodizing plays by decades may appear natural. But I think it is worth considering another way of categorizing information about title pages. It seems plausible that the Jonson and Shakespeare folios modified the ways in which printers, readers, and perhaps even authors regarded playtexts. The year *Tamburlaine* was printed, 1590, seems an appropriate starting date for analyzing printed plays for the public theater. The dates of the Jonson (1616), Shakespeare (1623), and Beaumont and Fletcher (1647) collections mark other boundaries. If we let the dates of these major events in publication define our periods, we see an even clearer trend toward generic designations.

Table 2. Professional plays, excluding collections, periodized by notable publications

| Time interval | # plays printed | # title pages indicating genre | % title pages indicating genres |
|---|---|---|---|
| 1590–1616 | 176 | 105 | 60% |
| 1617–1623 | 16 | 13 | 81% |
| 1624–1647 | 143 | 108 | 76% |
| 1648–1662 | 69 | 64 | 93% |
| Total | 414 | 299 | 72% |

*Note:* Chi square value = 31.1 (degrees of freedom = 4, $N = 414$); $p < .0001$. This indicates a statistically significant change over time in the rate of use of generic terms.

Table 2 seems most interesting as a "before and after" story. If we regard 1617–1623 as a time of transition, and simply think of the "before Jonson collection" period and the "after Jonson and Shakespeare folio" periods, we see a fairly striking change, which accelerates in the years after 1648.[21] Between 1590 and 1616, 60 percent of 176 plays were designated by genre.[22] From 1624 to 1647, 76 percent of 143 plays were so designated, and from 1648 to 1662 (a clear break point in Greg's list), 93 percent of 69 plays. Whether the Jonson, Shakespeare, and Beaumont and Fletcher collections are a cause of change or themselves responses to the same causes operating on single-play editions, we cannot tell from numbers. But the appearance of printed plays in collections seems associated with an increasing likelihood that when plays are printed singly, they will be designated by genre.

Let us think about the qualities that collections may have conferred upon plays. It is not news that Ben Jonson's 1616 *Workes* was an important event in the history of both printing and authorship. Douglas Brooks quite remarkably links Jonson's volume to the 1616 publication of the *Works* of King James: authorship and royal authority appear in tandem. Brooks also shows how the printing house practices inferable from the masques in Jonson's volume suggest that Jonson thought his authority over his plays for the professional theater was greater than his authority over masques performed at court by aristocratic amateurs. Without contesting Brooks's conclusions, I want to suggest that Jonson's 1616 folio may have exerted considerable influence on the subsequent appearance of printed plays by other authors and from other venues.

Sequence does not, of course, demonstrate causation; perhaps Jonson's volume, the Shakespeare folio, and subsequent single-play printed editions were all responding to similar forces within their culture. Yet the clarity of the pattern revealed in table 2 is striking. The appearance—in both senses of the word—of Jonson's *Workes* seems worth considering both as an effect of changes in the cultures of theater and print and as a contributory cause of such changes.

As Brooks points out, the *Workes* sends a mixed message. The classical arch ornamenting its title page not only proclaims the importance of the volume and its author but also implies a set of affiliations both ancient and theatrical (see fig. 9-2, page 218). Atop the arch is a representation of a Roman theater. Above that stands a figure labeled "tragicomoedia"; on either side are a satyr labeled "satvr" and a shepherd labeled "pastor." Whether these two figures denote "satire" and "pastoral" may be debated, but there can be no debate about the larger figures in niches on either side of the arch, "tragoedia" and "comoedia." Below "tragedy" is a picture labeled "plaustrvm" showing a figure in a cart, followed by a goat (presumably the figure is Tragedy); on the other side, labeled "visorium," is a circular amphitheater with a chorus dancing around a sacrifice to Bacchus. The images of theaters seem to emphasize that the volume contains pieces that have been performed. And the labeled figures link the performances with generic categories—at the very least, with tragedy, comedy, and the curiously unclassical tragicomedy. Genre seems to be working in two ways at once: it both elevates plays by associating them with classical precedent and links them to a tradition not just of readership but of performance as well.

Unlike the Shakespeare or Beaumont and Fletcher folios, Jonson's *Workes* provides each play with its own title page. Each of these pages specifies a genre, and each specifies an acting company and the year of first performance. A page that repeats information about genre, date, and acting company follows each play; these pages then list the names of the actors and note that the Master of the Revels allowed the performances. It would be hard to say whether the volume in the reader's hands gains more authority from its connection with the name of Ben Jonson, the history of licensed performance by known actors at a specific time, or its generic affiliations with the history of classical theater. Nonetheless, I suggest that the Jonson folio accelerates a modification in the meaning of generic terms on the title pages of plays. Generic terms take on some of the glamour of "works." The Jonson collection helped create the context for the dignity accorded to genre, and conferred by genre, on the title pages of the Shakespeare and Beaumont and Fletcher collections.

The aftermath of the Jonson collection suggests a changing relationship between the reading experience and attending the theater. After Jonson's *Workes* we see more plays printed in collections, with the pace accelerating after 1630. Unlike cheap single-play quartos, these collections are above all "readerly" texts. They invite their purchaser to review a body of work or remember a period in the theatrical past; they do not appear to envision a purchaser who wants to recall or anticipate a contemporary experience in the living theater. Printing thirty-six plays in three editions of the Shakespeare folio (indeed, more when the third folio adds what we now think of as apocrypha), thirty-four in the 1647 Beaumont and Fletcher folio, and multiple scripts in other collections suggests printers believed that there was a reading public for old plays even after their performance ceased as a living tradition.[23] Whether or not Peter Blayney is correct in his claim that plays were printed as a way of advertising stage productions, his argument is unlikely to be pertinent to expensive folio volumes containing large numbers of plays—and especially in the case of volumes published after the theaters were closed.[24]

Curiously, generic designation does not seem linked to other qualities of plays that one might think conferred status or prestige. If having a genre makes a play "literary," one would expect a relationship between having a generic designation and having an author's name on the title page. Yet statistical analysis shows no such relationship. We ordinarily think of plays performed by boys and plays performed indoors as appealing to a more elite—and perhaps more literary—audience than plays performed by men in the outdoor public theaters. Yet from 1616 on, there is no significant difference in the likelihood of indoor or outdoor plays, adult or children's performances, being designated by genre. To be sure, one might argue that by 1616 any distinction between "elite" and "popular" audience has begun to disappear. But even between 1590 and 1616, plays whose title pages describe an adult, outdoor theatrical provenance are more—not less—likely than plays for boys to mention a genre on their title pages.

Tallying the presence or absence of generic terms on title pages tells only part of the story. In the sixteenth century we find a much greater variety of generic terms than "comedy," "tragedy," and "history." Indeed, title pages usually make use of multiple terms, on the *Cambyses* model. Lyly's *Campaspe* (1584), for example, is a "most excellent comedy" on its title page and a "tragical comedy" in its running title. It takes nine different phrases on title pages to categorize the nine (of ten) professional plays printed before 1589 that have generic designations. Qualifying adjectives frequently appear, such as "excellent and pleasant comedy" or "moral and pitiful comedy." Between 1590 and 1616, fifty different phrases categorize the 105 of 176 plays with designations. Often, as before, the descriptors include adjectives such as "lamentable" or "pleasant conceited history." Sometimes we find a phrase such as "Roman tragedy." Between 1617 and 1623, eight phrases categorize 13 of 16 plays; between 1624 and 1647, 28 phrases categorize 108 of 143 plays; between 1648 and 1662, 13 phrases categorize 64 of 69 plays. Some once common terms, such as "interlude" or "moral play," virtually disappear in the seventeenth century. In part, the changes reflect the fading away of the old, "tragicall history," moralizing use of generic categories to validate fictions and the rise of a new way of validating stories by treating them as literature, on the model of ancient texts. By 1623, most plays identified by genre use a single word—"tragedy" or "comedy" or "tragicomedy." As generic designations grow more frequent, the range of words used to designate genres grows narrower.

I now turn to a related but distinct subject. We know that terms such as "comedy," "tragedy," and "history" are commonplace outside theatrical or literary contexts. What is the relationship between the use of those terms in non-theatrical and theatrical texts? What do we find when we look at all printed texts, not just at printed plays? One can search the tens of thousands of titles in the on-line *English Short Title Catalogue* (*ESTC*) for appearances in titles of the words "tragedy," "comedy," and "history."[25] Some analysis of ESTC information is useful for thinking about what generic terms mean in an emerging print culture.

Table 3 shows the frequency with which "tragedy," "comedy," and "history" appear in all titles listed in the on-line *English Short Title Catalogue*. These numbers reflect the results of "title word" searches that examine every word in a title (not just a short title) as well as running titles.[26] Note that I have periodized the data in a way which postulates that it is worth comparing printed books before 1590—when the printing of plays was relatively uncommon and the professional theater in its infancy—with the periods I analyzed in the preceding section. The number of titles printed per year increases dramatically over the years covered in this table, and the time periods are of uneven duration. For both reasons, I focus on the rate per thousand titles printed at which each genre appears. (I also include, in parentheses, the absolute number of titles with the generic designation.)

TABLE 3. Titles with generic terms per thousand *ESTC* titles

| Time interval | "Tragedy" | "Comedy" | "History" | Total *ESTC* titles |
|---|---|---|---|---|
| 1475–1589 | 7.3 (89) | 2.7 (33) | 30.3 (372) | 12,272 |
| 1590–1616 | 15.5 (159) | 6.9 (71) | 42.5 (437) | 10,247 |
| 1617–1623 | 9.6 (37) | 4.9 (19) | 36.3 (140) | 3,860 |
| 1624–1647 | 7.2 (178) | 4.6 (116) | 27.0 (669) | 24,744 |
| 1648–1662 | 7.2 (167) | 4.3 (101) | 36.8 (855) | 23,223 |

*Note:* Titles including more than one generic term are counted in multiple categories.

Between 1475 and 1589 titles with some form of the word "tragedy" appear at a frequency of 7.3 per thousand. (The word might be "tragic," "tragical," or "tragedy.") Between 1590 and 1616 the frequency grows to 15.5 per thousand. After 1617 the frequency drops. Although the rates differ, the same pattern repeats for various forms of the words "comic" or "comedy." For "history" as well, the frequency of appearance peaks between 1590 and 1616 and then falls off. What, if anything, do these changes have to do with the printing of plays?

I suggest that the printing of plays itself contributes both to the development of the market for printed books and to the ways in which generic terms such as "comedy" and "tragedy" appear on the title pages of nontheatrical works. The data we have been examining are consistent with that possibility. It will help our understanding to estimate what proportion of plays constituted the total number of printed books, and how that proportion changed over time. One cannot electronically search the online *ESTC* for plays, and a hand count is impractical. But I have counted plays among the *ESTC* titles that use the words "comedy" or "tragedy"; the results appear in columns 2 and 3 of table 4. (The proportion of plays among titles using the word "history"—1.2 per thousand titles between 1590 and 1616—is small enough to be safely ignored.) While we know that the sum of columns 2 and 3 (which appears in parentheses in column 5) understates the actual number of plays printed, that sum can serve as a reasonable surrogate to enable us to trace changes in the frequency of plays over time. And the changes are suggestive. As we can see in column 5 of table 4, before 1590 plays appear at a rate of about 4 per thousand titles. That rate jumps to nearly 16 between 1590 and 1616; by 1624- 1647 the rate drops to about 9 per thousand. The rate at which plays are printed does not keep pace with the increase in the overall number of books. As a check, I have performed the same kind of calculations using data from W. W. Greg on the number of printed plays for professional actors; those numbers appear in column 6. We see the same pattern: about 17 plays per thousand titles between 1590 and 1616; about 6 between 1624 and 1647.

TABLE 4. Estimated proportion of plays among printed books

| 1<br>Time interval | 2<br>Plays with "tragedy" in title | 3<br>Plays with "comedy" in title | 4<br>Total *ESTC* titles | 5<br>Frequency of plays (*ESTC* estimate) per thousand *ESTC* titles | 6<br>Frequency of plays (Greg, from table 2) per thousand *ESTC* titles |
|---|---|---|---|---|---|
| 1475–1589 | 29 | 25 | 12,272 | 4.4 (54) | |
| 1590–1616 | 97 | 65 | 10,247 | 15.8 (162) | 17.1 (176) |
| 1617–1623 | 24 | 19 | 3,860 | 11.1 (43) | 4.1 (16) |
| 1624–1647 | 108 | 113 | 24,744 | 8.9 (221) | 5.8 (143) |
| 1648–1662 | 106 | 90 | 23,223 | 8.4 (196) | 3.0 (69) |

*Note:* Figures in columns 5 and 6 are estimates developed for analyzing trends, not actual numbers of plays. Column 5 includes plays of all kinds that use "tragedy" or "comedy" in their titles; column 6 excludes plays in collections and includes only plays for professional performance.

Even allowing for the uncertainties of estimation, we can say with confidence that between 1590 and 1616 a higher proportion of printed titles were plays than earlier or later in the period I am studying. During the most exciting years in the history of the English stage, the proportion of playtexts among printed books surged. If printed plays are an effect of what we used to call "the Shakespearean moment," they are also potentially a cause of changes in the book trade itself. One presumes that these printed plays found readers, and in doing so they may have increased the reading audience for printed books of all kinds. Readers who read plays presumably continued to read books of other kinds, with expectations modified by play-reading. A book trade devoting more of its energies to printing plays may have modified its practices because of the expectations of an audience increasingly accustomed to play-reading. And we can see what appears to be the impact of such changed expectations in the way the word "tragedy" is used in the titles of non-theatrical publications during the time of the English Civil War.

Nigel Smith writes that after performances of plays were suppressed in 1642, "the theatrical migrated into pamphlets and newsbooks," and, moreover, that "the dramatic forms which had seen life on the stage before 1642 were taken into the printed pamphlet."[27] Susan Wiseman shows how "news" reported in staged plays in the 1620s and 1630s reemerged in printed dialogues and theatricalized pamphlets after the closing of the theaters.[28] In the titles of these texts, we see that by the mid-seventeenth century, the word "tragedy" often has a meaning derived from its use in the theater.

In the sixteenth century, "tragedy" often seems a synonym for "death"—often but not always the death of one who behaves badly. The term, especially when used alone, seems to refer to an event in a story rather than to a story's shape, implications, or form. As professional theater flourishes and printed plays become common, non-theatrical texts that use the word "tragedy" in their titles seem to expect their readers to recognize an allusion to plays. Let me illustrate my point with two verse narratives describing the death of a clergyman, one from the mid-sixteenth century and one from a hundred years later, and with another Civil War text describing the slaying of two royalists.

The full title tells what one needs to know about the 1548 work by Sir David Lindsay: *The Tragical death of Dauid Beato[n] Bishoppe of sainct Andrewes in Scotland. Wherunto is ioyned the martyrdom of maister George Wyseharte gentleman, for whose sake the aforesayed bishoppe was not longe after slayne. Wherein thou maist learne what a burnynge charitie they shewed not only towards him: but vnto al suche as come to their hãdes for the blessed Gospels sake.*[29] David Beaton, bishop of St. Andrews and cardinal of Scotland, was killed after ordering the death of the Protestant "heretic" George Wishart. Both the title page and Robert Burrant's prefatory narrative describe Beaton's death as a "tragedy," and the use of the term makes clear that what is meant by "tragedy" is an instructive story about the fall of a person of high estate. Lindsay begins his poem by saying that he is imitating Boccaccio, and he explicitly locates the story of Beaton's death in the tradition of Boccaccio's *de casibus* narratives. Beaton appears to Lindsay in a dream and recounts his own misdeeds, both boasting of his power and defining his power and behavior as illegitimate. Lindsay's poem concludes with sections advising priests and kings how to avoid the mistakes Beaton made. Notably, the words "tragic" and "tragicall" are used often to describe Beaton's death, and never used to describe the heroic martyrdom of Wishart. Burrant's preface sets tragic stories in a context beginning with the fall of Adam and including a long list of biblical royal miscreants. "Tragedy," in this volume, is a genre, not just a noun, but has no connection with theater.

A century later the picture is very different. Robert Wild writes a poem about the death in 1651 of a royalist minister, *The Tragedy of Christopher Love at Tower Hill.*[30] Love was a royalist minister executed by the Parliamentarians.[31] Not only is Wild's poem on his death called a tragedy, but also it is divided into five sections called "acts." Describing Love's death in "Act IV," the poem refers to the execution platform as a "fatall Stage." The section called "Act V" begins, "*Love* lyes a bleeding, and the world shall see / Heaven Act a part In this black Tragedie." (Wild's pun presumably echoes the subtitle of Beaumont and Fletcher's *Philaster, or, Love Lies a-Bleeding.*) Unlike Lindsay's tale of martyrdom, this one presents the word "tragedy" as very much a theatrical term. An anonymous 1648 royalist tract shows similar awareness of theater, though it is not divided into acts. It mingles theatrical language and biblical allegory to inveigh against the killing by the parliamentary leaders Fairfax and Ireton of two royalists who had in good faith surrendered. Once again the full title reveals what we need to know: *The Crvel Tragedy Or Inhumane Bvtchery, of Hamor and Shechem, with other their Adherents. Acted by Simeon and Levi, in Shechem, a City in Succoth a County or Lordship in Canaan. Lately revived and reacted heere in England, by Fairfax and Ireton, upon the persons of Sir Charles Lucas and Sir George Lisle, in Colchester, the 28. Aug. 1648. Presented to publicke view in Meditations, discoursing the former, discovering the latter, and comparing the circumstances of both, and Dedicated to the honoured memory of the two last named Worthies.*[32] Fairfax and Ireton are several times described as "actors in that tragedy at Colchester," and the writer calls for revenge. A final poem concludes with an echo of the ghost of Don Andrea at the end of act 3 in Kyd's *Spanish Tragedy*, "Revenge! Awake!"

I am not arguing that the word "tragedy" in the sixteenth century was never theatrical (for one thing, Seneca was an ever-present example), nor do I claim that in the seventeenth century the word had entirely lost the meanings it had in Boccaccio's *de casibus* narratives. Interesting words always have a range of connotations. But the range shifts for tragedy. Of course, some of that shift comes about because of theatrical performances and the remembered experiences of audiences in the theater. But especially at a time when the theaters were closed, much of the energy for the shift must have been transmitted by the culture of print.[33]

I argued earlier that the use of generic terms on title pages may have been part of the same quest for non-theatrical prestige that led Jonson to call his plays "works." But another effect of that usage was to associate the terms "comedy" and "tragedy" more explicitly with English stage plays. As theater flourished in the first forty years of the seventeenth century, plays became more readily available as metaphors for public and political events. And as the body of printed plays grew, generic terms associated with printed plays may have helped provide a vocabulary for some theatricalizing of public discourse. As more and more plays find their way into print, an increasing number of the plays have generic phrases on their title pages. As the decades go on, the range of generic terms narrows and is increasingly dominated by the words "comedy" and "tragedy" and their variants. Moreover, this change seems associated with treating plays as "works"—as texts conferring status on their authors and their readers. The labels "comedy" and "tragedy" on the title pages of plays seem to have had an effect not just on the perceived status of plays but also on the ways the words were used as metaphors in other texts. The Andrew Marvell who in his "Horatian Ode" described that royal martyr, Charles, as a "Royal Actor" upon a "tragic scaffold" had no doubt read as well as seen plays.

## NOTES

This project was made possible by advice and assistance from Janice A. Gifford, professor of statistics at Mount Holyoke College. My research assistant, Jessie Babcock '03, compiled the database.

1. *Mr. William Shakespeares comedies, histories, & tragedies* (London: Isaac Jaggard and Ed. Blount [at the charges of W. Jaggard, Ed. Blount, J. Smithweeke, and W. Aspley], 1623).

2. *Comedies and Tragedies written by Francis Beavmont and John Fletcher Gentlemen* (London: for Humphrey Robinson and Humphrey Moseley, 1647).

3. Thomas Preston, *A lamentable tragedy mixed ful of pleasant mirth, conteyning the life of Cambises king of Percia* (London: John Allde, 1570?).

4. Peter W. M. Blayney sorts out the roles of publishers, printers, and booksellers while acknowledging that the first term is anachronistic. See Blayney, "The Publication of Playbooks," in *A New History of Early English Drama*, ed. John D. Cox and David Scott Kastan (New York: Columbia University Press, 1997), 383–422.

5. E. K. Chambers, *The Elizabethan Stage*, 4 vols. (Oxford: Clarendon, 1923), 2:87.

6. Ibid., 4:274.

7. Ibid., 2:208.

8. Ibid., 2:188.

9. Malone Society, *Collections*, vol. 2, pt. 3 (Oxford: Oxford University Press, 1931), 384.

10. *Henslowe's Diary*, ed. R. A Foakes and R. T. Rickert (Cambridge: Cambridge University Press, 1961).

11. See *A Warning for Fair Women: A Critical Edition*, ed. Charles Dale Cannon (The Hague: Mouton, 1975).

12. Contemporary references make clear that posted "playbills" publicized performances of plays. Playbills appear to have been written by hand, not printed, and the only surviving example announces a bearbaiting. The document offers no information about whether playbills ordinarily used generic terms. See Andrew Gurr, *The Shakespearean Stage, 1574–1642*, 3rd ed. (Cambridge: Cambridge University Press, 1992), 11.

13. W. W. Greg, *A Bibliography of the English Printed Drama to the Restoration*, 4 vols. (London: Bibliographical Society, 1939–59).

14. For a powerful exploration of this larger issue in a broader context, see Julie Stone Peters, *The Theatre of the Book, 1480–1880: Print, Text, and Performance in Europe* (Oxford: Oxford University Press, 2000). Peters suggests that generic terms on title pages may have seemed more aristocratic than the laborious-sounding "works" (207).

15. James P. Saeger and Christopher J. Fassler, "The London Professional Theater, 1576–1642: A Catalogue and Analysis of the Extant Printed Plays," *Research Opportunities in Renaissance Drama* 34 (1995): 63–109.

16. Alan B. Farmer and Zachary Lesser, "Vile Arts: The Marketing of English Printed Drama, 1512–1660," *Research Opportunities in Renaissance Drama* 39 (2000): 77–165. See especially the graph on 83.

17. Jeffrey Masten, *Textual Intercourse: Collaboration, Authorship, and Sexualities in Renaissance Drama* (Cambridge: Cambridge University Press, 1997), 116–17.

18. Douglas A. Brooks, *From Playhouse to Printing House: Drama and Authorship in Early Modern England* (Cambridge: Cambridge University Press, 2000).

19. Lukas Erne believes the case to be different for Shakespeare, but even Erne acknowledges that Shakespeare's plays—unlike closet drama—had their initial life on the stage. See Erne, *Shakespeare as Literary Dramatist* (Cambridge: Cambridge University Press, 2003).

20. Saeger and Fassler make this assertion without distinguishing between single-play editions and collections; Farmer and Lesser qualify the generalization by distinguishing between plays for indoor and outdoor theaters.

21. Notably, table 2 shows the same pattern as table 1.

22. The proportion of plays Henslowe designates by genre is far smaller than the 72 percent so designated among printed plays of the professional theater in the 1590s (see table 1) or the 60 percent between 1590 and 1616.

23. On this aspect of the market for printed plays, see Alan B. Farmer and Zachary Lesser, "The Popularity of Playbooks Revisited," *Shakespeare Quarterly* 56 (2005): 1–32.

24. Blayney, "Publication of Playbooks," 386.

25. The *ESTC* is available at http://eureka.ohio.rlg.org.

26. Search terms in "title word" field (? is a wild card indicator): "trag?"; "comed? or comic?"; "histor? or hystor?" Titles are classified as "plays" if they are listed as such in the Greg or Harbage-Schoenbaum bibliographies. Items being counted are individual printings with distinct STC or Wing numbers. Collections including multiple plays are counted only once. Volumes including non-dramatic texts are included in counts if they also include plays. Especially before 1616, it is common for volumes to include multiple genre words in titles. In those cases the volume is counted under each category in which it appears.

27. Nigel Smith, *Literature and Revolution in England, 1640–1660* (New Haven: Yale University Press, 1994), 11, 75.

28. Susan Wiseman, *Drama and Politics in the English Civil War* (Cambridge: Cambridge University Press, 1998), 19–25. On the crossover between news and play publishing, see chapter 6 by Alan Farmer in this volume.

29. *The Tragical death of Dauid Beato[n]* (London: John Daye, and William Seres, [1548]).

30. Robert Wild, *The Tragedy of Christopher Love at Tower Hill August 22. 1651* (London, 1651).

31. In her excellent book on Royalist literature, Lois Potter says that Wild's poem was not printed until the Restoration. A 1651 broadside version is reproduced in *Early English Books Online* (Wing W2149a) The dating issue is irrelevant to Potter's argument and my own. See Lois Potter, *Secret Rites and Secret Writing: Royalist Literature, 1641–1660* (Cambridge: Cambridge University Press, 1989), 151–52.

32. *The Crvel Tragedy Or Inhumane Bvtchery, of Hamor and Shechem* ([London], 1648).

33. Elizabeth Sauer in chapter 4 of this volume discusses the political uses by Parliament of the closet drama *Tyrannicall-Government Anatomized.*

EIGHT

# The Masque in/as Print

LAUREN SHOHET

As preparations unfolded for the long-exiled Charles II to return triumphantly to London in 1660, a masque titled *The Subjects Joy for the Kings Restoration, Cheerfully Made Known in a Sacred Masque* was already in print by the time he landed at Dover.[1] The cultural logic of welcoming the king with a masque is clear: as the Restoration heals the breach in continuity of Stuart rule, Charles should be celebrated in the same genre used so famously for festive occasions of state by his parents and grandparents. The masques of Charles's forebears—the elaborate emblematic entertainments produced at the courts of Charles I and Queen Henrietta Maria and of James I and Queen Anna to introduce evenings of festive dancing—have been the focus of much discussion in recent decades, with historians and literary critics alike exploring masque performances as central articulations of Stuart culture. Some scholars have emphasized the efficacy of masque as an instrument of absolutist monarchy; others have understood masques more as "tools of cultural and political negotiation" available to a range of (elite) voices engaged in political dialogue.[2] Shared by almost all masque scholarship to date, however, has been an overwhelming emphasis on masque as a performance genre.[3]

The 1660 *Subjects Joy*, however, offered itself in print before performance: George Thomason purchased a copy on May 17, a week before Charles landed at Dover and nearly two weeks before the king came to London. Indeed, despite the text's invocation of a performance (it offers prefatory remarks as "private Speech of the Author, in Society with his Friends, to entertain the Time before the Masque begun"), this may have been a closet masque, since we have no record outside the masque text of performance having been undertaken.[4] Beyond the mere chronology of print preceding performance, *The Subjects Joy* thematically emphasizes masque as a print form. At the masque's conclusion, the figure Psyche approaches the king to present him with the text of the very masque she is enacting: "Psyche (with an observant haste), goes to present the King, with the Masque, in writing."[5] Insofar as the main matter of the masque—and hence of the text Psyche hands over—recounts the biblical story of Jeroboam's revolt against Moses, Psyche's presenting the king with this text about rebellion formally mimics the writers and publishers of pamphlets, petitions, and broadsides so active since the 1640s. Moreover, when, in anticipation rather than recollection of historical fact (or perhaps in violation of it), the masque text represents Psyche having interacted with the "king"—a king in text only, at the time of publication; a king granted authority *by* the masque rather than granting authority *to* it; a king fêted by a masque spontaneously offered without royal commission or control—we see masque mediating complex relationships between monarchs and subjects, between producers and receivers, in ways more characteristic of print culture than of our customary, performance-based notions of masque as a form wherein "the mysterious powers of kingship" manifest their glory to docile spectators.[6]

This emphasis on masque as a print form initially might seem specific to the Restoration context of *The Subjects Joy*. But many masques enjoyed robust lives as print artifacts from the beginning of the seventeenth century.[7] Masque criticism has not fully acknowledged masque's presence as a bi-medial form, its dramatic occasions consistently delivered into print. Court masque lived a double life: as an elite, private, densely emblematic performance form, saturated with insider knowledge, but one that was conveyed regularly into a nascent print public sphere. Indeed, print could supplant performance: King James canceled the 1624 court performance of the controversial *Neptune's Triumph* (inflected by coded disagreement about Spanish policy), but the masque was published in quarto nonetheless. Its circulation—with or without the blessing of its patrons—is confirmed by its listing in bookseller Edward Archer's catalogue in 1656.[8] This example demonstrates how considering masque uniquely as a performance form leaves the genre too firmly in the grasp of producers. Martin Butler argues that the "colliding priorities" of *Neptune's Triumph* were resolved "in the most absolute way imaginable: James simply refused to allow the masque to be performed."[9] But remembering that many masques circulated as material texts allows us to consider masque more broadly: in this instance, how the publication of *Neptune's*

*Triumph* brought the debate over Spanish policy into the sphere of print even as the king denied it courtly rehearsal.

Considering masque's textual life can provide a useful counterweight to our performance-based discussions of masque. Not only can a history of masque publication illuminate the bibliographic aspects of the genre that we often ignore entirely, but such a history can draw our attention to questions about masque reception in ways that potentially inflect our understanding of masque performance as well (since the latter has admitted little consideration of receivers).[10] Drawing masque into our inquiries about early modern reading can be mutually useful for both masque scholarship and the history of the book. Evidence that masque circulated through a variety of distribution networks yields an intriguing picture of events we have thought of as exclusively aristocratic being disseminated to a wider, more public audience. Although some *manuscript* copies of masques were elaborately decorated, the majority of masques were printed in small, affordable quartos; some masques were included among collections of works by such popular writers as Campion, Daniel, Jonson, and Carew. Indeed, masque's overlay of performance, insider gossip about performance, public gossip about performance, manuscript circulation, and print circulation offers an ideal place to heed Roger Chartier's call for book history to "question the long-recognized contrast between the completely oral and gestural forms . . . and the circulation of writing."[11] The import of multiple reading frames for masque emerges still more fully when we consider that court masques often encoded information about political policy *du jour*—and this in the decades before the distribution of political news became legal.[12] Furthermore, insofar as seventeenth-century masque reading encompasses literary, journalistic, and other readerly modes of reception at a moment of tumultuous historical change, investigating material masque can help us consider the relationship *between* modes of reading and historical change. This full project lies, of course, beyond the scope of the present essay. Here, my concern is to offer evidence about masque printing, circulation, and reading in an effort to establish the importance of masque as material text. Exploring masque publication 1603–1642 lets us consider the picture of masque that emerges when we think about readers and readings of masques in the years that saw simultaneous assertions of absolutist monarchal theory (whose relationship to masque has been well studied) and developing articulations of public politics (whose relationship to masque has not).[13]

From the earliest years of James's reign, masque texts circulated both within the court community and more widely. Throughout the Jacobean era, epistles from court enclosed masque texts for their recipients to read, or alluded to the coming publication of these texts. Courtier Dudley Carleton's letter to John Chamberlain about Queen Anna's second masque, the Twelfth Night 1605 *Masque of Blackness*, declines to describe the device in detail because "there is a pamphlet in press which will save me that pains."[14] Edward Sherburn enclosed a text of *Pleasure Reconciled to Virtue* with a letter to Carleton in 1618; Sherburn writes, "The Maske which was had on twelvth night wherein the Prince was one your Lordship will perceive the conceipt by perusing this little book."[15] Although Nathaniel Brent declined to send Carleton the text of *For the Honour of Wales* (a new version of *Pleasure*, also 1618), his remarks indicate that he could well have done so: "The princes masque was shewed againe at Court on Tuesday night with som few additions . . . without deserving so great honour as to be sent to your Lordship."[16] Epistolary circulation of masque texts also was undertaken outside the court: immediately after the first performance of *The Triumph of Peace* in 1634, Inns of Court gentleman Thomas Coke sent a copy to his father in the provinces, writing, "I Have sent you a booke of our Masque which was presented on munday last with much applause and commendation."[17]

Masque texts, then, were among the information reported throughout the networks of interested readers who consumed the court gossip, political information, and opinions that in the Stuart era were just taking a form we might recognize as "news." As panegyric, court masques might not at first glance seem promising sources for the novel political content whence "news" derives its name. But examining court masques in conjunction with questions about the history of reading suggests that the traditional critical sense of court masque as straightforward propaganda may be oversimplified. Most broadly, recalling that masques have *readers* (in the literal sense for textual encounters, in the figurative sense for both textual and theatrical iterations) reminds us that interpretive encounters are complex negotiations among producers, artifacts, and receivers. As Hans Robert Jauss remarks, "in the triangle of author, work, and public the last is no passive part, no chain of mere reactions, but rather itself an energy formative of history."[18] As well-trained humanist readers, the courtly and gentlemanly recipients of circulating masque texts were well positioned to observe the propagandistic elements of court masque with a critical eye, rather than merely acquiescing to laudatory proclamations.

With the critical distance such training offers, receivers can evaluate representations, cross-read different moments within a piece, look for gaps and silences, watch masques thematizing their own functions. For instance, when Ben Jonson's 1608 *Masque of Beautie* features a moving "*Island* floting on a calme water," then closes with the benediction "let your state, the while, / Be fixed as the Isle," the potential (if likely unintended) irony of "the Isle" referring either to Britain or to the clearly *unfixed* "Isle" of the masque scene can be just as available to contemporary receivers as it is to us.[19] Even the most ideologically motivated of absolutist masque spectacles, that is, contain more information of potential political interest when we acknowledge that receivers may *reflect upon* the ideological performance rather than be assumed to be merely subject to it.[20]

A second strand of court masque's significance to an emergent reading public is observable in masques that are explicitly edgier than the *Masque of Beautie*. The 1616 *Golden Age Restored* (Jonson), for example, refracts political changes at court. The masque depicts a Golden Age of virtue supplanting an Iron Age of vice at just the moment when King James's erstwhile favorite, Robert Carr, earl of Somerset, was imprisoned on suspicion of conspiracy to commit murder. As Martin Butler and David Lindley have illuminated, *The Golden Age Restored* topically reflects on the question of the king's intentions regarding Carr's trial. By celebrating the decline of an "Iron Age" that "distinctly registers the concatenation of crimes of which Somerset stood accused," Butler and Lindley argue that the masque signals the king's intention to let the current criminal investigation run its course (or, in Butler and Lindley's argument, Jonson's hope that James had so decided).[21] Considering masque's textual life shows how such vexed and indeed newsworthy issues as factional reorganization at court or the king's relationship to the judiciary can reach readers outside the court as well. Rumor and speculation ran wild about nearly every aspect of the Somerset case—but the only representation of the king's own position available in print was the *Golden Age* text sold in 1616 as part of Jonson's *Workes*. Interested parties with access to the London-based trade in illegal manuscripts could and did purchase copies of Chief Justice Edward Coke's speech to Parliament that sought to elicit James's assent to the legal proceedings, but the sole source of legal print representations of the king's position (purchasable by all, with or without connections to the patronage-based chain of manuscript circulation) was, interestingly, a masque.[22]

Not only those masques we understand today to be topically charged contain political news. Readers of even the blandest masques can receive information of political interest when we redefine the masque "text" in more historically contextualized ways. Leeds Barroll has argued persuasively that contemporaries would have taken the most significant political "text" of court masques to be the list of participating masquers (augmented, in epistolary accounts, by reports of which guests were honored with the first invitations to dance). Barroll argues that Queen Anna's scripting of masque participation, for instance, "was highly political . . . determining the interplay of court alliances or political overtures."[23] Barroll claims that a masque like the 1604 *Vision of the Twelve Goddesses* (scripted by Samuel Daniel) was read not only for the spectacle of queenship created in the text, but also as Anna's well-choreographed balancing of Howard and Essex factions, pointedly selecting masquers whose husbands had been important in James's recently securing the English crown, and signaling "the Stuart Crown's new approach to Essex Plot conspirators."[24] Epistolary recorders of masque events consistently identify masquers and honored dancers; significantly, published accounts usually do as well, offering wider audiences access to this part of the "text." Scripting (and publishing) this kind of political masque text extended well beyond Anna's queenship. For instance, Martin Butler discusses Charles's 1640 effort in *Salmacida Spolia* (Davenant) to use masque as "part of an ongoing political dialogue between the crown and its servants," here liberally including among the masquers "either moderate critics or future opponents of the king."[25] We can add to Butler's observation that the publication of *Salmacida Spolia* serves to report this political negotiation—pressing news indeed—to the reading public.

In considering masque books' relationship to an emergent public sphere, one finds it striking that the most intensively published masque of the 1630s, the 1634 Inns of Court *Triumph of Peace* (Shirley), was also one of the most thorough in its commentary on political questions of interest to a wide range of readers. This masque, which went through three quarto printings within a year (probably yielding three thousand copies), represents Irene (Peace), Eunomia (Law), and Diche (Justice) as the parents of the Inns of Court lawyers; they preside over songs and dances offered to their own "parents," Jove and Themis (King Charles and Queen Henrietta Maria).[26] Glancing at the dynastic masques often performed for weddings, which present genealogy more literally (recall how Milton's Ludlow masque concludes with the presentation of the

Lady and her brothers to the Earl and Countess of Bridgewater: "Heer behold so goodly grown / Three fair branches of your own"), we see that the *Triumph of Peace* metaphorizes genealogy to make the lawyers the grandchildren of the monarchs, who in turn are complimented, perhaps coercively, as the source of law and justice.[27] On one level, then, the masque plumbs the relationships between law and state that become increasingly pressing throughout the 1630s and 1640s. To the gentry, invested in the relationship between the legal profession and the monarchy, the broad publication of this masque would disseminate statements of something like "public" interest.

Moreover, this masque also more specifically engages one immediate issue touching upon monarchs and lawyers—and specifically the Inns of Court and the urban community more generally: the prosecution of lawyer William Prynne, whom the monarchs took to have criticized the queen's court theatricals in his treatise *Histrio-Mastix*. One of the masque producers, Bulstrode Whitelock, wrote that the Inns undertook *Triumph of Peace* to "manifest the difference of their opinion, from Mr. *Prynne's* new learning, and serve to confute his *Histrio-Mastix* against interludes."[28]

Broadening the masque's commentary on issues of public interest yet further, the expansive antimasques feature a variety of London figures, balancing the masque-proper discourse of law and state with antimasque discourse of middling-sort goods, services, and conditions of life. One antimasque features London craftsmen who explain that they have constructed the scenery and costumes for the masque spectacle itself: displaying, that is, how the masque spectacle of ethereal harmony depends on materials and goods they have provided. In another antimasque, tradesmen parade novel (if parodically presented) inventions for improving productivity. Whitelock took this antimasque as a commentary on recent crown actions regarding commercial monopolies, writing that "by [the antimasque of inventors], an information was covertly given to the King of the unfitness and ridiculousness of these projects against the law."[29] Yet another antimasque speaks to another topical issue of broad interest: the widely flouted, but recently reaffirmed, prohibition on gentry residing in London. As Lawrence Venuti has demonstrated, the antimasque of Opinion and Fancy parody precisely the behaviors recently cited by the crown as consequences of gentry forsaking their country obligations for urban pleasures.[30] These examples of ways the masque provides legible, if encoded, information of public interest, in a very wide-selling format, show how print masque can enter into something resembling news dissemination—and in ways that, by their very encoding, demand critical reading.

Given masque's finger on the pulse of cultural and political changes at court, and its potential to represent courtly negotiations in potentially nuanced ways to a reading and gossiping public, the tendency to consider the long-known publication record of court masques of solely esoteric interest seems misguided. Early masque scriptors remark the consistent market for print versions of masques from court—a readerly appetite that should be of interest not only to bibliographers but also to students of the history of reading and the emergence of public opinion. As masque scriptor Samuel Daniel writes in the reader's preface to the 1610 *Tethys' Festival* (produced by Queen Anna, for Henry's accession as Prince of Wales), "it is expected (according now to the custome) that I, being imployed in the busines, should publish a description and forme of the late Maske."[31] Daniel's phrase "according now to the custome" confirms that masque publication was expected, and indeed suggests that we should continue looking for more published Jacobean era masques than we have yet found. Similarly, masque scriptor Thomas Campion claims a market demand for masque texts to be made available: his preface to the *Lords' Masque* (for Princess Elizabeth's wedding festivities in 1613–14) asserts that "I have now taken occasion to satisfie many who long since were desirous that the Lords maske should be published."[32] Campion's claim that an audience has "long since" desired masque publication (like Daniel's invocation of the "late Maske") reveals that masque texts were not consumed only simultaneously with performance.

Table 1 offers a minimal sketch of masque publication 1603–1642; for reasons detailed shortly, masque publication substantially exceeded these instances. Although this list offers a minimal starting point, issues of medium (print versus manuscript), durability, and licensing practice complicate the investigation of material masque. Indeed, it is worth laying out some of the difficulties in recovering the record for masque books because in many ways they offer a usefully unexceptional object of study. In their modest size and cost, in the relative insignificance that often kept them from being considered weighty enough to catalogue or annotate, and in their bridging of elite and popular audiences, masques belong to the invisible majority of early modern books. The evanescence of the material record, and the subtlety of the evidence it can present, is suggested by Dudley Carleton's implication, cited earlier, that the forthcoming text of

TABLE 1. Individual masques entered in Stationers' Register and/or printed in separate, surviving format

| Performance date | | Scriptor | First printing |
|---|---|---|---|
| 1604 | *Vision of the Twelve Goddesses* | Daniel | 1604 |
| 1605 | *Masque of Blackness* (with *Beauty, Haddington*) | Jonson | 1608 |
| 1606 | *Hymenaei* | Jonson | 1606 |
| 1606 | *Challenge of the Four Knights Errant* | — | 1610 |
| 1606 | *Entertainment of King Christian IV* | various | 1606 |
| 1607 | *Lord Hay's Masque* (Hay wedding) | Campion | 1607 |
| 1608 | *Masque of Beauty* (with *Blackness, Haddington*) | Jonson | 1608 |
| 1608 | *Haddington Masque* | Jonson | 1608 |
| 1609 | *Masque of Queens* | Jonson | 1609 |
| 1610 | *Tethys' Festival* (*Order and Solemnitie*) | Daniel | 1610 |
| 1613 | *Lords' Masque* | Campion | 1613 |
| 1613 | *Masque of the Inner Temple and Gray's Inn* | Beaumont | n.d. |
| 1613 | *Memorable Masque* | Chapman | n.d. |
| 1613 | *Heaven's Blessing* | — | 1613 |
| 1613 | *Caversham Entertainment* (*Entertainment at Cawsome House*) | Campion | 1613 |
| 1614 | *Masque of Squires* | Campion | 1614 |
| 1614 | *Masque of Flowers* | various | 1614 |
| 1617 | *Lovers Made Men* | Jonson | 1617 |
| 1619 | *Inner Temple Masque* (*Masque of Heroes*) | Middleton | 1619 |
| 1620 | *Triumphs of Peace* | Squire | 1620 |
| 1620 | *Courtly Masque* (*World Toss'd at Tennis*) | Middleton | 1620 |
| 1622 | *Masque of Augurs* | Jonson | n.d. |
| 1623 | *Time Vindicated* | Jonson | 1623 |
| 1624 | *Neptune's Triumph* | Jonson | 1624 |
| 1625 | *Fortunate Isles* | Jonson | 1625 |
| 1630 | *Love's Triumph through Callipolis* | Jonson | 1630 |
| 1631 | *Chloridia* | Jonson | n.d. |
| 1631 | *Albion's Triumph* | Townshend | 1631 |
| 1631 | *Tempe Restored* | Davenant | 1631 |
| 1634 | *Triumph of Peace* | Shirley | 1634 |
| 1634 | *Coelum Britannicum* | Carew | 1634 |
| 1635 | *Temple of Love* | Davenant | 1635 |
| 1636 | *Triumphs of the Prince d'Amour* | Davenant | 1636 |
| 1636 | *Corona Minervae* | Kinnaston | 1636 |
| 1636 | *Entertainment at Richmond* | Jonson | 1636 |
| 1637 | *Microcosmus* | Nabbes | 1637 |
| 1634 | *Mask at Ludlow* (*Comus*) | Milton | 1637 |
| 1638 | *Britannia Triumphans* | Davenant | 1638 |
| 1638 | *Luminalia* | Davenant | 1638 |
| 1638 | *Spring's Glory* | Nabbes | 1638 |
| 1640 | *Salmacida Spolia* | Davenant | 1640 |
| 1640 | *Mascarade du Ciel* | J. Sadler | 1640 |
| 1640 | *Loves Mistresse, or The Queenes Masque* | Heywood | 1640 |
| 1642 | *King's Entertainment . . . at Lincoln* | — | 1642 |

*Blackness* will be a print artifact: "a pamphlet in press." No 1605 print text of *Blackness* survives. Carleton may simply have been mistaken; other possible ways to account for this provide a useful window into several characteristics of masque printing, and indeed the printing of "ephemera" in general. Establishing publication history from surviving libraries or catalogues of dispersed or lost collections is difficult. Printed masques were short books, usually small quartos, and many were printed on lower-quality paper (although others were not). Early modern purchasers of small books often left them unbound so that their paper might be recycled for household use, or purchasers might bind them together with other miscellaneous small works that rendered them unlikely to be catalogued in ways we can decipher. Dramatic genre can exacerbate this problem: in seventeenth-century libraries, small books generally, but perhaps small dramatic texts in particular, often were considered ephemera and were not catalogued.[33]

A further difficulty in establishing a "publication" history for early modern texts lies in the anachronism of our distinction between print (our sine qua non for publication) and manuscript. But Sherburne's and Brent's letters on *Pleasure* and *Wales*, cited earlier, leave open the question of whether the masques they enclosed were print or manuscript copies. Since they refer to masques we cannot confirm to have been printed before their inclusion in the second folio of Jonson's *Workes* (1640), the courtiers may well have been referring to manuscript texts. Manuscript form need not indicate, however, that these masques remained closed to a public readership. Even masques that were not printed were scribally published, and recent scholarship detailing the extent of scribal publication suggests that we should not assume that the circulation of any masque in manuscript must, by virtue of its medium, have been tightly circumscribed. Indeed, Harold Love demonstrates that many texts are disseminated by manuscript publication throughout the seventeenth century; even masques that are never printed can enjoy commercial publication and be offered for sale, often at the same booksellers' shops that carry print material.[34]

Nor can we reliably infer a full print history from imprints or licensing records, as has often been assumed. Printing (or some printing) was regulated by the Stationers' Company, and this guild was responsible for seeing that texts (or some texts) were licensed for publication by appropriate crown or church authorities. Entry in the *Stationers' Register* also established the publisher's legal rights to a text. Earlier bibliographers—centrally, for masque, W. W. Greg and the Oxford *Ben Jonson* editors C. H.

Herford and Percy and Evelyn Simpson—took lack of entry in the Stationers' records, particularly when combined with the absence of an imprint giving the name and location of the publisher, as a definitive sign of a masque's having been published privately, serving only as souvenirs for the primary audience. Yet ongoing investigations of printing and publishing in seventeenth-century England raise questions about these inferences. Analyzing the significant number of unregistered printings—indeed, Greg's own later work shows that a third of books published in this period were not registered—Leo Kirschbaum deduces that entry was optional.[35] Peter Blayney argues that licensing requirements obtained largely for books that could be expected to run into some trouble; "books that could offend nobody . . . were often published without authority, and no stationer is known to have been punished for failing to have an inoffensive text perused and allowed."[36] Furthermore, nothing that held a royal patent required licensing. As royally commissioned pieces, court masques may well have been taken to enjoy such status implicitly. These difficulties in recovering the material record for masque publication, then, suggest that we take the information we *can* establish as the lower limit of what was, in all likelihood, a more extended practice.

Complaints of piracy and brisk successions of reprints for certain masques indicate a lively commercial interest in the genre. Queen Anna's 1604 Christmas masque, the *Vision of the Twelve Goddesses*, was published twice that year: an unauthorized quarto from Edward Allde, and an octavo from Simon Waterson. In the latter, Daniel writes:

> In respect of the unmannerly presumption of an indiscreet Printer, who without warrant hath divulged the late shewe at Court, presented the eight of *January*, by the Queenes Maiestie and her Ladies; and the same very disorderly set forth: I thought it not amisse, seeing it would otherwise passe abroad, to describe the whole forme thereof in all points as it was then performed, and as the world wel knows very worthily performed.[37]

Daniel wonderfully betrays here the tensions between a vision of masque as private, aristocratic form ("divulged" through "indiscretion" and "presumption") and a model of masque as public, print genre—which deserves promulgation by a reliable source (Daniel), and which is moreover already public knowledge ("as the world wel knows"). Extending the irony, Daniel's exercise in public enlightenment comes in his dedication of the print text to a major aristocratic patron: Lucy, Countess of Bedford.

Masques were not competition-worthy properties only when they were new, but rather retained commercial potential over time. Twenty years after the performances of *The Gypsies Metamorphosed*, in 1640, its print text came out not only in the second folio of Jonson's *Workes* but also in a variant, duodecimo version from John Benson. The jockeying for rights to the previously unpublished masques in Jonson's 1640 *Workes* confirms commercial interest in masque rights.[38]

If editions from different printers, with differing degrees of authorial participation, imply that publishers thought of some masques as potential moneymakers, multiple editions from the same printer show that print runs sold out. For instance, the *Memorable Maske* (presented in 1613 by the gentlemen of the Middle Temple and Lincoln's Inn for the Palatine wedding festivities, scripted by Chapman) is preserved in two different quarto editions. Both published by George Norton, they appear to date from 1613 and 1614.[39] Likewise, the *Masque of the Inner Temple and Gray's Inn* (for the same occasion, scripted by Beaumont, published by Norton) survives in two different quarto issues from 1613. Publisher George Eld put out two editions of his collection of Thomas Middleton's civic masques, *Honorable Entertainments*, during 1621. As noted earlier, the 1634 *Triumph of Peace* was published three times within the year. The survival of a number of extant variant manuscripts of several masques, including Jonson's 1616 *Christmas His Show*, Jonson's 1621 *Gypsies Metamorphosed*, and Mildmay Fane's 1640 *Raguaillo d'Oceano*, indicates that a much larger number of contemporary manuscripts probably existed; the extent of the variants for some of these suggests that they may have been commercially, scribally published.

Some of the examples of well-published masques I offer here are associated with occasions that excited great public interest, such as Princess Elizabeth's Palatine wedding of 1613–14 or Prince Henry's investiture in 1610; reasons for readerly interest in their texts may include a commemorative or social-news function. Other well-published masques, such as *The Triumph of Peace*, contained major public processions within their productions; people who witnessed the most public portion of such festivities may have had a particular interest in reading the text of other parts. But the extent of readerly interest over time—evidenced in the Jonson examples discussed earlier, or in the reprint between 1610 and 1615 of some of the 1604 Jacobean accession pageantry—shows that masque texts were understood to retain interest after their performances were well past.[40] This suggests that people read masques for a variety of reasons and in a variety of ways, an observation that would seem too banal to mention in a discussion of modern reading but which is not always given due weight when we consider the experiences of past readers.

At the most concrete level, different material formats for masque printing create different experiences for readers. Readers encountered some masques in cheap separates, others in voluminous collections; some bound with other commemorations of an event, others bound with poetry and others still with plays; some in quick scribal copies, some in elaborate manuscripts, some in print. Many masques are issued separately, most often as quartos. Others are issued as parts of booklets printing together several aspects of one event: *Tethys' Festival*, for example, was printed in *The order and solemnities of the creation of Prince Henrie, Prince of Wales, Whereunto is annexed the Royal Maske* (published by William Stansby, in two editions during 1610), which also gives an account of Henry's investiture ceremony and the civic pageant *London's Love to the Royal Prince Henry*. Other masques are issued as part of anthologies containing additional works by the same scriptor: Samuel Daniel's *Certaine Small Workes* (1607 and 1611) contained the masque *Vision of the Twelve Goddesses* (1604); Beaumont and Fletcher's *Comedies and Tragedies* (1647) includes the *Mask of the Inner Temple and Gray's Inn* (1613, with two quarto editions that same year); and of course Ben Jonson's *Workes* (1616 and 1640) contains most of his masques. The inclusion of masques among other poetic or dramatic works raises further questions about both reader demand and implied models of genre and oeuvre.[41] When masque reprints are included among collections, we cannot know how much demand was excited by the masques themselves. But their inclusion is certainly notable; for example, Daniel's *Certaine Small Workes* does not aim for completeness, and hence the inclusion of *Twelve Goddesses* bears remark. Moreover, as James Knowles has shown, given masques certainly *can* be excluded from "Collected Works" that give an appearance of comprehensiveness, as when Jonson left two early Cecil masques (the Burse entertainment and the Salisbury House masque) out of the 1616 *Workes*.[42] Thus, conversely, *inclusion* is also noteworthy. The variety of these formats, these scriptors, and the readers they imply all adduce further evidence that masque publication and masque reading cannot be accounted for by a single, simple model of reception.

Although modern scholarship often occludes the existence of masque as a print genre, the seventeenth century considered it to be one. The appearance of the term "masque" as a category in contemporary catalogues demonstrates that contemporaries recognized print masque as a legible genre. When Robert Burton willed to the Bodleian Library any books in his collection that the Bodleian lacked, the librarian listed sixty-six of the new acquisitions under the heading "Maskes, Comedies, & Tragedies."[43] Furthermore, the representation of masque in commercial lists puts pressure on the long-standing notion that printed court masques should be understood only as privately produced souvenir copies. Bookseller Edward Archer's 1656 catalogue offers "An Exact and perfect Catalogue of all the Plaies that were ever printed; together, with all the Authors names; and what are Comedies, Histories, Interludes, Masks, Pastorels, Tragedies: And all these Plaies you may either have at the Signe of the *Adam and Eve*, in Little Britain; or, at the *Ben Johnson's* Head in Thredneedle-street, over against the Exchange."[44] Purchasers certainly know from such imprints where to find these books.

Genres begin to emerge in mid-century catalogues as information consumers might require. Archer offers his purchasers a genre code for each text in his catalogue, one of which is "M" for "masque."[45] (See table 2.) An important feature here (one shared by other booksellers' catalogues, such as Francis Kirkman's of 1661 and 1671) is the listing of individual Jonson masques that we do not know to have had separate quarto issue. This includes both masques performed prior to publication of the 1616 *Workes* (for instance, the 1611 *Oberon* or, in Kirkman, the 1613 *Irish Masque*) and masques performed between the 1616 and 1640 editions of the *Workes* (for example, the 1617 *Vision of Delight*, the 1621 *Masque of Gypsies*, or, in Kirkman, the 1624 *Mask of Owls*). This reminds us that books were generally sold unbound; extant partial and out-of-order bindings of the *Workes* show that some purchasers bought portions of the book at a time, sometimes binding them irregularly, and presumably sometimes not binding them—or ever completing their purchase—at all.[46] Whether separate listings for these masques indicate that purchasers continued to acquire portions of the *Workes* into the second half of the century, or whether particular masques were taken as sufficiently desirable to excite buyers' interest in the complete collection, their separate listings clearly indicate that a purchasing, reading public was understood to be interested in individual court masques. Individual masques were not encountered merely as a by-product of reading the *Workes*. Similarly indicating interest in individual masques are listings in William London's 1658 catalogue that specify the inclusion of masques among mixed-genre works. (See table 3.)

TABLE 2. Texts given "M" designation in Archer's 1656 catalogue (bracketed authors not given in Archer)

| | |
|---|---|
| Shirly [sic] | *Contention for honor and riches* |
| [Jonson?] | *Characters* [perhaps *Blackness and Beauty*][a] |
| Shirly | *Cupid and Death* |
| Shirly | *Duke's Mistress* |
| [Jonson] | *Fortunate Isles*[b] |
| [Jonson] | *Hymenaei* |
| Daniel | *Hymen's Triumph* |
| — | *King and Queen Intert*[*ainment*] |
| Haywood | *Loves Mistress* |
| [Jonson?] | *Loves Triumph* [*through Callipolis*?] |
| — | *Lovers, a mask* |
| [Beaumont] | *Mask at at* [sic] *Graies-Inn* |
| [J. Sadler] | *Masquard D ciel* |
| [Jonson] | *Metamorphosed Gypsy* |
| [Nabbes] | *Microcosmus* |
| [Jonson] | *Neptune's Triumph* |
| [Jonson] | *Oberon* |
| [Jonson] | *Pleasure Reconciled* |
| Thomas Nabbs [sic] | *Springs glory* |
| [Davenant] | *Temple of Love* |
| [Shirley] | *Triumph of Beauty* |
| Shirly | *Triumph of Peace* |
| [Jonson] | *Vision of Delight* |

[a]One version of this text was called *The Characters of the Queen's Two masques, the one of Blackness, the other of Beauty*.
[b]There is also an entry for "Fortunate Isles" as a "C[omedy]."

If booksellers' data allow us to deduce some information about the market for masques, other (unfortunately rather scattered) sources help fill in a bit more information about who owned printed masque texts. Humphrey Dyson's records of his book purchases between 1610 and 1630 are one useful resource, both because they itemize books collected by one bibliophile, and because his recording of their prices gives some sense of these texts' affordability. Francis Johnson's study of book prices indicates that "in the early seventeenth century, masques usually sold at 3*d*., even though they consisted of no more than two sheets. Longer masques, requiring three or more sheets for their printing, were usually sold at 4*d*."[47] Dyson's least expensive purchases, at 2*d*, include three Jonsonian court masques; the most expensive, at 6*d*, include two of his three accession accounts. (For calibration, note that a loaf of bread cost 1*d* at this time.)[48] (See table 4.)

TABLE 3. Masques included in William London's 1658 catalogue

| in category "Poems" | format |
|---|---|
| Mr *Curews* [Carew's] Poems, with a masque [*Coelum Britannicum*] | 8° |
| Horrace, *de arte poeticoe*, englished by *B. Johnson*, an execration against *Vulcan*, a mask of Gipsies | 12° |
| Mr *Milton's* Poems with a mask before the Earl of *Bridgwater* [*Comus*] | 12° |
| Mr *Shirls* Poems with a mask, the triumph of beauty | 8° |
| **in category "Playes"** | |
| Mr *Beamont* [sic], and *Flecher*. 34. Plays, Comedies, and Tragedies, with a mask [*Masque of the Inner Temple and Gray's Inn*] | 2° |
| Mr *Shirley*. Triumph of Peace | 4° |
| Sr. *W. Davenant*. Triumphs of Prince *de amour. Masque* | 4° |
| The famous comedy, and masque of *Pellus* and *Thetis*, by *J. Howel* Esq. | 4° |

These masque quartos appear, then, to be fairly inexpensive (averaging well under Peter Blayney's estimate of an average price of unbound books of 6*d*).

Masque texts of recoverable provenance suggest a widespread ownership for masques.[49] Sir Richard Paulet offers an example of a provincial commoner who owned masque texts. A member of the House of Commons from Herriard Park, Hampshire, Paulet owned *Tethys' Festival*.[50] Robert Burton, a London commoner (author of *The Anatomy of Melancholy*), owned a quarto copy of the 1624 *Fortunate Isles*. Richard Browne, a boy actor in *Cupid's Banishment* (a Deptford Ladies' Hall masque of 1617, attended by the queen), owned a printed text of the masque, which eventually became part of the library of diarist John Evelyn, Browne's son-in-law.[51] Evidence of academic readers comes from the manuscript of a Cambridge miscellany now in the Folger collection, which contains *Christmas His Show*; penned on the flyleaf in what appears to be a seventeenth-century hand is "Mock-maske. For Christmas before the kinge. 1615."[52] Examples of prominent aristocrats who owned masque texts include the second earl of Bridgewater, Thomas Egerton (the younger brother in Milton's *Comus*, and member of a family who danced in several court masques); his library included a quarto of Jonson's accession pageant, twelve of Jonson's masques in the 1640 *Workes*, and a quarto of the *Fortunate Isles*.

Masque texts indicate their writers' expectations that some readers will approach the masque without prior knowledge of its performance

Table 4. Humphrey Dyson's purchases of masques and entertainments, 1610–1630

| | | | |
|---|---|---|---|
| 2*d* | Fenton | *King James His Welcome* | 1603 |
| | Dugdale | *The Time Triumphant* | 1604 |
| | anon. | *Entertainment to Prince Charles* | 1623 |
| | Jonson | *Fortunate Isles* | 1624 |
| | Jonson | *Loves Triumph through Callipolis* | 1630 |
| | Jonson | *Chloridia* | 1630 |
| 3*d* | Daniel | *Discription of a Royall Masque* [*12 Goddesses*] | 1604 |
| | Campion | *Caversham Entertainment* | 1613 |
| | — | *Marriage of Frederick and Lady Elizabeth* | 1612 |
| 4*d* | [Munday] | *London's Love* | 1610 |
| | Beaumont | *Maske of Inner Temple and Gray's Inn* | 1613 |
| | Chapman | *Mask of Middle Temple and Lincoln's Inn* | 1613 |
| | Campion | *Maske of St. Stephens Day* (incl. music) | 1614 |
| | — | *Mask of Flowers* | 1614 |
| | Middleton | *Inner-Temple Masque* | 1619 |
| 6*d* | Dekker | *Entertainment to King James* | 1603 |
| | T.M. | *Entertainment of His Majesties* | 1603 |

*Note:* Data taken from Francis Johnson, "Notes on English Retail Book-Prices, 1550–1640," *The Library,* ser. 5, 2 (1950).

circumstances, while other readers will experience the masque text in conjunction with their memories of performance. Campion indicates in the published account of the 1613 *Entertainment at Cawsome House* (put on by Lord Knollys for Queen Anna) that "for as much as this late Entertainment hath beene much desired in writing, both of such as were present at the performance thereof, as also of many which are yet strangers both to the busines and place, it shall be convenient, in this generall publication, a little to touch at the description and situation of *Cawsome* seate."[53] Daniel's *Tethys* preface "To the Reader" similarly invokes two kinds of receivers, one reading the masque text in relationship to recalling the performance, the other reading it without having attended: the print record of the masque should both "preserve the memory thereof" and "satisfy their desires, who could have no other notice, but by others report of what was done."[54] Richard Paulet offers an example of a reader using the masque to extend access to an elite event. He reports in his diary that after taking the oath of allegiance with other Commons members on June 5, 1610, he "came to the Court, walking in the garden to see those that went into the Mask that night."[55]

Provenance records, material characteristics, and publication history, then, suggest a range of cultural uses for masque and readerly approaches to it. Masques that offer prefaces to readers provide another kind of evidence about masque reading, evidence that confirms both that masque writers considered readerly encounter to be significant and distinctive enough to address, and that masque reading cannot be flattened to a single mode or approach embraced by every receiver. We cannot delimit how early modern readers engaged any text, since reading always involves dynamic kinds of agency that cannot be predicted, controlled, or comprehensively recovered. After all, contemporary with the very masques examined here, the Star Chamber's prosecution of polemicist William Prynne indicted Prynne's failure to regard how independent and unpredictable readers can be, arguing that an author must be aware that "hee doth not accompanye his booke, to make his intencion knowne to all that reades it."[56]

But, even if we cannot determine with certainty how every reader would approach a given text, these masques do allow us to examine their inscriptions of various potential readerly responses. Campion's print masques yield particularly useful examples of multiple, overlaid inscriptions of possible readerly modes. Campion's amazingly dense performance detail suggests a reportage function (since it seems unlikely that anticipation of re-creating events in their homes could account for expected readerly interest in the information provided about, say, the optimal angle between sackbuts and shawms in the text of Lord Hay's 1607 wedding masque). To give only a small excerpt, Campion reports:

> The greate hall . . . received this division, and order: The upper part, where the cloth and chaire of State were plac'd, had scaffoldes and seates on eyther side continued to the skreene . . . the right hand whereof were consorted then Musitions, with Basse and Meane lutes, a Bandora, double Sackbott, and an Harpsicord, with two treble Violins; on the other side somewhat neerer the skreene were plac't 9 Violins and three Lutes; and to answere both the Consorts (as it were in a triangle) sixe Cornets, and sixe Chappell voyces, were seated almost right against them, in a place raised higher in respect of the pearcing sound of those Instruments; eighteen foote from the skreene, an other Stage was raised higher by a yearde then that which was prepared for dancing.[57]

Such detail certainly can offer readers a "you were there" experience. But journalistic re-creation is not the only function such passages can serve. Campion himself implies something perhaps more literary, indeed mock heroic, in the copiousness of his scene description: "As in battailes, so in all other actions that are to bee reported, the first, and most necessary part is the discription of the place, with his opportunities, and properties, whether they be naturall or artificiall."[58] The relationship this creates between the preface's narratorial persona and the reader is complex: shared wonder at the scale of the event, perhaps also a bit of amusement at its epic proportions, a briskly pedagogic moment (also a bit self-deprecating?) as the narrator instructs the reader in appropriate strategy for the chronicler.

Modes of readerly response are perhaps even more multiple in Campion's performance details from the masque itself. A passage describing a glorious stage effect gone awry has simultaneous dramatic, reportorial, and self-fashioning aspects for the authorial persona. At the end of the first formal dance, the text gives the sublime design wherein the five-voice, four-player band of "Sylvans" begins the "song of transformation" that will turn golden trees into masquers. As they sing,

> that part of the stage whereon the first trees stoode began to yeeld, and the three formost trees gently to sincke, and this was effected by an Ingin plac't under that stage. When the trees had sunke a yarde they cleft in three parts, and the Maskers appeared out of the tops of them; the trees were sodainly convayed away, the first three Maskers were raysed againe by the Ingin.[59]

Campion provides a marginal note, however: in performance the transformation was not quite so stunning as the one he has just helped his reader imagine. Instead, "either by the simplicity, negligence, or conspiracy of the painter, the passing away of the trees was somewhat hazarded; the patterne of them the same day having bene showne with much admiration, and the 9 trees beeing left unsett together even to the same night."[60] Providing this deflating news just after the reader has visualized a wonderful transformation accurately chronicles the performance event, to be sure. Beyond this, it may contribute to a sense—with which Ben Jonson would concur—of the reader's encounter with the performance as scripted being potentially cleaner than an audience's encounter with the hazards of theatrical realization. *Only* the reader, that is, "sees" the effect as it was meant to be instead of as it was. Additionally, whether amused or exasperated, Campion's comment creates a relationship between the authorial persona and the reader.

In some ways, reports dense with performance detail position the authorial persona as gracious dispenser of aristocratic information to the hungry reader. In other ways, the textual personae create an intimacy with the reader that can convey a solidarity of taste and understanding in the face of messy performance problems and aristocratic dimness. Thomas Dekker includes speeches in the *Magnificent Entertainment* quarto of Jacobean accession pageantry (1604), then concedes, in an afterword to the reader, that "Reader, you must understand, that a regard, being had that his Maiestie should not be wearied with teadious speeches: A great part of those which are in this Booke set downe, were left unspoken: So that thou doest here receive them as they should have bene delivered, not as they were."[61] Similarly, Jonson records in the *Hymenaei* text (1606) that "this song, of which, then, onely one *staffe* was sung; but because I made it both in *forme*, and *matter* to emulate that kind of *poeme*, which was call'd *Epithalamium* . . . I have here set it downe whole."[62] Both Dekker's and Jonson's readers, then, have access to an experience that the performance audience was not privileged to enjoy.[63]

George Chapman's *Memorable Maske* (one of the Inns of Court masques for the 1613 Palatine wedding, issued 1613 and 1614) directly addresses the reader with a complaint not about collaborators or other hitches in the performance, but rather about the process of book production. Breaking seamlessly into the description of the Temple of Honour (with no material signal of discontinuity), Chapman complains of not being given the opportunity to proof the printers' pages:

> These following should in duty haue had their proper places, after euery fitted speech of the Actors, but being preuented by the vnexpected haste of the Printer, which he neuer let me know, and neuer sending me a proofe, till he had past those speeches, I had no reason to imagine hee could haue been so forward. His fault is therefore to be supplied by the obseruation, and reference of the Reader, who will easily perceiue, where they were to bee inserted.[64]

Proffering an alliance with the clever reader against the unmannerly printer (whose unexpected haste suggests a publisher's sense of immediate consumer desire), Chapman produces a text that requires a certain amount of mental cutting and pasting to align descriptions with the apposite text. Similarly, readers need to cross-reference entrances as represented in the text with entrances as they must have occurred chronologically: "After the speech of *Plutus*, (who as you may see after, first entred), the middle part of the Rocke began to moue."[65] Interestingly, the 1614 edition does not make any of the changes Chapman claims to have wished to make in the first edition.[66]

If it requires readerly labor to parse the discontinuous text of the *Memorable Maske*, Campion produces a discontinuous text of a different kind when he prints music from the *Lord Hay's Masque* at the end of the text. Like the activity Chapman requires for any readers wishing fully to imagine the courtly performance, any of Campion's readers who wishes to hear or imagine the masque songs in their proper places must bookmark, index, and cross-reference the text. Campion also suggests that readers may use different parts of the text differently when he appends to the songs "the last three Ayres [which] were devised onely for dauncing, yet they are here set forth with words that they may be sung to the Lute or Violl."[67] Out of sequence, the songs serve not to inform the reader what happened at court, but rather to be more useful for domestic re-creation. Campion's redeploying music from court masques in domestic settings—a practice common far beyond Campion, as suggested by the number of instrumental pieces titled after masque productions in both lute and harpsichord collections—brings masque practice into private homes, just as printing moves masque from the Banqueting House into the hands of booksellers and book buyers. As material text, masque delivers courtly event into the active, judgmental purview of readers.[68]

The publication—the making public—of masque texts allows us to return with a fresh eye to the bibliographic aspect of masque that has been uniquely emphasized in previous scholarship: the court-distributed copies of printed masques. I have argued against assuming that printed masques were produced *only* for court distribution, but presentation of copies at masque events indubitably occurred. Since some presentation and souvenir copies of masque texts were manuscripts, we are now in a position to ask why others were not. If the print runs of some or all of the un-imprinted masques were indeed small, printing was not an economical choice; this suggests that we must consider the cultural as well as the economic logic of print presentation.[69] We must, that is, *read* the "printness" of print presentation. In the opposite situation of accounting for scribal duplication in circumstances wherein print texts also were available, Harold Love notes that scribal publication sometimes is preferred when it connotes "privileged information, not meant to be available to all enquirers," thus "bonding groups of like-minded individuals into a community."[70] Conversely, we might note, one available connotation of print duplication is its formal evocation of a more public world. The possibilities for debate encoded in masque texts suggest that print readers can use masque as the opportunity for evaluation and scrutiny as much as passive wonderment. We cannot determine the precise effects of some masques' being distributed in print while others were given out in manuscript (and some were not published at all), but neither could their primary producers or patrons. We *can* say with certainty that masque was one of the kinds of writing that fully inhabited both manuscript and print practice. When a masque is printed as a book, then, we might profitably consider how its material form might impact its meanings. We can investigate, in Love's terms, "how modes of communication contributed to the framing of myths of legitimacy"—and also, perhaps, how these modes contributed to undoing those frames.[71]

## NOTES

Research for this essay was undertaken with the support of fellowships from the Folger Shakespeare Library and the Huntington Library; I am most grateful for the financial support and the willingly shared expertise of the staffs of both libraries.

1. Anthony Sadler, *The Subjects Joy* (London: for James Davis, 1660). Sadler, whom Dale Randall calls a "rambling-headed divine," was the author of sundry eclectic texts. See Randall, *Winter Fruit: English Drama, 1642–1660* (Lexington: University Press of Kentucky, 1995), 369.

2. James Knowles, "The 'Running Masque' Recovered: A Masque for the Marquess of Buckingham (*c.* 1619–20)," *English Manuscript Studies* 8 (2000): 79. For an absolutist view of masque, see especially Jonathan Goldberg, *James I and the Politics of Literature: Jonson, Shakespeare, Donne, and Their Contemporaries* (Baltimore: Johns Hopkins University Press, 1983); Stephen Orgel, *The Illusion of Power: Political Theater in the English Renaissance* (Berkeley: University of California Press, 1975); and Graham Parry, *The Golden Age Restor'd: The Culture of the Stuart Court, 1603–42* (New York: St. Martin's, 1981). Martin Butler summarizes the usefulness of masque for New Historicist inquiry, which tends to emphasize masque's absolutist ideology, by noting that masque offers "works of art in which spectacle most emphatically became a tool of state . . . symptomatic of the ineluctable magnetism by which kingly absolutism pulled its age's representational forms into its own orbit." Martin Butler, "Courtly Negotiations," in *The Politics of the Stuart Court Masque*, ed. David Bevington and Peter Holbrook (Cambridge: Cambridge University Press, 1998), 21. For a less absolutist—but still firmly aristocratic—view of masque's functions, see especially Butler's *Theatre and Crisis, 1632–1642* (Cambridge: Cambridge University Press, 1984); Kevin Sharpe, *Criticism and Compliment: The Politics of Literature in the England of Charles I* (Cambridge: Cambridge University Press, 1987); and Knowles, whose work has elucidated many aspects of the life of the masque beyond the purview of court.

3. The major exception here would be Jonson scholars' interest in Jonsonian texts as projects that advance a model of authorial presence. In a way, this body of work also emphasizes "performance," although here the sense is metaphorical, by focusing on production instead of reception. See especially Joseph Loewenstein, "Printing and the

'Multitudinous Presse': The Contentious Texts of Jonson's Masques," in *Ben Jonson's 1616 Folio*, ed. Jennifer Brady and W. H. Herendeen (Newark: University of Delaware Press, 1991), 168–91; Loewenstein, "The Script in the Marketplace," in *Representing the English Renaissance*, ed. Stephen Greenblatt (Berkeley: University of California Press, 1988), 265–78; Loewenstein, *Jonson and Possessive Authorship* (Cambridge: Cambridge University Press, 2002); and Stephen Orgel, "Marginal Jonson," in Bevington and Holbrook, *Politics of the Stuart Court Masque*, 144–75

4. Sadler, *Subjects Joy*, B.

5. Ibid., 39.

6. Graham Parry, "Entertainments at Court," in *A New History of Early English Drama*, ed. John D. Cox and David Scott Kastan (New York: Columbia University Press, 1997), 202.

7. For a discussion of printing even earlier, Elizabethan pageants, see Wendy Wall, *The Imprint of Gender: Authorship and Publication in the English Renaissance* (Ithaca: Cornell University Press, 1993), 111–68.

8. *Neptune's Triumph* is one of the masques that has been assumed to have been printed privately, for limited distribution to its primary audience, rather than for sale to the public. As discussed later, however, these assumptions may be unfounded; moreover, even if it was not intended for public sale, copies made their way into commercial circulation.

9. Butler, "Courtly Negotiations," 35, 36. *Neptune's Triumph* was, according to its title page, "celebrated in a masque, at the Court, on the Twelfth night [January 6], 1623 [/4]."

10. One exceptional instance where masque texts have been quite thoroughly studied is the *Gypsies Metamorphosed*. This was scripted by Jonson in 1621, was offered to King James in a series of performances at different venues, and exists in an unusually large number and variety of manuscript copies (one example is discussed by Marta Straznicky in chapter 3 of this volume). The fact that W. W. Greg's and Dale Randall's books on this phenomenon are cited mostly by bibliographic scholars, and have not been greatly visible in studies of masque, demonstrates the emphasis of modern masque scholarship on performance, and the need for intersecting study of masque and the history of material texts. See Greg, *The "Masque of Gipsies" in the Burley, Belvoir, and Windsor Versions: An Attempt at Reconstruction* (London: Oxford University Press, 1952); and Randall, *Jonson's Gypsies Unmasked: Background and Theme of "The gypsies metamorphos'd"* (Durham: Duke University Press, 1975). Jerzy Limon, in *The Masque of Stuart Culture* (Newark: University of Delaware Press, 1990), does attend to material masque, but by way of postulating a distinction between "literary masque" and "masque-in-performance" that limits masque's possible meanings and uses to producers' intentions. Furthermore, Limon's argument rests on some questionable assumptions. For example, he follows Herford and Simpson's taking any entry in the Stationers' Register that predates performance to signal souvenir printing. There is indeed good evidence that texts often were distributed at performances, but not that this was the unique use to which such a printing was put; it is difficult, for instance, to see why imprint information would be offered, or licensing undertaken, if not to advance the commercial ends of directing purchasers to the booksellers or protecting publishers' rights. Furthermore, Limon claims that any masque giving its stage directions in the present tense is provided only for participants and audience members, with accounts of masque intended for publication serving only as records of a singular event that has already happened, indicated by past-tense verbs. This overreading of tense as evidence is shaky for several reasons. First, some masques were presented many times, in different relationship to issue date. Second, the different self-presentations of scrip-

tors such as Jonson, Daniel, and Campion suggest that we should read their tenses quite differently. The abstraction of the present tense may signal very different things for Jonson-the-king's-servant and for Daniel-beloved-of-poetry-readers. Finally, texts may not have been produced for such a segmented market as these notions assume.

11. Roger Chartier, "Texts, Printing, Readings," in *The New Cultural History*, ed. Lynn Hunt (Berkeley: University of California Press, 1989), 170.

12. Public discussion of matters of state was statutorily prohibited in Stuart England, although these laws were circumvented in various ways. On early "news," see especially David Zaret, *Origins of Democratic Culture: Printing, Petitions, and the Public Sphere in Early Modern England* (Princeton: Princeton University Press, 2000); Richard Cust, "News and Politics in Early-Seventeenth-Century England," *Past and Present* 112 (1986): 60–90; F. J. Levy, "How Information Spread among the Gentry, 1550–1640," *Journal of British Studies* 22 (1982): 20–24; and Joad Raymond, ed., *News, Newspapers, and Society in Early Modern Britain* (London: Cass, 1999). On relationships between early news and drama printing, see Alan Farmer (chapter 6) in this volume; F. J. Levy, "Staging the News," in *Print, Manuscript, and Performance: The Changing Relations of the Media in Early Modern England*, ed. Arthur F. Marotti and Michael D. Bristol (Columbus: Ohio State University Press, 2000), 252–78; and Stuart Sherman, "Eyes and Ears, News and Plays: The Argument of Ben Jonson's *Staple*," in *The Politics of Information in Early Modern Europe*, ed. Brendan Dooley and Sabrina Baron (London: Routledge, 2001), 23–40.

13. The nature and extent of civil society or a public sphere in seventeenth-century Britain is much contested, although most scholars agree that major changes occur between 1603 and 1660. See especially Craig Calhoun, ed., *Habermas and the Public Sphere* (Cambridge: MIT Press, 1992); Brendan Dooley, "News and Doubt in Early Modern Culture; or, Are We Having a Public Sphere Yet?" in Dooley and Baron, *Politics of Information*, 275–90; Zaret, *Origins*; Alexandra Halasz, *The Marketplace of Print: Pamphlets and the Public Sphere in Early Modern England* (Cambridge: Cambridge University Press, 1997); and Douglas Bruster, "The Structural Transformation of Print in Late Elizabethan England," in Marotti and Bristol, *Print, Manuscript, and Performance*, 49–89. Relationships between masque and civic pageants (both performances and books) constitute another important component of these interplays among court, city, and reading public; see Lauren Shohet, *Reading Masques: The English Masque and Public Culture in the Seventeenth Century* (New York: Oxford University Press, 2006).

14. Carleton to Chamberlain, January 7, 1605, in *State Papers of the Reign of James I, Great Britain, Public Records Office, The Complete Papers Domestic, 1509–1702* (hereafter *SP*) (Reading, England: Research Publications, 1993–1995), reel 14/12.

15. *SP* 14/95.

16. Brent to Carleton, February 21, 1618 (*SP* 14/96).

17. *Historical Manuscripts Collection* 12, appendix 2, pt. 2, 34, quoted in *Trois Masques à la cour de Charles 1er d'Angleterre*, intro., trans., and commentary Murray Lefkowitz (Paris : Éditions du Centre national de la recherche scientifique, 1970), 39.

18. Hans Robert Jauss, *Toward an Aesthetics of Reception*, trans. Timothy Bahti (Minneapolis: University of Minnesota Press, 1982), 19.

19. *The Complete Works of Ben Jonson*, ed. C. H. Herford and Percy and Evelyn Simpson, 11 vols. (Oxford: Clarendon, 1925–52), 7:186, 194.

20. For a more complete discussion of the critical elision of reception from masque studies, see Lauren Shohet, "Interpreting *The Irish Masque at Court* and in Print," *Journal for Early Modern Cultural Studies* 1, 2 (Fall–Winter 2001): 42–65.

21. Martin Butler and David Lindley, "Restoring Astraea: Jonson's Masque for the Fall of Somerset," *English Literary History* 61 (1994): 816.

22. Despite the technical illegality of disseminating parliamentary speeches, "separates" of these texts circulated widely from the time of Elizabeth onward; Notestein and Relf find that for the Stuart Parliaments, separates survive in "untold numbers." Wallace Notestein and Frances Relf, eds., *Commons Debates for 1629* (Minneapolis: University of Minnesota Press, 1921), xii.

23. Leeds Barroll, *Anna of Denmark, Queen of England: A Cultural Biography* (Philadelphia: University of Pennsylvania Press, 2001), 75, 86.

24. Ibid., 96.

25. Martin Butler, "Politics and the Masque: *Salmacida Spolia*," in *Literature and the English Civil War,* ed. Thomas Healy and Jonathan Sawday (Cambridge: Cambridge University Press, 1990), 60, 65.

26. The estimate of three thousand copies is G. E. Bentley's; see *The Jacobean and Caroline Stage*, 7 vols. (Oxford: Clarendon, 1941–68), 7:1162.

27. *The Complete Poetry of John Milton*, 2nd ed., ed. John T. Shawcross (New York: Anchor, 1971), ll. 968–69.

28. Lefkowitz, *Trois Masques*, 30.

29. Ibid. Whitelock claims that encoded critique was the intention of Attorney General Loy; Orgel and Strong are less certain that this attribution is accurate. See Stephen Orgel and Roy Strong, *Inigo Jones: The Theatre of the Stuart Court,* 2 vols. (Berkeley: University of California Press, 1973), 1:64–65.

30. Lawrence Venuti, "The Politics of Allusion: The Gentry and Shirley's *The Triumph of Peace,*" *English Literary Renaissance* 16 (1986): 182–205.

31. Samuel Daniel, *Complete Works in Verse and Prose*, ed. Alexander Grosart, 5 vols. (New York: Russell and Russell, 1963), 2:305.

32. *The Works of Thomas Campion: Complete Songs, Masques, and Treatises with a Selection of the Latin Verse*, ed. Walter R. Davis (Garden City, N.Y.: Doubleday, 1967), 249.

33. E. S. Leedham-Green writes that many early modern libraries contained more light literature (the category that would include drama) than they catalogue (*Books in Cambridge Inventories: Book-Lists from Vice-Chancellor's Court Probate Inventories in the Tudor and Stuart Periods*, 2 vols. [Cambridge: Cambridge University Press, 1986], 1:xiii). Heidi Brayman Hackel cautions that "the absence of a title from an inventory . . . does not necessarily indicate the absence of a book from a collection" ("'Rowme' of Its Own: Printed Drama in Early Libraries," in Cox and Kastan, *New History of Early English Drama*, 125). On ephemera, see also Margaret Spufford, *Small Books and Pleasant Histories: Popular Fiction and Its Readership in Seventeenth-Century England* (Athens: University of Georgia Press, 1982).

34. Harold Love, *The Culture and Commerce of Texts: Scribal Publication in Seventeenth-Century England* (Amherst: University of Massachusetts Press, 1998).

35. W. W. Greg, "Entrance, License, and Publication," *The Library*, ser. 4, 25 (1944–45): 1–22; Leo Kirschbaum, *Shakespeare and the Stationers* (Columbus: Ohio State University Press, 1955). See also Maureen Bell, "Entrance in the Stationers' Register," *The Library*, ser. 6, 16 (1994): 50–54.

36. Peter W. M. Blayney, "The Publication of Playbooks," in Cox and Kastan, *New History of Early English Drama*, 397.

37. Samuel Daniel, *Vision of the 12. Goddesses* (London: T[homas] C[reede] for Simon Waterson, 1604), A3.

38. John Benson registered *Gipsies* on February 20, 1640, just before the folio appeared; Crooke and Sergier registered *Augurs, Time Vindicated, Neptune's Triumph,* and *Pan's Anniversary* ("with sundry Elegies and other Poems by Benjamin Johnson") on March 20, 1640—even though publisher Richard Bishop held a competing claim to

these through partial right to Jonson's *Workes* which Bishop had purchased from Elizabeth Stansby the previous year. See Edward Arber, ed., *A Transcript of the Registers of the Company of Stationers of London, 1554–1640*, 5 vols. (London: Privately printed, 1894), 4:474, 434.

39. Evidence for dating presented in W. W. Greg, *A Bibliography of the English Printed Drama to the Restoration*, 4 vols. (London: Bibliographical Society, 1939–59), 1:310. For details on establishing that dating, see R. B. McKerrow, *An Introduction to Bibliography for Literary Students*, intro. David McKitterick (1927; reprint, Bury St. Edmunds: St. Paul's Bibliographies, 1994), 192–93.

40. Stephen Harrison, *The Arch's of Triumph* (London: John Windet, 1604). This was "printed by John Windet" and "sold at the author's house in Lime-Street." The reprint is undated; Greg suggests 1610–15 as the likely range of dates based on the years of activity for bookseller George Humble, cited in the imprint.

41. For instance, what, if anything, should we make of some masques' inclusion among poetic works (such as Shirley's 1646 *Poems &c.*, which includes the 1634 *Triumph of Peace)* and others among dramatic (such as Beaumont and Fletcher's *Comedies and Tragedies*)? Marketing probably accounts for some of this: the kinds of works for which a given writer is known, and the somewhat different market connotations of the more culturally privileged genre of poetry versus "ephemeral" drama. Francis Johnson notes that "poetical works by well-known authors seem definitely to have sold at prices above the average" ("Notes on English Retail Book-Prices, 1550–1640," *The Library*, ser. 5, 2 [1950]: 91). Investigating this would require locating each scriptor's self-positioning in the realm of letters; Daniel, for example, appears invested in thinking of himself as a poet.

42. James Knowles, "'To raise a house of better frame': Jonson's Cecilian Entertainments," in *Patronage, Power, and Culture: The Early Cecils, 1558–1612*, ed. Pauline Croft (New Haven: Yale University Press, 2002), 181–98.

43. Nicolas Kiessling, *The Library of Robert Burton* (Oxford: Oxford Bibliographical Society, 1988), viii.

44. Philip Massinger, Thomas Middleton, and William Rowley, *The Excellent Comedy, called The Old Law* (London: for Edward Archer, 1656). The catalogue is on a separate quire, marked $(a)_1$, and its presence is signaled on the book's title page.

45. Interestingly, some entries give authors, while others do not. Most of the masques listed in the catalogue with no authorial attribution certainly have authors given on their title pages (and/or who were common knowledge, as in the Jonson pieces), so this information was available. Perhaps the included author names (which perhaps disproportionately represent playwrights active later in the century) indicate market appeal.

46. I owe this observation to James Knowles.

47. Johnson, "Notes on English Retail Book-Prices," 93. Blayney challenges many of Johnson's price estimates based on the belief that Johnson mistook wholesale for retail prices in sellers' price lists, but Blayney's reservations would not be relevant to the masques Johnson lists because all masques Johnson examined came from the private collection of Humphrey Dyson, with listed *purchase* prices.

48. Natascha Würzbach, *The Rise of the English Street Ballad, 1550–1650*, trans. Gayna Walls (Cambridge: Cambridge University Press, 1990).

49. The majority of books whose provenance we can trace belonged to higher-status major collectors, whose records are relatively more recoverable. But scholars who study seventeenth-century English reading more generally report that during this period "reading habits are not stratified into peasant, bourgeois and gentry." T. A. Birrell, "Reading as Pastime: The Place of Light Literature in Some Gentlemen's Libraries of the Seventeenth Century," in *Property of a Gentleman: The Formation, Organisation,*

*and Dispersal of the Private Library, 1620–1920*, ed. Robin Myers and Michael Harris (Winchester: St. Paul's Bibliographies, 1991), 113.

50. The purchase is recorded in Paulet's account book, Hampshire Records Office MS 44M69/E4/40. The same day Paulet purchased this book, the "Jesuytes Gospell," and the "apologie for the murther of the french king"; he records only the total purchase price for the three books as 12*d*. I am grateful to Eric Lindquist for sharing this information in advance of the publication of his edition of Paulet's papers.

51. Burton inscribed the British Library quarto of *Fortunate Isles*; for Browne, see C. E. McGee, ed., "*Cupid's Banishment (1618),*" *Renaissance Drama* 19 (1988): 227–64.

52. Folger MS J.a.1. For discussion of this manuscript, see Malone Society *Collections*, vol. 14 (Oxford: Oxford University Press, 1988).

53. Campion, *Works,* 235.

54. Daniel, *Complete Works*, 305.

55. Jervoise of Herriard Park MSS 44M69/F2/15/1, Hampshire Record Office. I thank Eric Lindquist for this reference.

56. *Documents Relating to the Prosecution of William Prynne in 1634 and 1637*, ed. S. R. Gardiner (London: Camden Society, 1877), 14, 16.

57. Campion, *Works,* 211.

58. Ibid. Campion may also envisage a readerly audience that overlapped with the readers of his musical treatises, who might have been interested in the acoustical issues addressed in the staging details.

59. Ibid., 221–22.

60. Ibid., 222. In the quarto, this note is in the margin of $C_3$, in italics. Its typeface and position on the page align it with earlier notes glossing mythological emblems. This information, that is, meets the eye in the same format as notes on, for example, Diana: "The Moone and Queen of Virgins, as saide to be regent & Impress of Night, and is therefore by Night defending her quarrel for the loss of the bride, her Virgin" (B4).

61. *The Dramatic Works of Thomas Dekker*, ed. Fredson Bowers, 4 vols. (Cambridge: Cambridge University Press, 1953–61), 2:303.

62. Herford and Simpson, *Works of Ben Jonson*, 7:225.

63. William Davenant included "songs" "to be printed, not sung" in *Salmacida Spolia* (*Dramatic Works,* ed. James Maidment and W. H. Logan, 5 vols. [Edinburgh: Paterson, 1872–74], 2.320). Similarly, Chapman appends a thematically appropriate but non-performative "Hymne to Hymen" to the *Memorable Maske* quarto.

64. George Chapman, *The Memorable Maske* (London: G. Eld, for George Norton, [1613]), B4v–C.

65. Ibid., a2.

66. The 1613 is STC 4981, with the address to the reader on a1v–a2; the 1614 is STC 4982, with address to the reader on C2v.

67. Campion, *Works,* 230. This section of the text also includes a song from the *Somerset Masque.*

68. Note Daniel on the readerly encounter with print as censurable, discussable, and contentious: "the way of censure whereunto I see all publications (of what nature soever) are liable" (*Complete Works*, 305–6).

69. Peter Blayney states that scribal duplication was less expensive than print duplication for runs of under a hundred copies or so (personal communication, June 2001).

70. Love, *Culture and Commerce*, 177.

71. Ibid., 157–58.

NINE

# Inky Kin: Reading in the Age of Gutenberg Paternity

DOUGLAS A. BROOKS

> A madman is not only a man who thinks he is a rooster, but also a man who thinks he is directly a man—that is to say, this material body he feels directly as his own.
>
> Slavoj Žižek, *The Plague of Fantasies*

Given the focus in this part of the book on the intersections between dramas—many of which were written to be viewed in performance, not read[1]—and the early modern publishing industry, I want to concentrate in this chapter on a play that we might agree is rather readerly: Richard Brome's *The Antipodes.*[2]

## Needing Spectacles

The plot of Brome's play is centered largely on a character named Peregrine whose pathological obsession with reading travel narratives began, as his long-worrying father (Joyless) makes clear, when he was just a child:

*Joyless:* In tender years he always lov'd to read
Reports of travels and of voyages.
And when young boys like him would tire themselves
With sports and pastimes and restore their spirits
Again by meat and sleep, he would whole days
And nights (sometimes by stealth) be on such books
As might convey his fancy all round the world.

(1.1.31–37)

Now that Peregrine is a grown man "Of five and twenty" years his single-minded passion for reading threatens to undermine the dynastic future of the family name, for he has shown no conjugal interest in Martha, the wife he married "divers years since." Peregrine, to borrow a coinage of Jeffrey Masten's, prefers textual intercourse.[3] In fact, so profound is his marital negligence that Martha is naïvely compelled to interrogate another woman about the mysteries of procreation:

*Martha:* Pray tell me, for I think Nobody hears us,
How came you by your babes? I cannot think
Your husband got them you.
. . . . . . . . . . . . . . . . . . . . . . . . . . . . . . . . . . . . . . . .
For were I now to die, I cannot guess
What a man does in child-getting. I remember
A wanton maid once lay with me, and kiss'd
And clipp'd and clapp'd me strangely, and then wish'd
That I had been a man to have got her with child.
What must I then ha' done, or, good now, tell me,
What has your husband done to you?
(1.1.245–47, 251–57)

Certainly this passage has a homoerotic subtext which, in a different critical context, would be worth exploring; but my immediate interest in Martha's lack of schooling in the facts of life is somewhat superficial. Peregrine's bookish interests apparently interfere with his conjugal duties. Indeed, given the nature of Joyless's concern and the seriousness of Martha's reproductive dilemma, it could be argued that here, near the end of act 1, scene 1, reading has disrupted the relationship between a father and son, and threatens to prevent the son from ever becoming a father.

Reading and husbanding, *The Antipodes* suggests, appear to be incompatible activities—an incompatibility first intimated (in English at least) in the prologue to the *Wife of Bath's Tale* and currently evidenced by the correlation in many societies between low literacy rates and high birthrates. All is not lost, though, for in its proto-psychoanalytic wisdom, *The Antipodes* offers up a play-within-the-play as the remedy for Peregrine's reading disorder. This dramatic strategy will enable Peregrine to exorcise Mandeville's ghost on stage and to reenact his marriage to Martha as a courtly ceremony in which a royal heir is at stake in their coupling. Freud attended a production of an earlier London drama that featured a play-within-the-play and found Oedipus; Peregrine goes to a production of *The Antipodes* and finds Martha: the potency of a book's impact on his impotence is significantly dissipated once the curative power of performance is brought to bear on the specific circumstances of his malady: drama as Viagra. If only Hamlet had been less well read . . .[4]

In *The Antipodes*, then, Brome would seem to be pitting ink against kin, book against play, reading against playing, the closet against the stage—and for Peregrine, hanging in the balance of this conflict is his future as a husband and potential father. By act 4, spectators/readers of the play who might side with reading in this contest are poised to win, because Peregrine's peculiar madness appears to be contagious and spreading. Inevitably conflating us with Peregrine, a stage direction near the beginning of the act signals—to the play's audience and the play-within-the-play's audience—the following literatory event:

> *Enter an* OLD WOMAN, *reading* [*a handbill*];
> *to her young* MAID [*with a book*].
>
> (4.1.5–6)

This stage direction, this textual dumbshow-in-a-glance that silently disembodies a bit of acting and translates it onto the printed page for a future reading audience, constitutes something like a microcosm of the entire play inasmuch as it suggests the confrontation between watching a play and reading a text. (The bracketed insertions made by the play's editors further clarify the nature of the confrontation, inasmuch as they specify two very different types of texts: the former, indicating a printed handbill used by theaters to advertise plays, belongs to the world of the stage; the latter, indicating a book, belongs to the world of the page.) The Doctor, the most knowledgeable member of the-play-within-the-play's audience, indicates that something important is happening at this point when he tells Peregrine, "Stand close, sir, and observe" (4.1.7). Indeed, the moment the old woman begins to speak, one of the play's central concerns becomes legible:

> What though
> My sight be gone beyond the reach of spectacles
> In any print but this, and though I cannot—
> No, no, I cannot—read your meditations,
> [*strikes down* MAID's *book*]
> Yet I can see the royal game play'd over and over,
> And tell which dog does best, without my spectacles.
> And though I could not, yet I love the noise;
> The noise revives me, and the Bear-garden scent
> Refresheth much my smelling.
>
> (4.1.17–23)

An old woman who can barely see to read anything smaller than the large—presumably, black-letter—type of printed handbills luxuriates in the fleshy entertainments that often preceded the performance of a play, while a maid who has presumably not yet luxuriated in the flesh prefers a book.[5]

The opposition that structures this scene, as we might expect by now, is stage versus page, the comparative quietude of reading versus the smell and noise of dying bears at the playhouses. Once upon a time, of course, the distinction between books and dying animals was less clear. After the invention of the codex a century or so before the Christian era, this new technology served for nearly 1,500 years as the main point of convergence between flesh and book. Indeed, it must have been very difficult to ignore the embodiment of the word when using a parchment codex: the difference in color between the flesh side and the hair side of any given page served as a constant reminder that one was handling the skin of a dead animal.[6] For Peregrine and the play's audience, however, reading and theater also meet in the two meanings of the word "spectacles" (staged entertainments and lenses for correcting imperfect vision); and it is hard not to think of the rusted outlines of eyeglasses that have been preserved on a few pages of some 1623 Shakespeare folios—the book that contributed so much to seventeenth-century efforts to translate Shakespeare's plays from the stage to the page.[7]

Subsequently, another character in the play-within-the-play offers a different version of the juxtaposition implied by the old woman's reference to spectacles:

> *Gentleman:* Nay, prithee, be not angry.
> [*arranges cloak on* SERVINGMAN's arm]
> Thus; and now
> Be sure you bear't at no such distance but
> As't may be known appendix to this book.
>
> (4.1.44–47)

Books prevent Martha from bearing children, and an old woman prefers dying bears to books. Here, in something like an acting tutorial that begins with the Gentleman instructing his servingman to "Publish it, sirrah. Oh, presumptuous slave, / Display it on one arm!" (4.1.42–43), bearing a cloak is linked to a textual apparatus (appendix) that is also a body part. Furthermore, in the quoted passage I think we can glimpse what is perhaps an erudite allusion to a key moment in the New Testament when books, cloaks, and flesh share a page. Remarkably, the only Greek writer of the first century AD to mention the parchment codex is Paul in 2 Timothy 4:13: "The cloak that I left at Troas with Carpus, when thou comest, bring with thee, and the books, but especially the parchments [*membranas*]."[8] Paul's choice of words here to refer to the recent invention, the Latinate *membranas* phonetically transcribed into Greek,[9] begins to suggest why shortly after its introduction the parchment codex generated a number of rhetorical, metaphorical, and conceptual convergences between the body and the book.[10]

As the play written for the sake of curing Peregrine of his compulsive reading habits proceeds, references to various forms of reading and reading materials abound. Nevertheless, since reading is what ails him, it is only fitting that in the end, the theater carries the day. Both the play-within-the-play and the play that houses it conclude with a kind of mini-masque in which Dischord and its faction run amok for a few moments before the approach of Harmony and its followers abruptly ends their brief, chaotic reign. Accordingly, the frame play ends with an epilogue that brings the doctor and his patient back on stage to tout one other Viagric element of the theater that will presumably ensure that Peregrine finds his way back to Martha's bed after three years of marital celibacy—the audience:

*Doctor:* Whether my cure be perfect yet or no
It lies not in my doctorship to know.
Your approbation may more raise the man
Than all the College of Physicians can,
And more health from your fair hands may be won
Than by the strokings of the seventh son.
*Peregrine:* And from our travels in th'Antipodes
We are not yet arriv'd from off the seas;
But on the waves of desp'rate fears we roam
Until your gentler hands do waft us home.

Nearly twenty-five years earlier another adventurer whose love of books and excessive reading got him into trouble similarly appealed to an audience to help him return home:

Let me not,
Since I have my Dukedom got,
And pardon'd the deceiuer, dwell

In this bare Island, by your Spell,
But release me from my bands
With the helpe of your good hands.[11]

In an early study of the shifting relations between the stage and the page in the early modern period, Doris Fenton argues that a rupture of sorts occurred in 1616 which bifurcated the first era of the professional theater in England (1576 to 1642) into two distinct phases. Focusing on the presence of direct audience addresses in dramatic texts, Fenton notes that approximately two-thirds of the extant drama written before 1616 featured such addresses. After 1616 the use of such addresses by playwrights declined steeply, a change Fenton attributes to an evolving textual self-consciousness in the early modern English theater industry.[12] Thus, while these two direct theatrical addresses are thematically very similar, in light of Fenton's analysis we might expect them to be somehow different. In fact, there is one significant difference between the two plays' epilogues that is entirely consistent with Fenton's findings. In the earlier (pre-1616) play, when Prospero addresses the theater audience he gets the last word; in the latter, Peregrine's address to the audience is not the final direct address of the play. Rather, in the dramatic text that has come down to us, someone else addresses a very different kind of audience, and, in doing so, somewhat undermines the primary argument of the play that has just come to an end. As Peregrine heads off stage to give his poor wife her first—long overdue—lesson in the facts of life, the author of the play that dramatizes their bizarre story steps forward on the page to give readers the facts of the book:

> Courteous Reader,
> You shall find in this book more than was presented upon the stage, and left out of the presentation for superfluous length (as some of the players pretended). I thought good all should be inserted according to the allowed original, and as it was at first intended for the Cockpit stage, in the right of my most deserving friend Mr William Beston, unto whom it properly appertained. And so I leave it to thy perusal as it was generally applauded and well acted at Salisbury Court.
> Farewell,
> Ri. Brome

Published for the first time in 1640, some two years after it was initially performed, the quarto text of *The Antipodes* ends with the name of its author signing (in print!) an address he has written for his prospective readers. And there's the rub: immediately after the theater has apparently succeeded in persuading Peregrine to give up his travel books, Brome tries to persuade future readers of Peregrine's plight to purchase a book about traveling by claiming it is superior to the version that was presented on stage. Players left things out of the "presentation" because they decided it was of a "superfluous length"; the occasion of publication has enabled the author to reassert his control over the play and restore it "according to the allowed original." Thus, a play about the perils of reading for paternity and the curative powers of the theater will be reinvigorated for readers not long after its life on stage has come to an end. I will have more to say with regard to what *The Antipodes* may be reporting to us about drama and reading as the first era of the professional theater in England is about to be eclipsed. For now, however, I want briefly to sketch out a historical context for understanding Brome's reader address, as well as the printed play's other paratexts.

## The Place of the Page

Adrian Johns has observed that "when early modern readers determined a book not to be worthy of credit, they could do so on a number of grounds. It was in the attribution of "piracy," however, that the issues of credibility and print particularly converged."[13] Focusing more specifically on issues of drama publication, I have argued elsewhere that the construction of individual authorship within the largely collaborative conditions of the early modern theater frequently necessitated the production of an oppositional relation between the stage and the page, and that one precedent for this effort can be found in strategies used by printers to distinguish between their texts and those of a competitor.[14] As early as 1590, Richard Jones, the printer of a quarto edition of Marlowe's two *Tamburlaine the Great* plays, had introduced a comparably oppositional structure in his note "To the Gentlemen Readers: and others that take pleasure in reading Histories"—though the opposition was no longer between himself and another printer he was accusing of piracy. Rather, a new opposition had emerged that is still viable fifty years later when Brome signs off on the publication of his playscript. Hoping that his printed edition of the plays "wil be now no lesse acceptable vnto you to read after your serious affaires and studies, then they haue bene (lately) delightful for many of you to see, when the same were shewed in London vpon stages," Jones proceeds to describe how publication has enabled him to take a few authorial liberties with a work he didn't write:

> I haue (purposely) omitted and left out some fond and friuolous Iestures, digressing (and in my poore opinion) far vnmeet for the matter, which I thought, might seeme more tedious vnto the wise, than any way els to be regarded, though (happly) they haue bene of some vaine co[n]ceited fondlings greatly gaped at, what times they were shewed vpon the stage in their graced deformities.[15]

Both Jones and Brome claim that the published play is to be distinguished from the play that was previously performed, though they approach the distinction very differently: Jones takes things out, Brome puts things back.

In general, early addresses "To the Reader" reveal that printers and readers, if not yet authors, valued authentic and reader-friendly texts. That all of these early addresses preoccupied with textual matters were written by printers[16] and directed at readers seems only logical. And yet, the fact that playwrights eventually took over the self-consciously important textual space of the reader address indicates that the space could be appropriated[17]—an appropriation that points to a significant transition in the history of the relation between the early modern stage and page. Jonson, as has often been remarked, substantially reinforced the oppositional relation between the theater and the text in the preface to *Sejanus* by differentiating between "this Booke" and the play "which was acted on the publike Stage." Quite aware, like Jones, of the transformative power of publication, Jonson did not disguise his preference for print.

No surprise then that Jonson was one of the first English playwrights to commandeer the space of the address previously occupied by printers in the note "To the Reader" included almost as an afterthought to the 1602 quarto edition of *Poetaster or The Arraignment*:

> Here (Reader) in place of the Epilogue, was meant to thee an Apology from the Author, with his reasons for the publishing of this booke: but (since he is no lesse restrain'd, then thou depriv'd of it, by Authoritie) hee praies thee to thinke charitably of what thou hast read, till thou maist heare him speake what hee hath written.[18]

Is this the printer speaking on behalf of Jonson, as the location of the address after the main text would suggest, or is this Jonson speaking on his own behalf in the third person within a discursive textual space previously reserved for printers? Either way the address captures and frames a threshold moment in Jonson's career as it constitutes the first time his authorship will be linked to the purposeful publication of a play.

What I hope this brief digression on the space of the dramatic author's address suggests is that in 1640 Brome's address to the "courteous reader," appearing at the end of the book, is something of an anomaly. Indeed, its colonization of the space usually reserved at this point in the history of printed dramatic texts for the transcription of a theatrical epilogue makes the text's privileging of its current reader over its prior spectator, the printed play over the performed play, all the more obvious. If, following Fenton, we credit this privileging of the book over the theater to an increasing text-consciousness, the symptoms of which—according to her analysis—can be clearly recognized after 1616, then perhaps the published text of *The Antipodes* offers up another clue or so about the drama and its readers.

For at least a century, the publication of Jonson's folio *Workes* in 1616 has been viewed by scholars of Renaissance drama as constituting a profound shift in the complex relation between playhouse and printing house in England.[19] During the past few decades, the 1616 folio has figured prominently in studies of early modern authorship, often being treated as a singular achievement of emergent authorial awareness—especially with regard to the meaning of print.[20] Summing up the current scholarly consensus on the Jonson folio, Elizabeth Hanson observes, "In many recent accounts of his career, Jonson's location of his authorship in the printed book heralds the proprietary author, who is linked through implication and theoretical filiation to possessive individualism, modern subjectivity, and bourgeois culture."[21] By 1640, when Brome's play was first published, the author who had done so much to transform acting scripts into reading texts had been dead for three years.[22] And yet, in the printed text of *The Antipodes* (written a year before Jonson's death), in the space so frequently reserved for the author's address to the reader, the following opening lines of a commendatory verse appear instead:

> To censuring Critics on the approved Comedy,
> *The Antipodes*
> Jonson's Alive! The world admiring stands,
> And to declare his welcome there, shake hands,
> Apollo's pensioners may wipe their eyes
> And stifle their abortive elegies;

> Taylor his goose quill may abjure again,
> And to make paper dear, scribbling refrain;
> For sure there's cause of neither.

Thus, a play whose title, at least for readers familiar with Mandeville's writings, promises travel to exotic lands begins with that most anti-theatricalist and bookish of playwrights, then refers to another rather bookish writer—John Taylor, who, like Peregrine, was also obsessed with a set of travel narratives—and even offers up a partial list of the tools of the writer's trade. Only in the last line of this verse, some fifteen lines later—after we have been told to "praise each line / Of his *Volpone*, *Sejanus*, and *Catiline*"—do we learn that Jonson is dead, but still "sojourns in his Brome's *Antipodes*." In a subsequent commendatory verse, the next and last page of textual apparatus before the "Dramatis Personae," the writer actually seems to have come down with the same illness that threatens the well-being of the play's hero. Addressed this time "To the Author on his Comedy, / *The Antipodes,*" rather than to the play's "censuring Critics," the verse begins:

> Steer'd by the hand of Fate o'er swelling seas,
> Methought I landed on th'Antipodes,
> Where I was straight a stranger; for 'tis thus:
> Their feet do tread against the tread of us.
> My scull mistook; thy book, being in my hand,
> Hurried my soul to th'Antipodean strand,
> Where I did feast my fancy and mine eyes
> With such variety of rarities.

What performance, one wonders, might cure this poor reader of his affliction? Like Peregrine, he seems to suffer from an ailment that—with a nod to Edward Said—we might call the "textliness of the world." Nor, for that matter, do the writers of these verses indicate that they have seen a performance of the play, or even that the play was ever performed. Indeed, for both writers, *The Antipodes* is always already a book to be read, and the only reference to its stage life—"generally applauded and well-acted at Salisbury Court"—appears, strangely enough, as the last line of the book, that is, the last line of Brome's address "to the reader."

When, however, we move just beyond the printed text of Brome's play to the broader historical conditions under which it appeared, then it becomes obvious that the plot's privileging of performance over reading, its faith in the curative powers of the theater, specifically the capacity to bring a life-affirming conjugal harmony to lives threatened by discord, is either something of a last hurrah or a fantasy of one. First, there is the fact that when Brome was writing the play, the theaters were closed by an outbreak of the plague, and remained closed from May 1636 to October 1637. It is a little hard to consider the play's promotion of a theatrical remedy without also recalling that it was written during a time when the theater represented a particularly dangerous site for the spread of contagion. Then, no more than four years after the play was performed in 1638 and two years after it was published, the performance of plays in London's theaters would for all practical purposes be banned for the next two decades. Having gotten his cure while the getting was still good, Peregrine couldn't have had better timing. For the theater, however, time was about to run out.

Moreover, the play's narrative privileging of the theater over the book comes, paradoxically enough, at a time when printed dramatic texts were poised to eclipse performed play scripts in prominence. One clue to the changing status of printed drama as the closing of the theaters forced plays back into the closet can be gleaned from the status of dramatic authorship at that moment. If, as seems clear from a number of recent studies,[23] dramatic texts were more likely to be author-ized when they made their way from the playhouse to the printing house, and by extension into the hands of readers, then it stands to reason that what was good for the early modern publishing industry may also have been good for authors and their readers. An examination of Stationers' Register entries for dramatic texts bears this out. Only during the last full decade of the professional stage (1631–40), when the publication of dramatic texts soars, does the number of attributed entries (ninety-one) surpass the number of anonymous entries (sixty-two). Such an abrupt increase in the recording of authors' names by the Stationers' Company suggests two important concomitant developments with regard to the relationship between the theater and the book that the printed text of Brome's play dramatizes: not only had the authorship of dramatic texts become an important factor in the regulation of their publication, but also the locus of a play's authority had shifted from the collaborative conditions of the theater to the individualized agency of the author—an agency that was much better suited to the marketing practices of the book trade. And the newly heightened status of the dramatic author would only be enhanced during the next two decades when the closing of the theaters in 1642 temporarily foreclosed future links between a given play and a given playing company and/or playhouse. In short, the time was very right for Brome to place an author's address to the readers of *The Antipodes* after the two epilogues directed at an audience that was about to be rendered obsolete. Indeed, that the play ends with an account of its passage from the playhouse to the printing house by instructing us first about what audiences must do to make the play's elixir of love fully function, then about what the author had to do to make the play suitable for readers, seems remarkably prescient.

I turn now from what the published text of *The Antipodes* and its paratexts say about the relation between stage and page to the complex links between books, reproduction, and paternity—links that, as I noted earlier, Brome's play suggestively thematizes.

## After Death Do Us Part

At an important early moment in his *Mechanick Exercises, or the Doctrine of Handy-Works Applied to the Art of Printing*, published in London in 1683, Joseph Moxon offers a detailed description of "the office of the Master Printer." While informing the reader that "a Master Printer provides a fount (or fund) of letter of all bodies," Moxon suddenly expresses an uncharacteristic bit of uncertainty in the following note: "It is not clear whether our word 'body' or its French and German equivalents (corps, Kegel) first attached themselves to the dimension of the type or to the part of the mold which determines it."[24] The history of writing technologies has always been deeply engaged with the body, from the time of the earliest invention when clay served as both the material base of cuneiform and the matter out of which the Sumerian gods fashioned the first humans in the earliest extant creation narratives, to the January 2004 issue of *Wired*—a magazine devoted to the computer industry—which features as its "exclusive" womb-red cover story "The Making of a Human Clone: 7 Days Inside a Maverick Embryo Lab."[25] And, of course, the early modern printer relied on a matrix (a womb) to produce type, each of which—Moxon's illustrations of type make clear—is a little human. As Margreta de Grazia observes, "Typefounders and printers have always regarded the single moveable type character as a human being standing erect, each type having a body, a face, beard, neck, shoulder, back, belly, and feet."[26] The fact that all of these erect beings have beards suggests that typefounders' wombs carried only sons to term.

Whereas manuscript culture largely relied on a primal scene of sorts in which the scribe's pen had its way with the virginal page, each printed book was a collection of memories of inked bodies no longer present: an originary absence that, grammatologically speaking, underwrote a graphic presence and thus made the early modern book a kind of mausoleum or monument. The early modern London book trade was a deadly business, one that traded in bodies and orphaned texts. Some acknowledgment of the macabre, embodied nature of print is articulated in the elegiac pronouncements of John Heminge and Henry Condell in their address "To the great variety readers" of the 1623 Shakespeare folio. Lamenting "that the Author himselfe had [not] liv'd to have set forth, and overseen his owne writings," Heminge and Condell offer their readers Shakespeare's remains "cur'd, and perfect of their limbes."[27]

More than a decade before his death would be transformed into the occasion of his material birth as an author, Shakespeare briefly alluded to some of the conceptual systems that made such a transformation possible, and he did so in the context of an orphaned character named, appropriately enough, Posthumous. A British war hero in the conflict with Rome who has been mistakenly imprisoned by British forces, Posthumous falls asleep and dreams one of the strangest bits of stage business in Shakespeare's canon. In the dream, his family, beginning with the dead father he never knew, assembles around him, bemoans his suffering, then appeals to Jupiter to "take off his miseries" (*Cymbeline,* TLN 3120). That relief, when promptly doled out by Jupiter, comes oddly enough in the form of a tablet given to the apparitional family with the instructions that they lay it "vpon his breast" (TLN 3145). Although we may pass over the subtle connection here between the resurrection of the dead and the miraculous appearance of a text, Posthumous himself compels us to look more closely. Upon waking up from a dream peopled by the father who died while he was in the womb, the mother from whom he was untimely ripped, and Lucina, the goddess of childbirth, Posthumous asserts, "Sleepe, thou hast been a Grandsire, and begot / A Father to me" (TLN 3160–61). Upon discovering the tablet a few lines later, he remarks, "A book? O rare one, / Be not, as is our fangled world, a Garment / Nobler then that it covers" (TLN 3170–72).

Given that the play in which Posthumous sleeps and wakes is set in Roman Britain at the time of Christ's birth, then the book that so delights him must be a rare one indeed, a very recent technological innovation known as the parchment codex, which, as I noted earlier, was referred to by Paul as "membranas." And yet, his fear that the noble cover of the book passed on to him from beyond the grave belies its less than noble contents suggests that Posthumous has been compelled to ventriloquize a characteristically Shakespearean anachronism. Evidence from extant codices and paintings of their earliest users indicates that the noble cover was a later fashion development in the history of scribal publication. Thus, I suspect that Shakespeare had books produced and sold by London stationers in mind when he wrote those lines.

I rely on this suspicion to shift attention briefly from Posthumous's concern with noble covers to the paratexts of a self-avowed crude book that would have been very much at home on Peregrine's bookshelf next to his copy of *Mandeville's Travels*. The book I have in mind is the 1611 edition of *Coryats Crudities.*[28] It is not difficult to see in the *Crudities* an act of "possessive authorship" that Joseph Loewenstein attributes in its purest form to Jonson. Rather, we need only to juxtapose the title page of the 1611 *Crudities* (fig. 9-1) with the title page of the 1616 *Workes* (fig. 9-2) to sense that Jonson must have figured out something about authorial self-promotion in print from this earlier publishing venture. Furthermore, William Stansby, who printed the 1611 *Crudities*, would subsequently be called upon to print the 1616 Jonson folio.

What interests me most about the 1611 edition of the *Crudities* here, however, is what appears on its second title page (fig. 9-3), a page that, I want to suggest, played an extraordinarily important role in generating Thomas Coryate's authorial persona. To begin with, the second page is the first to indicate the details of the text's production: "London: Printed by W.S. Anno Domini 1611." Then there are the opening lines of the page, which inform readers that this is not an edition of a text by a single author but rather a volume that gathers related texts by more than one author. In much the same way that Jonson, Shakespeare, and Beaumont and Fletcher will be author-ized through the publication of collections (even multiauthor collections in the case of both the Shakespeare folio and the Beaumont and Fletcher folio), Coryate makes his grand authorial debut within a hodgepodge of travel narratives. But what is particularly striking about this collection is how the contents of the volume are narrated: "THREE CRVDE VEINES ARE PRESENTED IN This BOOKE following (besides the fore-said CRVDITIES) no lesse flowing in the body of the BOOKE, then the CRVDITIES *themselues, two of* Rhetoricke and one of POESIE." Decades before William Harvey theorized the circulation of the

FIG. 9-1. Thomas Coryate, *Coryats Crudities* (London, 1611), frontispiece. By permission of The Huntington Library, San Marino, California.

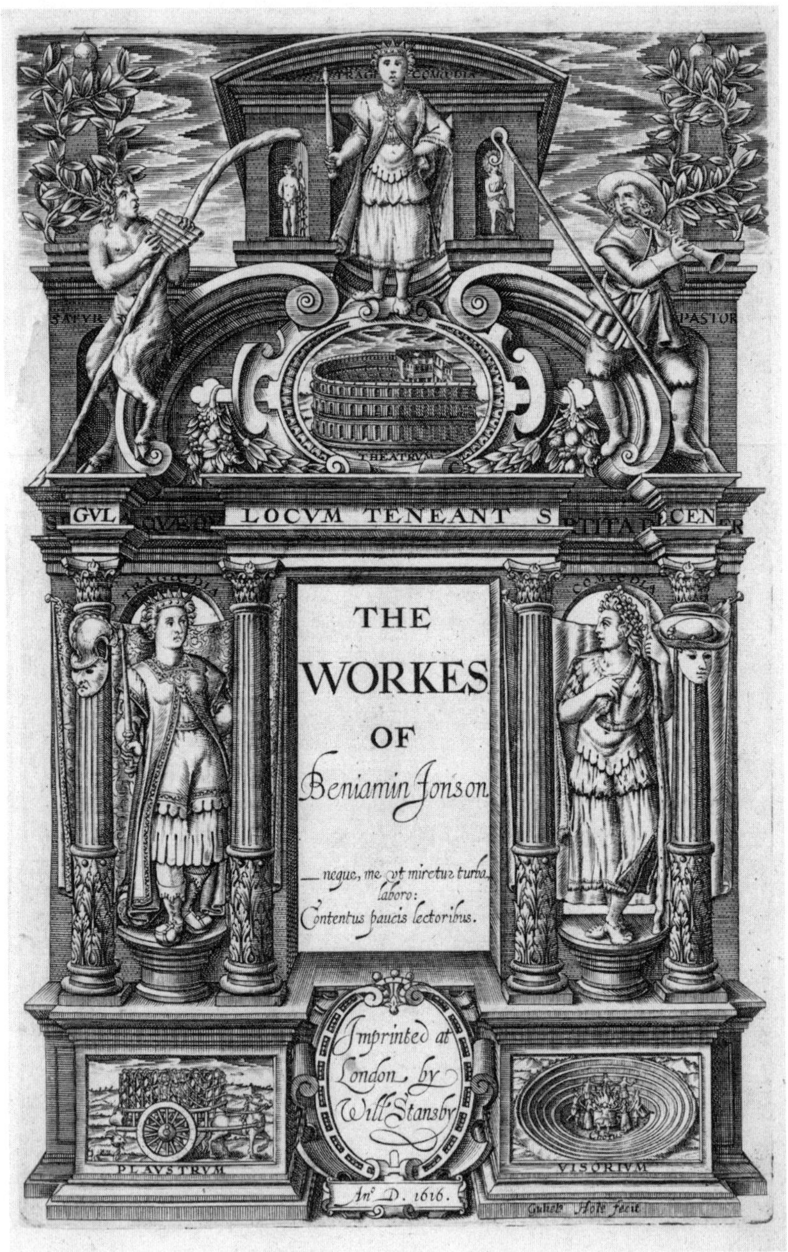


Fig. 9-2. Ben Jonson, *The Workes of Beniamin Jonson* (London, 1616), frontispiece. By permission of The Huntington Library, San Marino, California.

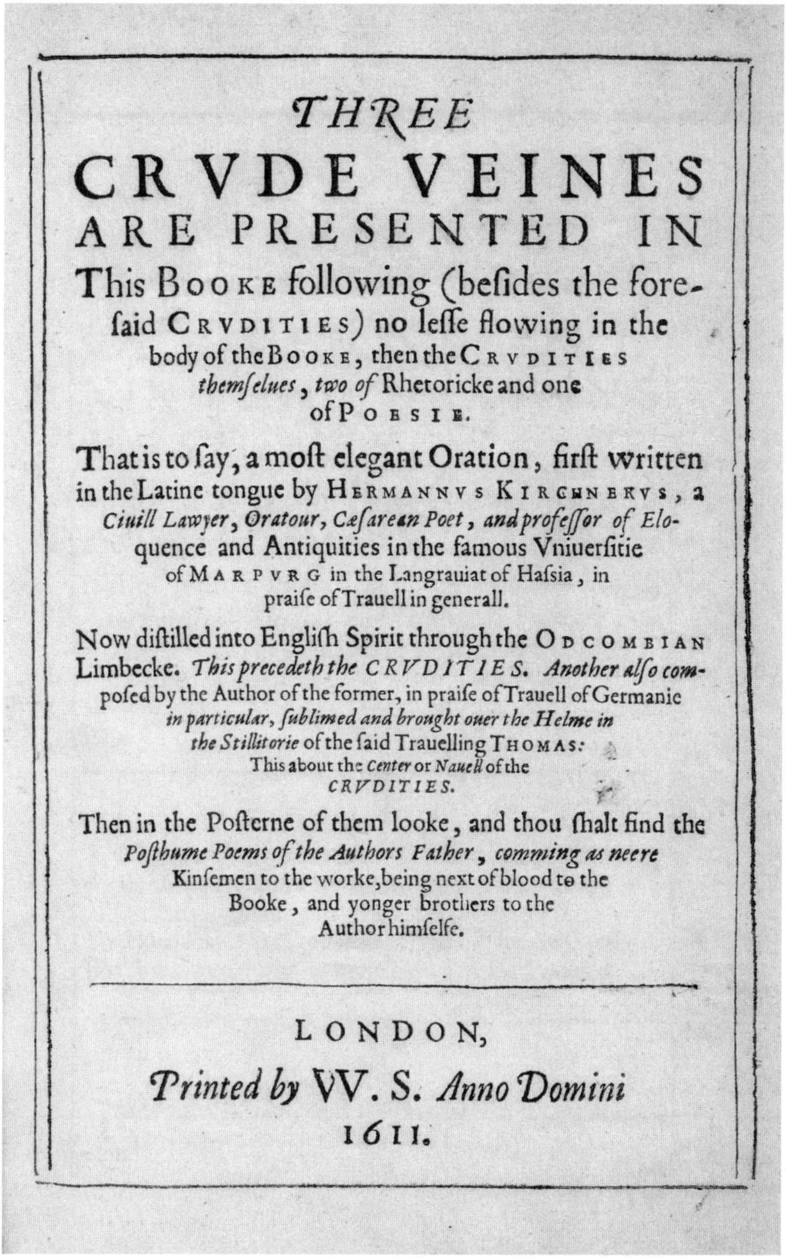

THREE

CRVDE VEINES ARE PRESENTED IN This Booke following (besides the foresaid Crvdities) no lesse flowing in the body of the Booke, then the Crvdities *themselues*, *two of* Rhetoricke and one of Poesie.

That is to say, a most elegant Oration, first written in the Latine tongue by Hermannvs Kirchnervs, a *Ciuill Lawyer, Oratour, Cæsarean Poet, and professor of Eloquence* and Antiquities in the famous Vniuersitie of Marpvrg in the Langrauiat of Hassia, in praise of Trauell in generall.

Now distilled into English Spirit through the Odcombian Limbecke. *This precedeth the CRVDITIES. Another also com*posed by the Author of the former, in praise of Trauell of Germanie *in particular, sublimed and brought ouer the Helme in the Stillitorie* of the said Trauelling Thomas: This about the *Center* or *Nauell* of the *CRVDITIES*.

Then in the Posterne of them looke, and thou shalt find the *Posthume Poems of the Authors Father, comming as neere* Kinsemen to the worke, being next of blood to the Booke, and yonger brothers to the Author himselfe.

LONDON,

*Printed by* VV. S. *Anno Domini* 1611.

Fig. 9-3. Thomas Coryate, *Coryats Crudities* (London, 1611), imprint and contents page. By permission of The Huntington Library, San Marino, California.

blood, this book seems almost to be alive, the veins of its body flowing with what we might call Coryate crude. If Coryate's authorial persona becomes so readily available for appropriation by future writers,[29] this availability can be traced in part to the fact that Coryate is initially exposed to the world via a complex set of transfusions from other narratives and writers, one of whom, we shall see momentarily, appears to come from his father.

Referring to the emergence of the early modern author function, Robert Weimann observes that "the ties between product and producer had by this stage become so close and personal that the process of appropriation was often sanctioned by metaphors of procreation. . . . [T]he political economy of the product (the text in the marketplace, the book as a unit of exchange-value) could be almost obliterated in the biological metaphor of procreation, which suggested the process of 'bringing forth one's own.'"[30] One such obliteration seems to be under way in the political economy of bringing forth the *Crudities* to market. No doubt the bizarre and outrageous authorial persona Coryate crafted for himself contributed significantly to the longevity of a posthumous career that produced several travel narratives under his name during the next two centuries; but I also suspect that the proto-biologist effort of this publishing venture to link him to other travel writers contributed a great deal to Coryate's eventual transformation into a kind of Mandeville figure, an empty authorial signifier that comes to signify almost anything associated with the particular literary genre of the travel narrative. Accordingly, I think we need to hold William Stansby equally responsible for the construction of Coryate's authorship, as his proto-Jonsonian fingerprints can be spotted all over the 1611 edition of the *Crudities*.

In this context, what seems most remarkable about the second title page I've been dwelling on is the description of the fourth and last book included in the edition: "Then in the Posterne of them looke, and thou shalt find the *Posthume Poems of the Authors Father*, coming as neere Kinsmen to the worke, being next of blood to the booke, and yonger brothers to the Author himselfe." The father referred to here is George Coryate, of whose work no extant text remains except that which is included in the *Crudities*. As with Shakespeare's Posthumous, the resurrection of a dead father is implicated in the appearance of a book, and just in case we miss the reproductive point—the links between ink and kin—Jonson amplifies it in the dedicatory acrostic he writes for the 1611 edition of the *Crudities*:

C ome forth thou bonnie bouncing booke then, daughter
O f *Tom of Odcombe* that *odde* Ioviall Author,
R ather his sonne I should have cal'd thee, Why?
Y es thou wert borne out of his travelling thigh
A s well as from his braines, and claimest thereby
T o be his *Bacchus* as his *Pallas:* bee
E uer his thighes *Male* then, and his braines *Shee.*

(A3r)

Coryate's father writes a book that is "next of blood to the booke" his son writes, and the son gives birth to a daughter—and/or perhaps a son—that is a "bouncing" book. Having spent ten sonnets extolling the physical beauty of a certain young man and instructing him to procreate so that said beauty will not be lost, Shakespeare concludes the next sonnet by advising him, "Thou shouldst print more, not let that copy die."[31] As Ann and John O. Thompson have shown, Shakespeare frequently relied on words and phrases pertaining to the early modern publishing industry throughout his career when it came to matters of biological reproduction;[32] and Richard Wilson observes that in the later plays, especially the romances, Shakespeare turned increasingly to "the proprietorial rights and productive relations" of the London book trade to express his character's concerns about procreation, the legitimacy of sons, and patriarchal authority.[33]

The frequency of conceptual and/or lexical conflations of parenting and printing—and there are dozens of them—in Shakespeare's work suggests just how readily metaphors of textual reproduction could be appropriated for the discourse of human reproduction. In the case of the acrostic Jonson devises to represent Coryate's act of literary production, however, the metaphorical cross-fertilization goes in the opposite direction. For Shakespeare, who wrote almost nothing about authorship or publication, books and print provided a ready set of terms with which to represent the facts of life. By contrast, for Jonson, who wrote often and in depth about authorship and publication, the facts of life provided him with a ready set of terms with which to characterize the material being in the world of his (and other authors') works. Jonson does, of course, write of children, but textual reproduction metaphors are conspicuous in their absence. Even in epigram 45 ("On My First Son"), which meditates on fatherhood and loss, Jonson famously calls the dead son "his best piece of poetry," but makes no mention of the poem-child's textuality. Or, to return to the opposition that structures *The*

*Antipodes*, a playwright closely affiliated with the stage sees children in terms of print; a playwright closely affiliated with the page sees print in terms of children.

I can't prove it, but I am tempted to speculate that Stansby wrote the material on the second title page of the *Crudities*. After all, as the printer/publisher, Stansby was taking a substantial risk in underwriting the costs of producing a text by a writer who was about to make his authorial debut in print. Therefore, Stansby had the greatest interest in devising a successful approach to marketing the book, and he might rightly have viewed the bundling of several travel narratives into one volume as constituting both a good way of lending a new entry into the travel writing business some much-needed credibility and a smart bit of value-added retailing. And while I'm feeling tempted to speculate, I also want to suggest that Jonson was responding to Stansby's description of the relation between the *Crudities* and Coryate's father's book as he set out to depict the nature of the son's authorial accomplishment. By 1611, Jonson—who may already have started to think about publishing a collection of his own—has learned much from Stansby's approach to marketing books and their authors. Thus, he may well be following Stansby's lead as he writes an acrostic based on the author's name in order to describe the authorship of a text that will soon be inexorably linked to that name.

As for what Stansby's approach is, I think it can best be characterized—to borrow from the rhetoric of the publishing venture itself—as crude commodity fetishism. In the first volume of *Capital,* Marx famously intimates that there is a significant relation between "the whole mystery of commodities, all of the magic and necromancy that surrounds the products of labour on the basis of commodity production," and the rather ghoulish logic of the fetish, in which objects associated with the dead come to be imbued with magical powers not inherent in the objects themselves.[34] And so at this early stage in the capitalist game when the workings of commodity production have not yet been completely hidden, printed books—lifeless bodies with no inherent powers of their own—often appear in the world accompanied by acknowledgments of the dead ancestors that imbue them with their peculiar magic, or as oedipal textual children poised to take the places of the fathers who bring them into the world with the help of midwives/stationers. And if authorship, the form of fetishism that so successfully facilitates the commodification of printed books, is so often represented within proto-biologistic narratives of reproduction, it is partly because such narratives of fathers and children, of blood and kinsmen, constitute the epistemological foundations of ancestor worship and life after death. In this sense, posthumous authorship, the veneration of objects attributed to an author after his or her death, is the most transparent form of the commodity fetishism that emerged from the early modern publishing industry. When Posthumous awakes, he naïvely observes, "Sleepe, thou hast been a Grandsire, and begot / A Father to me." In fact, it is the book placed on his chest that awakens him and triggers the recollection of a visit from the dead. Such book-driven visitations were a commonplace in the London book trade.

## *Ex Utero* or The Matrix Unloaded

Margreta de Grazia observes that "in the English Renaissance, comparisons of mechanical and sexual reproduction, imprints and children seem to multiply. . . . The textual imprint as child recurs in preliminaries to early modern books, putting into play the semantics shared by biological and textual reproduction."[35] One of the earliest extant examples of the semantic intercourse between biological and textual reproduction can be found in the letter Gargantua writes to his son Pantagruel in Rabelais's first published work (1533).[36] In this brief—and uncharacteristically serious—episode, a father writes his "most dear son" that of all God's embellishments of "human nature," the greatest is "the one by which we can, in this mortal state, acquire a kind of immortality and, in the course of this transitory life, perpetuate our name and seed: which we do by lineage sprung from us in lawful marriage."[37] Next, having confided that "I might seem to have desired nothing but to leave you, after my death, as a mirror representing the person of me your father," Gargantua makes this rather odd assertion: "The elegant and accurate art of printing, which is now in use, was invented in my time, by divine inspiration."[38] Two different methods of God-given reproduction are brought together courtesy of a father, a son, and a mirror, suggesting that the fundamental conceptual link between the two methods is the promise (or perhaps fantasy) of producing identical copies. It is worth noting that Gargantua's missive follows a chapter devoted to cataloguing "the fine Books in the Library of Saint Victor's."[39]

As many of the examples I have examined here suggest, the conceptual, semantic, and metaphorical ties that bind printing and parenting become significantly strengthened as the burgeoning early modern publishing industry comes into its own. In this light, *The Antipodes* stands out as something of an anomaly. Certainly the published drama's paratexts work hard to market the book of the play sub rosa, according to "the whole mystery of commodities," resurrecting the dead—printed drama's earliest and most vocal proponent, Ben Jonson—in the first of its two commendatory verses and privileging the printed play over the performed play in Brome's concluding address to the reader. But there is no biology lurking here. No texts-as-babies cry out to be taken home with a prospective buyer; no author apologizes here for the premature birth of a text untimely exposed to the world by a greedy printer. In fact, the play itself makes the disjunction of books and babies, of reading and reproducing, one of its principal themes, even as it privileges the power of the stage over the power of the page. How might we account for these innovations?

I want to conclude by answering this question from the perspectives of both sexual and textual reproduction, the two sides of the same metaphorical coin that constitutes the main interpretive investment of this essay. In the case of sexual reproduction, I would argue that Brome's play is responding to an important moment in the history of patriarchal culture when the reign of Gutenberg paternity, nearly two hundred years on the throne, has finally consolidated its authority. If, as Friedrich A. Kittler observes, the paternal contribution to reproduction was once chiefly articulated in terms of "an omnipresent metaphor [that] equated women with the white sheet of nature or virginity onto which a very male stylus could then inscribe the glory of its authorship,"[40] it is also true that the invention of the printing press provided stiff competition for the primal scribal scene in terms of the proto-biological effort to understand and put into words those reproductive functions that remained largely invisible and unknowable till the nineteenth century. And although scribal publication continued to be a vibrant medium well into the eighteenth century, the early modern father—compelled to await the certitude of scientific evidence that blood "types" and DNA testing would someday offer him—had pretty much completed the conceptual, semantic, and metaphorical transition from scribal technology to print technology by the middle of the seventeenth century. As such, the Gutenberg Father, armed with upgraded technological notions of paternity, may well have had a vested interest in covering his epistemological tracks. Not to do so, in some sense, would have called attention to the fundamental absence at the core of paternity and paternal authority, as well as many of the cultural structures relied on to maintain them in their privileged position. Thus, although Brome's play intimates links between fathers and books, literacy and legitimacy, ink and kin—links that are concisely expressed in Shakespeare's sonnets, in plays such as *Cymbeline* and *The Winter's Tale,* and in the paratexts of books such as the *Crudities*—it nevertheless thematizes their disjunction and mutual exclusion by making them the before and after of Peregrine's rather Jonsonian/humoral malady. We've come a long way in the century that separates *The Antipodes* from the letter Gargantua writes to Pantagruel.

In the case of textual reproduction, I would argue that the various embodiments that enabled the fetishistic commodification of printed books in the emergent book trade have been deployed so often by the time *The Antipodes* is published that they have lost a bit of their marketing magic. In short, as Peregrine might have guessed, by 1640 these two interrelated discursive systems—these *mentalités,* Foucault might have called them—have traveled far and wide and are in need of a respite.

## NOTES

An early version of this chapter was circulated in a Shakespeare Association of America seminar led by Marta Straznicky. I am grateful to her for inviting me to expand that paper and for her comments on subsequent drafts. I am also very fortunate to have had the opportunity to circulate and present a full-length version to the Melbern G. Glasscock Center for Humanities Research Colloquium at Texas A&M University. I thank the following members of that colloquium for very helpful comments and suggestions: James Rosenheim, Don Dixon, Hilaire Kallendorf, Gary Stringer, Donnalee Dox, Ilan Mitchell-Smith, and Larson Powell.

1. Lukas Erne has, of course, notoriously called into question this assertion, especially in the context of Shakespeare, who, he argues, produced reading texts for publication that had to be shortened subsequently for performance. See his *Shakespeare as Literary Dramatist* (Cambridge: Cambridge University Press, 2003).

2. Richard Brome, *The Antipodes: a Comedie* (London: J. Okes, for Francis Constable, 1640). I will be using the Globe Quarto edition, ed. David Scott Kastan and Richard Proudfoot (New York: Theater Arts Books/Routledge, 2000), cited parenthetically in the text.

3. Jeffrey Masten, *Textual Intercourse: Collaboration, Authorship, and Sexualities in Renaissance Drama* (Cambridge: Cambridge University Press, 1997).

4. On Hamlet's reading habits, see Eve Rachele Sanders's astute analysis in *Gender and Literacy on Stage in Early Modern England* (Cambridge: Cambridge University Press, 1998), 57–88.

5. On early modern rhetorical conflations of book and flesh, see Gordon Williams, *Shakespeare, Sex, and the Print Revolution* (London: Athlone Press, 1996), 46–55.

6. See Colin H. Roberts and T. C. Skeat, *The Birth of the Codex* (London: Oxford University Press, 1983), 19–22.

7. Peter W. M. Blayney includes some of these images in *The First Folio of Shakespeare* (Washington, D.C.: Folger Library Publications, 1991).

8. Quoted in Roberts and Skeat, *Birth*, 22.

9. Roberts and Skeat argue that Paul's use of the word *membranas* refers to the word (*membraneae*) used in contemporary Rome for parchment notebooks (ibid., 22).

10. On the history of these convergences, see my introduction to *Printing and Parenting in Early Modern England,* ed. Douglas A. Brooks (Aldershot: Ashgate, 2005), 1–23; and my essay "Bodies That Mattered: Technology, Embodiment, and Secretarial Mediation," in *Literary Secretaries/Secretarial Culture,* ed. Leah Price and Pam Thurschwell (Aldershot: Ashgate, 2005), 129–51. See also the essays in Dolores Warwick Frese and Katherine O'Brien O'Keefe, eds., *The Body and the Book* (Notre Dame: University of Notre Dame Press, 1997).

11. William Shakespeare, *The Tempest* (1623), cited from *The Norton Facsimile of the First Folio of Shakespeare*, prepared by Charlton Hinman, 2nd ed., with a new introduction by Peter W. M. Blayney (New York: Norton, 1996), TLN 2326–30. Quotations from Shakespeare are cited parenthetically by through line numbers (TLN) from this edition.

12. Doris Fenton, *The Extra-dramatic Moment in Elizabethan Plays before 1616* (Folcroft, Pa.: Folcroft Press, 1970), 8.

13. Adrian Johns, *The Nature of the Book: Print and Knowledge in the Making* (Chicago: University of Chicago Press, 1998), 32.

14. Douglas A. Brooks, *From Playhouse to Printing House: Drama and Authorship in Early Modern England* (Cambridge: Cambridge University Press, 2000).

15. Christopher Marlowe, *Tamburlaine the Great* (London: Richard Jhones, 1590), A2.

16. I am using the word "printer" here somewhat loosely to denote the printer and/or publisher of a given text. The distinction between printer and publisher was not yet firm in the early modern book trade.

17. On the "prehistory" of prefatorial addresses, see Gérard Genette, *Paratexts: Thresholds of Interpretation,* trans. Jane E. Lewin (Cambridge: Cambridge University Press, 1997), 163–70.

18. Ben Jonson, *Poetaster or The Arraignment* (London: [R. Bradock] for M. L[ownes], 1602), N1v.

19. G. E. Bentley, for example, remarks of Jonson's *Workes* that "probably no other publication before the Restoration did so much to raise the contemporary existence of the generally belittled form of plays" (*The Profession of Dramatist in Shakespeare's Time, 1590–1642* [Princeton: Princeton University Press, 1971], 55–56). More recently, significant research by Alan B. Farmer and Zachary Lesser has given us a much richer and more historically accurate portrait of this shift. See their "Vile Arts: The Marketing of English Printed Drama, 1512–1660," *Research Opportunities in Renaissance Drama* 39 (2000): 77–166. See also Lesser's astute essay "Walter Burre's *The Knight of the Burning Pestle,*" *English Literary Renaissance* 34 (1999): 335–61.

20. See, for example, Joseph Loewenstein, *Jonson and Possessive Authorship* (Cambridge: Cambridge University Press, 2002); Richard C. Newton, "Jonson and the (Re-) Invention of the Book," in *Classic and Cavalier: Essays on Jonson and the Sons of Ben,* ed. Claude J. Summers and Ted-Larry Pebworth (Pittsburgh: University of Pittsburgh Press, 1982), 31–58.

21. Elizabeth Hanson, *Discovering the Subject in Renaissance England* (Cambridge: Cambridge University Press, 1998), 120.

22. Brome had strong ties to Jonson. He was first employed as a servant in Jonson's household in 1614, later becoming a protégé and friend.

23. See, for example, David Scott Kastan, "Plays into Print: Shakespeare to His Earliest Readers," in *Books and Readers in Early Modern England: Material Studies*, ed. Jennifer Andersen and Elizabeth Sauer (Philadelphia: University of Pennsylvania Press, 2002), 23–41. For an overview of the impact of printing on authorship, see Wendy Wall, "Authorship and the Material Conditions of Writing," in *The Cambridge Companion to English Literature, 1500–1600*, ed. Arthur F. Kinney (Cambridge: Cambridge University Press, 2000), 64–89.

24. Joseph Moxon, *Mechanick Exercises, or the Doctrine of Handy-Works Applied to the Art of Printing (1683–84),* facsimile, ed. Herbert Davis and Harry Carter (New York: Dover Publications, 1958), 19.

25. For a discussion of these engagements, see Brooks, "Bodies That Mattered."

26. Margreta de Grazia, "Imprints: Shakespeare, Gutenberg, and Descartes," in *Alternative Shakespeares,* vol. 2, ed. Terence Hawkes (New York: Routledge, 1996), 74.

27. *Mr. William Shakespeares comedies, histories, & tragedies* (London: Isaac Jaggard and Ed. Blount [at the charges of W. Jaggard, Ed. Blount, J. Smithweeke, and W. Aspley], 1623), A3r.

28. *Coryats Crudities Hastily gobled vp in five Moneths trauells in France, Sauoy, Italy, Rhetia co[m]monly called the Grisons country, Heluetia aliàs Switzerland, some parts of high Germany, and the Netherlands; Newly digested in the hungry aire of Odcombe in the County of Somerset, & now dispersed to the nourishment of the trauelling Members of this Kingdome* (London: W[illiam] S[tansby] for the author, 1611).

29. The appropriation of Coryate's authorial persona can be said to commence as early as 1612, when John Taylor—who appears in the commendatory verse of *The Antipodes* that proclaims "Jonson's alive!"—addresses the first poem of his first collection of poems, *The Sculler,* "To Tom Coriat." A year later, Taylor published another book, *Laugh and Be Fat: or A commentary upon the Odcombyan Banket*, which parodies the *Crudities.* The following year (1613) Taylor produced two more books about Coryate's travels: *Odcombs Complaint* and *The Eighth Wonder of the World.* Coryate returns as one of several world travelers in Taylor's *The Praise of Hemp-seed* (1623), and some of Coryate's notes and letters are published in Samuel Purchas's *Hakluytus Posthumous* in 1625. A subsequent text, *Another Traveller! Or Cursory Remarks and Critical Observations made upon a Journey through Part of the Netherlands In the Latter End of the Year 1766*, is ascribed to Coryate Junior. For a detailed study of Coryate's authorial afterlives in print, see M. G. Aune, "Thomas Coryate for the Ages: Constructing Authorship and Celebrity" (unpublished conference paper).

30. Robert Weimann, *Authority and Representation in Early Modern Discourse*, ed. David Hillman (Baltimore: Johns Hopkins University Press, 1996), 180.

31. Sonnet 11, in *Shakespeare's Sonnets*, ed. Katherine Duncan-Jones (Walton-on-Thames: Thomas Nelson, 1997), 133.

32. Ann Thompson and John O. Thompson, "Meaning, 'Seeing,' and Printing," in Brooks, *Printing and Parenting,* 50–77.

33. Richard Wilson, *Will Power: Essays on Shakespearean Authority* (Detroit: Wayne State University Press, 1993), 165.

34. Karl Marx, *Capital: A Critique of Political Economy,* vol. 1, trans. Ben Fowkes (New York: Vintage Books, 1977), 169. For a lucid analysis of the role of fetishism in Marx's thought, see William Pietz, "Fetishism and Materialism: The Limits of Theory in Marx," in *Fetishism as Cultural Discourse*, ed. Emily Apter and William Pietz (Ithaca: Cornell University Press, 1993), 119–51.

35. De Grazia, "Imprints," 74.

36. Marshall McLuhan points to the broader significance of the letter for understanding print culture: "Anybody who looks at the Gutenberg question at all, runs very soon into Gargantua's Letter to Pantagruel. Rabelais, long before Cervantes, produced an authentic myth or prefiguration of the whole complex of print technology. . . . *[P]antagruelion* [is] the symbol and image of printing from moveable type" (*The Gutenberg Galaxy* [Toronto: University of Toronto Press, 1962], 179–80).

37. François Rabelais, *Gargantua and Pantagruel,* trans. J. M. Cohen (New York: Penguin, 1955), 193.

38. Ibid., 194.

39. Ibid., 186–89.

40. Friedrich A. Kittler, *Gramophone, Film, Typewriter,* trans. Geoffrey Winthrop-Young and Michael White (Stanford: Stanford University Press, 1999), 186.

# Contributors

PETER BEREK is professor of English at Mount Holyoke College. He has published widely on early modern English drama in journals such as *Renaissance Quarterly, Shakespeare Quarterly, Studies in English Literature, Renaissance Drama*, and *Research Opportunities in Renaissance Drama.*

DOUGLAS A. BROOKS is associate professor of English at Texas A&M University and editor of *Shakespeare Yearbook.* He is the author of *From Playhouse to Printing House: Drama and Authorship in Early Modern England* (Cambridge University Press, 2000), and editor of a collection of essays, *Parenting and Printing in Early Modern England* (Ashgate, 2005). Brooks has published in *Medieval and Renaissance Drama in England, English Literary Renaissance, Philological Quarterly, Renaissance Drama, Studies in English Literature*, and *Poetics Today.*

CYNDIA SUSAN CLEGG is Distinguished Professor of English at Pepperdine University. Among many other publications, she is the author of "History of the Book: An Undisciplined Discipline?" *Renaissance Quarterly* 54 (2001): 221–45; "Liberty, License, and Authority: Press Censorship and Shakespeare," in *Companion to Shakespeare*, ed. David Scott Kastan (Blackwell, 1998), 464–85; and two books on early modern censorship, *Press Censorship in Elizabethan England* (Cambridge, 2000) and *Press Censorship in Jacobean England* (Cambridge, 2002).

ALAN B. FARMER is assistant professor of English at Ohio State University. He has published widely on drama and early modern print culture in *Shakespeare Quarterly, The Shakespearean International Yearbook,* vol. 2, *Where Are We Now in Shakespearean Studies?* (Ashgate, 2002), and *Research Opportunities in Renaissance Drama.* He is co-editor (with Adam Zucker) of *Localizing Caroline Drama, 1625–1642* (Palgrave, forthcoming).

ZACHARY LESSER is assistant professor of English at the University of Illinois, Urbana. He is the author of *Renaissance Drama and the Politics of Publication: Readings in the English Book Trade* (Cambridge University Press, 2004), as well as articles on early modern drama and print culture in *Shakespeare Quarterly, ELH, English Literary Renaissance*, and elsewhere.

LUCY MUNRO is lecturer in English at Keele University, Staffordshire. She is the author of *Children of the Queen's Revels: A Jacobean Theatre Repertory* (Cambridge University Press, 2005). She has edited *The Fleer* for Globe Quartos (2005), and is the author of "Early Modern Drama and the Repertory Approach," *Research Opportunities in Renaissance Drama* 42 (2003): 1–33; and "*The Knight of the Burning Pestle* and Generic Experimentation," in *Early Modern English Drama: A Critical Companion*, ed. Patrick Cheney, Andrew Hadfield, and Garret A. Sullivan (Oxford University Press, 2005).

ELIZABETH SAUER is professor of English at Brock University, St. Catharines, Ontario, where she holds a Chancellor's Chair for Research Excellence. She is author of *"Paper-contestations" and Textual Communities in England, 1640–1675* (University of Toronto Press, 2005), and *Barbarous Dissonance and Images of Voice in Milton's Epics* (McGill–Queen's University Press, 1996). Sauer has also coedited numerous collections of essays, including *Reading Early Modern Women*, with Helen Ostovich (Routledge, 2004), and *Books and Readers in Early Modern England: Material Studies*, with Jennifer Andersen (University of Pennsylvania Press, 2002). She is editing *Milton and Toleration* with Sharon Achinstein (Oxford University Press, forthcoming).

LAUREN SHOHET is associate professor of English at Villanova University. She is the author of *Reading Masques: The English Masque and Public Culture in the Seventeenth Century* (Oxford University Press, 2006). She has also published articles on Shakespeare, Milton, Jonson, and Pullman in *Milton Studies*, *Journal of Early Modern Cultural Studies*, *Shakespeare Studies*, and *Texas Studies in Language and Literature*, among other journals.

MARTA STRAZNICKY is associate professor of English at Queen's University, Kingston, Ontario. She is author of *Privacy, Playreading, and Women's Closet Drama, 1550–1700* (Cambridge University Press, 2004). She has published on early modern closet drama in *ELH*, *English Literary Renaissance*, and *Criticism* and contributed the chapter "Closet Drama" to *Companion to Renaissance Drama*, ed. Arthur F. Kinney (Blackwell, 2002).

# INDEX